CACTI
— THE —
ILLUSTRATED
DICTIONARY

CACTI
— THE —
ILLUSTRATED
DICTIONARY

ROD & KEN PRESTON-MAFHAM

BLANDFORD

First published in the United Kingdom in 1991 by
Blandford an imprint of Cassell plc
Villiers House, 41/47 Strand, London WC2N 5JE

Reprinted 1991, 1992
Copyright © 1991 Blandford
Text copyright © 1991 K.G. & R.A. Preston-Mafham
Photographs copyright © Premaphotos Wildlife and photographers credited on page 224

Distributed in the United States by
Sterling Publishing Co., Inc.
387 Park Avenue South, New York, N.Y. 10016−8810

Distributed in Australia by
Capricorn Link (Australia) Pty Ltd
P.O. Box 665, Lane Cove, NSW 2066

British Library Cataloguing in Publication Data
Preston-Mafham, Rod
  Cacti.
  1. Cacti
  I. Title II. Preston-Mafham, Ken
  583.47

  ISBN 0−7137−2092−1

Typeset by Setrite Typesetters Ltd
Printed and bound in Singapore by Kyodo Printing Co.

CONTENTS

ACKNOWLEDGEMENTS

We are deeply indebted to all those people — some of whom were complete strangers when we first made contact with them concerning this project — who have made freely available to us their cacti, their expertise and also their hospitality. Without access to their specialist collections, which mainly consist of fully documented material, this book would not have been a practical proposition. Our special thanks therefore go to the following — this book is as much theirs as ours: Elisabeth and Graham Charles, John Donald, Len Evans, Roger Ferryman, Peter Gavin, Graham Hole, Heinz Klein, Mike Muse, David Parker, Chris Pugh, 'Pip' Smart, Nigel Taylor and Sidney Woolcock.

We must further thank Graham Charles who, in addition to making his collection available to us, also took for us many excellent photographs. Indeed, on occasions his enthusiasm for the project seemed even greater than our own and this is reflected in the number of his pictures which we have been pleased to use. Further thanks go to Roger Ferryman and 'Pip' Smart for providing us with extra photographic material, Rene Geissler for lending us all his copies of the German cactus journal, KuaS, and John Donald for much advice.

We must also thank the long-suffering wives of some of the above, who had to put up with the loss of their spouses during the many hours spent discussing the ins and outs of cactus taxonomy!

Finally, special thanks go to RP-M's wife, Jean, for her assistance in the preparation of the manuscript.

INTRODUCTION

We have set out in this volume to attempt the impossible, that is to illustrate all of the globular cacti popularly collected by enthusiasts and to give them their correct scientific name.

Our concept of the term 'globular' has had to be expanded somewhat to avoid excluding the increasingly popular genus *Echinocereus*, which contains only a few truly globular members but without which the book would be of greatly reduced use to the average enthusiast. On the other hand, to avoid including the fairly large genus *Trichocereus*, which mainly contains large columnar plants with very restricted appeal, we have adopted a narrow generic concept. This has enabled us to include the globular plants of the genus *Echinopsis* in its old, restricted sense without also including *Trichocereus*, which is now generally united with *Echinopsis* but which is seldom seen as such in seed and plant lists.

We have also taken the difficult decision to maintain familiar, long-used genera such as *Lobivia* (now included in *Echinopsis*), and *Notocactus* (now included in *Parodia*). However, we should point out that not all professional and amateur botanists working on the Cactaceae accept the current conservative trend towards uniting genera in this way.

The above remarks also apply to current thinking on the thorny problem of how to define a species within the Cactaceae, a subject which has provoked – and continues to provoke – more heated argument amongst interested scientists and enthusiasts than any other topic. It seems to us that this is an argument which is unlikely ever to have a conclusive solution that is acceptable to all botanists throughout the world. The crux of the problem lies in the incredible variability to be observed both within and between individual populations of cacti in the wild. This is because the Cactaceae appear to be in a state of very active evolution compared with other plants.

In many cases an individual population will have a well-defined and unique set of characters which continually breed true both in the wild and in cultivation, enabling instant recognition of the species concerned. Where this is a species such as *Mammillaria plumosa*, which shows little variation over its fairly narrow range and has no close relationship with or tendency to intergrade into any other species, there is no problem.

However, with a species such as *Sulcorebutia glomerispina* or *S. tiraquensis* the situation is much more complex and difficult to resolve. Both are obviously closely related to what was in earlier times described as *S. steinbachii* and could indeed be regarded as varieties of the latter. To understand their relationship more fully requires a study of the plants in their natural habitat. *S. glomerispina*, for example, grows within a few miles of a very variable *S. steinbachii* population. *S. glomerispina*, however, maintains a relatively limited and well-defined set of characteristics, which originally led to its being described as a separate species from *S. steinbachii*. *S. glomerispina* remains distinct in cultivation and is worth acquiring on this account, but in purely botanical terms it is very doubtful if it should be treated as a separate species although it is maintained as such in the present work.

In fact the whole situation concerning a complex 'core' species such as *S. steinbachii* is very difficult to resolve satisfactorily, especially where plants are sufficiently distinct to be of interest to collectors. For example the gradation from *S. steinbachii* to *S. tiraquensis* seems to be via a series of plants currently enjoying specific or varietal status but which perhaps could be more properly regarded as forming a botanical cline (i.e., the gradual change in characteristics of a species along a geographical line, with the result that plants at either end of this line may superficially appear to be quite distinct species), within a single species, i.e., *S. steinbachii*.

Since this situation occurs commonly throughout the Cactaceae the decision as to whether or not these distinctive, self-maintaining populations should be considered as species in their own right (as most now are), or reduced to varieties of a single, widespread and extremely variable species (as is the current trend), is basically a subjective one. One botanist's species may therefore be another, equally well-qualified, botanist's variety.

In response to this never-ending problem we have decided to adopt a middle-of-the-road approach, which we hope combines common-sense with the need to satisfy the interests of the reader who will be familiar with the numerous specific names currently in use. The notes provided beneath the illustrations may help in understanding our decisions in this context as well as the relationships between plants.

The situation is further complicated by the extreme variation even within a single accepted species. Sometimes, within a discrete population, plants growing next to each other and often from the same seed pod can be of a surprisingly different appearance. Body colour and shape, spine number, length and colour, as well as the colour of the flower and petal shape, can vary so widely that the plants may at first sight appear to be a mixture of several different species, and consequently may be described as such. It is mistakes like this which have tended to give rise to many of the superfluous specific names which are shown in italics in the index.

Careful study of such a variable population may often reveal that in reality there is no such thing as the 'typical' plant, which a collector may have come to expect from his familiarity with the species in cultivation. This restricted concept of a species' characteristics has often been due to the small amount of living material originally imported which was frequently selected by the field collector for its uniform appearance.

In view of the above we have had some difficulty with certain species in illustrating a plant which adequately sums up the general characteristics of the species as it occurs in the wild. In some instances we have overcome this by showing two markedly different forms in the same plate. Where this is not possible, the reader is referred to the notes for information regarding the variability of the species. Where a species shows easily recognized named varieties and/or forms, these are also illustrated where space permits.

The large number of plants we have photographed in order to illustrate this volume have come both from our own collection and those of other helpful and enthusiastic collectors. As far as possible we have photographed material of known origin, either field-collected plants or plants grown from field-collected seed. Where possible we have taken advantage of access to well-grown vegetative propagations (or clones), from the original type plant. There are, however, a good number of species which show very little variation and for which material with field data is not easily available. For these we have used a picture of a plant as typically seen in cultivation.

The fact that we have considerably reduced the number of species does not in itself necessarily affect the numbers of collectable cacti. Previously, for example, the reader might have collected three different so-called species, based upon differences in flower colour alone. The present situation might be that he or she now obtains the same number of plants, each with a different flower colour, with long and short spines and with a hooked or straight central spine in order to have a true representation of a single species in the collection.

USING THE DICTIONARY

The book is divided into two sections: the first comprises a large number of plates with accompanying notes, set out in alphabetical order; the second is a cross-referencing index containing most of the names which have been in common use during the last 20 years.

When requiring information about a particular species, for example a name taken from a seed list, the reader should first search for it in the illustrated main section. If the name is not to be found there, it should then be sought in the index, where hopefully the equivalent, as illustrated in the book, will be found.

In both sections names may be found in **bold type** for species which we accept and in *normal italics* for those names which we regard as invalid synonyms. (We accept that some readers will disagree with some of our decisions, although these are based upon KGP-M's wide experience of the extreme variability of cacti in habitat).

Some of the names that we accept appear in inverted commas, which are used for three reasons. Firstly they indicate plants which we consider sufficiently distinct for inclusion in the book but which currently lack a valid description. Secondly, they indicate plants which have been validly described but not in the way in which we feel they should be used, for instance in the 'wrong' genus or at specific rather than varietal rank, or *vice versa*. Thirdly, some names in common use are invalid, that is to say, some mistake has been made in the original description, or material of the original plant has not been deposited in a herbarium. Until such time as these plants are validly described, their names will have to be maintained as in our opinion there are no viable alternatives. The new 'combinations' thus seen in inverted commas are purely for our own use to serve as indications of our own ideas and are NOT intended to be considered as validly published.

We anticipate that many people will use this book as a method of deciding which species from a plethora of many, perhaps unfamiliar names, would be worth purchasing from seed and plant lists.

Many lists contain numerous redundant or invalid names: for example, the reader may see a species listed as *Echinocereus caespitosus*. On looking this up in the index you will be referred to **Echinocereus reichenbachii**, which is now accepted as the correct name for this species. Your plant list may also include *Echinocereus baileyi* which the index will give as a variety of **E. reichenbachii**.

Some names in the index will be followed by the epithet 'status doubtful' and it is important to cactus collecting that these names are eventually taken out of use. In many instances they refer to species whose original descriptions were scant, habitats were vague or no material was deposited from which later collections could positively be identified. Some recent collections are reckoned to be rediscoveries of some of these 'lost' species, but to us it seems that much of this is wishful thinking and in most instances it would be better to describe a new species or variety rather than maintain a doubtful old name. We have tracked down as many of these spurious names as possible but the true identity of some of them has continued to elude us.

SOURCES OF THE PLANTS

We have included in code, in square brackets, as much information as is available to us with regard to the origin, nature and ownership of the plant. In a few cases we do not have this information. First, if known, comes the collector's code and number as follows:

B= Frau Muhr	L= Lau
SB= S. Brack	JL= J. Lambert
Card.= M. Cardenas	FO= F. Otero
JD= J. Donald	P= J. Piltz
OF= O. Ferrari	PM= Preston-Mafham
RMF= R. Ferryman	WR= W. Rausch
H= D. Hunt	Repp= W. Reppenhagen
DH= D. Herzog	FR= F. Ritter
HU= Horst-Uebelmann	Schl= H. Schlosser
K= H. Klein	HS= H. Swoboda
FK= F. Katterman	NPT= N. Taylor
HK= H. Kuentzler	DV= D. van Vliet
KK= K. Knize	MLV= M. Vereb
KR= W. Krahn	

Second is the origin of the plant: H = a plant photographed in habitat; IP = a plant imported from the wild or a vegetative propagation from such a plant; HS = a plant grown from seed collected in habitat; CS = a plant grown from commercial seed.

Third is the collection from which the plant was photographed:

EC= E. Charles	K= H. Klein
GC= G. Charles	M= M. Muse
ERC= Echinocereus Reference Collection	P= C. Pugh
	PM= Preston-Mafham
E= L. Evans	RM= R. Mottram
DHS= Donald/Hole/Smart	R= A. Rollason
F= R. Ferryman	W= S. Woolcock.
G= P. Gavin	

UNDERSTANDING THE NOTES

It may not be obvious why some entries contain virtually a full description of the plant while others mention only the briefest details. Within the space available for each entry we have given as much information as possible for the newer, lesser−known species and for those which show a large amount of variation. However, with less variable or more familiar species we are letting the illustrations of the plants speak for themselves, on the basis that a clear picture is worth a thousand words.

For those of you who are not fully versed in the naming of cactus species, the following diagram should help you understand more easily the information contained in the text. Where we have problems with space, species names have been abbreviated, but only after they have been mentioned in full at least once somewhere within the entry. Again, due to limited space, any particularly lengthy entry has been extended into a separate appendix.

Sizes given are only rough guides, for experience has shown us that the eventual size of a plant will often vary from collection to collection, depending upon how 'hard' the plants are grown, meaning how much food and water they are supplied with. Again, plants in cultivation often show a lesser development of spines than those to be found in the wild.

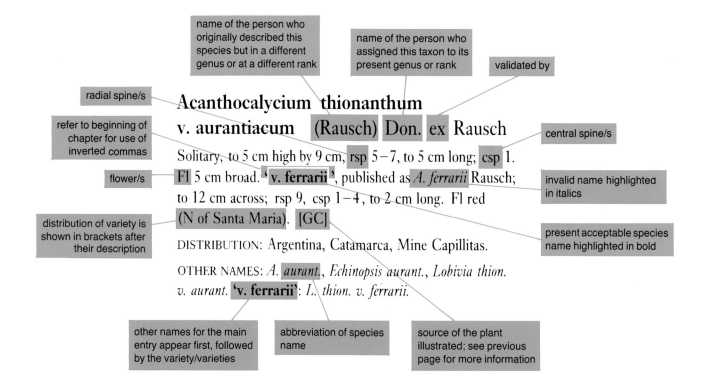

ILLUSTRATED
A-Z OF SPECIES

Acanthocalycium spiniflorum
(Sch.) Bkbg.

Solitary, to 60 cm high by 15 cm; spines 14–20. Fl pink.
v. klimpelianum (Werd. & Weidl.) Don. (illus.); to 10 cm
by 10 cm, spines fewer. Fl white (nr Cordoba). [B3/M]

DISTRIBUTION: Argentina, NW Cordoba.

OTHER NAMES: **v. klimpelianum**: *A. klimpelianum, A.
peitscherianum, Lobivia spin. & v. klimp.*

Acanthocalycium spiniflorum
fa. violaceum   (Werd.) Don.

Mainly differentiated from the species by its beautiful violet
coloured fl. [CS/PM]

DISTRIBUTION: Argentina, Cordoba.

OTHER NAMES: *A. violaceum, Lobivia spin. v. violacea.*

Acanthocalycium thionanthum
(Spcg.) Bkbg.

Solitary, to 12 cm high by 6–10 cm. **v. brevispinum** (Ritt.)
Don.; to 50 cm by 6 cm, spines darker and shorter. Fl
yellow (Cafayate). **v. chionanthum** (Speg.) Hoss; similar.
Fl white (Cachi-Cachipampa). [CS/PM]

DISTRIBUTION: Argentina, Salta, Cachi.

OTHER NAMES: *A. catamarcense*, '*A. griseum*', *Lobivia thion. v.
cat.* **vars.**: *A. brevis., A. chion., Lobivia thion. v. brevis., L.
thion. v. chion.*

Acanthocalycium thionanthum
v. aurantiacum   (Rausch) Don. ex Rausch

Solitary, to 5 cm high by 9 cm, rsp 5–7, to 5 cm long; csp 1.
Fl 5 cm broad. '**v. ferrarii**', published as *A. ferrarii* Rausch;
to 12 cm across; rsp 9, csp 1–4 to 2 cm long. Fl red (N of
Santa Maria). [GC]

DISTRIBUTION: Argentina, Catamarca, Mine Capillitas.

OTHER NAMES: *A. aurant., Echinopsis aurant., Lobivia thion.
v. aurant.* '**v. ferrarii**': *L. thion. v. ferrarii.*

Acanthocalycium thionanthum
v. glaucum   (Ritt.) Don. ex. Rausch

Solitary, to 15 cm high by 7 cm, grey-blue. Fl 6 cm across.
[CS/PM]

DISTRIBUTION: Argentina, Catamarca, between Belen and
Hualfin.

OTHER NAMES: *A. glaucum, Echinopsis glaucina, Lobivia
thion. v. glauca.*

'Acanthocalycium thionanthum
v. variiflorum'   (Bkbg.) Don.

Globular, to 10 cm across. Fl yellow or orange to red.
'**v. munita**', published as *Lobivia thion. v. munita* Rausch;
spines longer and more bent. Fl smaller (Cerro Zorrito).
[CS/PM]

DISTRIBUTION: Argentina, Tucuman, W of the Abra
de Infernillo.

OTHER NAMES: *A. variiflorum, Lobivia thion. v. variif.*

Ancistrocactus crassihamatus
(Web.) Benson

Solitary, to 20 cm or so high by 10–15 cm. Fl not opening widely, 2 cm long, purple. [IP/K]

DISTRIBUTION: Mexico, Queretaro.

OTHER NAMES: *Glandulicactus crassihamatus.*

Ancistrocactus scheeri   (S-D) B. & R.

Solitary, to 10 cm high by 6 cm. Fl to 2.5 cm long, greenish-yellow. [H]

DISTRIBUTION: Texas and N Mexico.

OTHER NAMES: *A. brevihamatus, A. megarhizus.*

Ancistrocactus uncinatus   (Gall.) Benson

Solitary, to 20 cm high by 7 cm. Csp to 4, to 9 cm long. Fl 2.5 cm long, brownish. **v. wrightii** (Englm.) Benson; csp 1, to 15 cm. Fl to 3.5 cm, purple (Texas to N Mexico, Chihuahua). [PM55/HS/PM]

DISTRIBUTION: Mexico, Chihuahua to San Luis Potosi.

OTHER NAMES: *Glandulicactus uncinatus.* **v. wrightii**: *G. unc. wrightii.*

Arequipa hempeliana   (Guerke) Oehme

Globular to elongated, spination extremely variable, often much denser than in the plant illustrated. [RMF30/IP/F]

DISTRIBUTION: N Chile and S Peru.

OTHER NAMES: All other species of *Arequipa*; *Borzicactus hempelianus, B. rettigii* & vars.

Ariocarpus agavoides   (Castan.) Anderson

Fairly easy from seed, reaches flowering size in seven years. [CS/GC]

DISTRIBUTION: Mexico, Tamaulipas.

OTHER NAMES: *Neogomesia agavoides.*

Ariocarpus fissuratus   (Englm.) Sch.

Extremely variable in body size, tubercle shape and sculpting. In **v. lloydii** (Rose) Anderson the tubercle furrow is only about half the length of the tubercle. [IP/P]

DISTRIBUTION: SW Texas and New Mexico.

OTHER NAMES: *Roseocactus fissuratus.* **v. lloydii**: *A. intermedius, A. lloydii, R. intermedius, R. lloydii.*

Ariocarpus kotschoubeyanus (Lem.) Sch.

There is also a white-flowered form. [IP/EC]

DISTRIBUTION: Mexico: Durango; Nuevo Leon; San Luis Potosi.

OTHER NAMES: *Roseocactus kotschoubeyanus.*

Ariocarpus retusus Scheidw.

Illustrated is a seed-grown plant. Tubercles smooth.
v. furfuraceus (Watson) Thomps. tubercles calloused. [CS/EC]

DISTRIBUTION: Mexico, widespread in San Luis Potosi, Coahuila and Nuevo Leon.

Ariocarpus scapharostrus Boed.

DISTRIBUTION: Mexico, Nuevo Leon. [IP/EC]

Ariocarpus trigonus (Web.) Sch.

A **v. elongatus** (S-D) Bkbg. with longer tubercles has been described. [IP/GC]

DISTRIBUTION: Mexico, Nuevo Leon.

Astrophytum asterias (Zucc.) Lem.

A fairly constant plant in cultivation; noticeable raised ribs usually indicate a hybrid with **A. capricorne**. [CS/EC]

DISTRIBUTION: NE Mexico and S Texas.

Astrophytum capricorne (Dietr.) B. & R.

Varies in the amount of flock on the surface and in the number and length of the twisted brown spines. Some forms may lack the red centre to the fl or the flock may be partly or wholly missing. [CS/PM]

DISTRIBUTION: N Mexico.

Astrophytum capricorne v. niveum (Kays.) Ok.

Included here as arguably the most beautiful of all of the forms to be found in the genus **Astrophytum**. [K161/IP/K]

DISTRIBUTION: N Mexico.

OTHER NAMES: *Astrophytum niveum*

Astrophytum coahuilense (Moell.) Kays.

Distinguished from the superficially similar **A. myriostigma** by its softer, dirtier flock and the red centre to the large flower. [CS/PM]

DISTRIBUTION: Mexico, Coahuila.

Astrophytum myriostigma Lem.

Many varieties/forms described for this species including the columnar **v. columnare** (Sch.) Tsuda, the four ribbed **v. quadricostatum** (Moell.) Baum and the flock-less **v. nudum** (R. Mey.) Bkbg. [CS/PM]

DISTRIBUTION: C to N highland areas of Mexico.

OTHER NAMES: Varieties may all have been referred to as full species at one time or another.

Astrophytum ornatum (DC.) Web.

Not illustrated here is the **v. mirbelii** (Lem.) Ok. with golden spines and more flock, and the **f. glabrescens** (Web.) Bkbg., dark green with little or no flock. [CS/GC]

DISTRIBUTION: Mexico, Hidalgo to Queretaro.

Astrophytum senile Fric

In **v. aureum** (Moell.) the young spines are pale yellow. [CS/EC]

DISTRIBUTION: N Mexico.

Aztekium ritteri (Boed.) Boed.

A very constant species now frequently grown from seed. [1P/F]

DISTRIBUTION: Mexico, Nuevo Leon.

Blossfeldia liliputana   Werd.

Tends to be difficult to grow on its own roots and is usually found as a grafted plant in collections. [H]

DISTRIBUTION: N Argentina and S Bolivia.

OTHER NAMES: *B. atroviridis, B. campaniflora, B. fechseri, B. minima, B. pedicellata.*

Copiapoa boliviana   (Pfeiff.) Ritt.

[KK/IP/GC]

DISTRIBUTION: Chile, hills in the area around Antofagasta.

OTHER NAMES: *Copiapoa atacamensis.*

Copiapoa bridgesii   (Pfeiff.) Bkbg.

Closely related to **C. marginata**. [PM261/H]

DISTRIBUTION: Chile, hills N of Chanaral Airfield.

Copiapoa calderana   Ritt.

Plants in habitat develop a greyish bloom not found on seed-grown plants in cultivation. [H]

DISTRIBUTION: Chile, coast N of Caldera.

OTHER NAMES: *C. lembckei.*

Copiapoa cinerascens   (S-D) B. & R.

Extremely variable in habitat where it exists in numerous closely spaced mini-populations differing in the number and size of heads, colour of epidermis and spine, length, thickness, number and colour. [PM210/H]

DISTRIBUTION: Chile, around Chanaral.

OTHER NAMES: *C. applanata.*

Copiapoa cinerea   (Phil.) B. & R.

The greyish-white bloom on the habitat plant illustrated under this species does not develop on seed-grown plants in cultivation. [PM198/H]

DISTRIBUTION: Chile, around Taltal.

OTHER NAMES: *C. tenebrosa.*

Copiapoa cinerea v. columna-alba (Ritt.) Bkbg.

Occurs as two closely adjacent populations in habitat differing markedly in spine length and colour and in body height. [KK622/IP/GC]

DISTRIBUTION: Chile, mainly in Pan de Azucar National Park, N of Taltal.

OTHER NAMES: *C. columna-alba* & *C. melanohystrix.*

Copiapoa cinerea v. haseltoniana (Bkbg.) N.P. Taylor

In habitat very variable in all of its characters except in its flowers. [PM202/H]

DISTRIBUTION: Chile, around Paposo.

OTHER NAMES: *C. haseltoniana, C. gigantea, C. cinerea v. gigantea* & *C. eremophila.*

Copiapoa dealbata   Ritt.

Forms huge multiheaded mounds in habitat. [H]

DISTRIBUTION: Chile, Carrizal Bajo.

OTHER NAMES: *C. carrizalensis* & *C. cinerea v. dealbata.*

Copiapoa desertorum   Ritt.

Clumping, stems to 50 cm high by 6−10 cm. Fl yellow. [RMF153/IP/F]

DISTRIBUTION: Chile, E of Cifuncho. **Copiapoa hornilloensis** Ritt. from the Cerro Hornillo, N of Esmeralda, may only be a variety of this species.

Copiapoa dura   Ritt.

Extremely variable in habitat, each population with its own distinctive set of characters. [PM230/H]

DISTRIBUTION: N Chile, around Totoral and Carrizal Bajo.

OTHER NAMES: *C. alticostata, C. cuprea.*

Copiapoa echinata   Ritt.

v. borealis Ritt. from Monte Amargo is a very distinctive plant with much stouter spination. [PM220/H]

DISTRIBUTION: Chile, N and S of Carrizal Bajo.

OTHER NAMES: **v. borealis**: *C. totoralensis.*

Copiapoa esmeraldana Ritt.

Plants in habitat are virtually buried and very difficult to find; however cultivated plants quickly become cylindrical and rather elongated. [CS/PM]

DISTRIBUTION: Chile, Esmeralda above coastal cliffs where they are much eaten by vicunas.

Copiapoa fiedlerana (Sch.) Bkbg.
[RMF183/IP/F]
DISTRIBUTION: Chile, Huasco.

OTHER NAMES: *C. pepiniana v. fiedleriana.*

Copiapoa grandiflora Ritt.

Clumping. [RMF164/IP/F]
DISTRIBUTION: Chile, Esmeralda.

Copiapoa humilis (Phil.) Hutch.

One of the most variable of all cacti in its body and spine characters. [IP/GC]

DISTRIBUTION: Coast of N Chile, e.g. Paposo.

OTHER NAMES: *C. longispina, C. paposoensis.*

Copiapoa hypogaea Ritt.

Very variable in spination, the **v. barquitensis** Ritt. from Barquito having longer and thinner spines. [CS/GC]

DISTRIBUTION: Chile, coastal mountains N of Chanaral.

OTHER NAMES: *C. mollicula, C. montana, C. rarissima.*
v. barquitensis: '*C. barquitensis*'.

Copiapoa krainziana Ritt.

In habitat seems to form hybrid swarms with **C. cinerea**. Some of these may be seen in cultivation labelled **C. krainziana** but these have hard spines rather than the soft almost hair-like spines typical of the latter species. [PM206/H]

DISTRIBUTION: Chile, coastal mountains N of Taltal.

OTHER NAMES: *C. scopulina.*

Copiapoa lauii Diers

The smallest of the copiapoas with heads less than 2 cm in diameter. Flowers more freely on its own roots. [RMF162/IP/F]

DISTRIBUTION: Chile, Esmeralda.

Copiapoa longistaminea Ritt.

Forms large, handsome, many-headed mounds in habitat. [H]

DISTRIBUTION: Chile, Esmeralda.

Copiapoa marginata (S-D) B. & R.

Distinctive for its long, dense, heavy spination; closely related to **C. bridgesii**. [PM219/H]

DISTRIBUTION: Chile, SW of Caldera, Morro Copiapo.

OTHER NAMES: *C. streptocaulon.*

Copiapoa megarhiza B. & R.

Rarely seen in cultivation. [RMF129/IP/F]

DISTRIBUTION: Chile, Copiapo valley.

OTHER NAMES: *C. megarhiza v. macrorhiza* Ritt.

Copiapoa olivana Ritt.

Globular to 7 cm broad. [RMF150/IP/F]

DISTRIBUTION: Chile, N of Taltal.

Copiapoa pendulina Ritt.

A very variable species. [H]

DISTRIBUTION: Chile, around Coquimbo and S to Frai Jorge and E to La Serena.

OTHER NAMES: *C. coquimbana* & *v. wagenknechtii, C. pseudocoquimbana* & vars., *C. serenana.*

Copiapoa rupestris Ritt.

Fl yellow. The plant named as **C. rubriflora** Ritt. occurs nearby and is probably just a red-flowered variant. [RMF 154/IP/F]

DISTRIBUTION: Chile, Cifuncho.

Copiapoa serpentisulcata Ritt.

A very distinctive and attractive plant; unhappily it is very rare in cultivation. Fl yellow. [PM212/H]

DISTRIBUTION: Chile, N of Chanaral.

Copiapoa solaris (Ritt.) Ritt.

A spectacularly spined species difficult in cultivation. Has been heavily collected from its narrow habitat. Fl yellow. [RMF43/IP/F]

DISTRIBUTION: Chile, El Cobre.

OTHER NAMES: *C. ferox, Pilocopiapoa solaris*.

Copiapoa tenuissima Ritt.

Another member of the **C. humilis** complex but very distinctive in its spination. [RMF318/IP/F]

DISTRIBUTION: Chile, coastal mountains S of Antofagasta.

Copiapoa tocopillana Ritt.

[RMF312/IP/F]

DISTRIBUTION: Chile, N of Tocopilla and S towards Antofagasta, the most northerly member of the genus.

Copiapoa vallenarensis Ritt.

Closely related to **C. pendulina** and **C. fiedleriana**. [H]

DISTRIBUTION: Chile, Vallenar to near Huasco.

Copiapoa variispinata Ritt.
[RMF53/IP/F]
DISTRIBUTION: Chile, N of Paposo.

Coryphantha andreae Purpus & Boed.
Fl yellow, 5–6 cm across. [CS/W]
DISTRIBUTION: Mexico, Vera Cruz.

Coryphantha bergeriana Boed.
Fl yellow, 7 cm across. [K102/IP/K]
DISTRIBUTION: Mexico, Nuevo Leon.

Coryphantha bernalensis Bremer.
Body to 10 cm high and 9 cm across. Fl 6 cm across.
DISTRIBUTION: Mexico, Queretaro, N of Bernal on the road to Toliman.

Coryphantha bumamma
(Ehrenbg.) B. & R.
Fl yellow, 5–6 cm across. [CS/W]
DISTRIBUTION: Mexico, Morelos and Guerrero States.

Coryphantha calipensis H. Bravo
[PM12/HS/PM]
DISTRIBUTION: Mexico, Puebla, near Calipan.

Coryphantha clavata (Scheidw.) Bkbg.

Fl yellow, 4 cm broad. **v. radicantissima** is more globular with a fl only 2.5 cm across. [K18/IP/K]

DISTRIBUTION: Mexico Hidalgo and just spreading into the adjacent states of Queretaro and Mexico DF.

OTHER NAMES: *C. raphidacantha.* Very similar but with more than one csp is **C. clava** (Pfeiff.) Lem. from Hidalgo.

Coryphantha compacta (Englm.) B. & R.
[K237/IP/K]

DISTRIBUTION: Mexico, Chihuahua, Cosihuiriachi.

Coryphantha connivens B. & R.

Fl yellow to 7 cm across. [CS/PM]

DISTRIBUTION: Mexico, near the capital city.

Coryphantha cornifera (DC) Lem.

Fl to 5 cm across, lemon yellow. [K18/IP/K]

DISTRIBUTION: Mexico, Hidalgo State around Ixmiquilpan.

Coryphantha delaetiana (Quehl) Berg.

Fl yellow plant eventually forming mats in habitat. [K215/IP/K]

DISTRIBUTION: Mexico, Coahuila State.

Coryphantha durangensis (Rge.) B. & R.
[CS/PM]

DISTRIBUTION: Mexico, Durango State.

Coryphantha echinus (Englm.) B. & R.
Fl yellow. [K231/IP/K]
DISTRIBUTION: USA, W Texas; N Mexico, Coahuila State.
OTHER NAMES: *C. cornifera v. echinus.*

Coryphantha elephantidens (Lem.) Lem.
[CS/PM]
DISTRIBUTION: Mexico, Michoacan State.

Coryphantha erecta (Lem.) Lem.
Fl up to 7.5 cm across, light yellow. [CS/PM]
DISTRIBUTION: Mexico, Hidalgo.

Coryphantha gladiispina (Boed.) Berg.
Fl yellow. [K127/IP/K]
DISTRIBUTION: Mexico, Coahuila, Parras.

Coryphantha gracilis Bremer & Lau
Solitary, occasionally sprouting to form small clumps.
Stems 8 cm high by 3.5–4 cm; rsp 12–18; csp 0. Fl
4–5 cm wide, pale yellow to cream. [L645/IP/K]
DISTRIBUTION: Mexico, Chihuahua, Delayo on hills E of
Rancho El Toro.

Coryphantha greenwoodii H. Bravo
Fl 5 cm broad, yellow with a fine brownish stripe.
Populations adjacent to the original show greater variation
in radial spine count, almost resembling a different species.
[K15/IP/K]
DISTRIBUTION: Mexico, Vera Cruz, Acultzingo Valley.

Coryphantha guerkeana (Boed.) B. & R.

Fl white. [K30/IP/K]

DISTRIBUTION: Mexico, near the city of Durango.

Coryphantha jalpanensis Buchenau

Fl pale yellow-green up to 1.2 cm across. [CS/W]

DISTRIBUTION: Mexico, Queretaro, hills around Jalpan.

Coryphantha lauii Bremer

Solitary, globose to elongate, 5 cm across; rsp 18–20, 9–13 mm long; csp 1, to 16 mm long. Fl 4.5 cm across, light yellow. [CS/W]

DISTRIBUTION: Mexico, Coahuila, 30 miles N of El Marte, 2000–2500 m.

Coryphantha longicornis Boed.

Fl yellow. [CS/W]

DISTRIBUTION: Mexico, N Durango.

OTHER NAMES: *C. grandis.*

Coryphantha macromeris Englm.

The plant illustrated is **v. runyonii** B. & R. which has fewer rsp and a smaller fl than the type. [CS/PM]

DISTRIBUTION: From W Texas and New Mexico in the N to Zacatecas State, Mexico in the S; **v. runyonii** Texas, Rio Grande.

OTHER NAMES: *Lepidocoryphantha macromeris.* **v. runyonii**: *L. runyonii.*

Coryphantha maiz-tablasensis Bkbg.

Fl yellowish. [K261/IP/K]

DISTRIBUTION: Mexico, San Luis Potosi, Ciudad Maiz.

Coryphantha melleospina Bravo
Distinctive but probably conspecific with **C. retusa.**
[K148–1/IP/K]

DISTRIBUTION: Mexico, Oaxaca, Huajuapan de Leon.

Coryphantha pallida B. & R.
Fl light yellow, 5–7 cm broad. [CS/W]

DISTRIBUTION: Mexico, Puebla, Tehuacan.

Coryphantha palmeri B. & R.
An extremely variable species, each population within its vast range differing in body size and spination to the extent that there is probably no such thing as a 'typical' plant. [IP/K]

DISTRIBUTION: Mexico: Durango, Zacatecas, Coahuila and San Luis Potosi States.

Coryphantha poselgeriana
(Dietr.) B. & R.
[CS/PM]

DISTRIBUTION: Mexico, Coahuila, nr. Saltillo.
OTHER NAMES: *C. kieferiana.*

Coryphantha poselgeriana v. valida
(Purpus) Heinr.
[CS/PM]

DISTRIBUTION: As for the species.

Coryphantha potosiana
(Jac.) Glass & Foster
[IP/K]

DISTRIBUTION: Mexico, San Luis Potosi.

Coryphantha pseudoechinus Boed.
Flower pink, 3 cm across. [CS/PM]
DISTRIBUTION: Mexico, Sierra de la Paila.
OTHER NAMES: *C. pusilliflora.*

Coryphantha pseudonickelsae Bkbg.
Fl 3.5 cm wide, pale yellow. [K160/IP/K]
DISTRIBUTION: Mexico, Durango State.

Coryphantha pulleineana (Bkbg.) Glass
[CS/PM]
DISTRIBUTION: Mexico, San Luis Potosi, near Matehuala.
OTHER NAMES: *Neolloydia pulleineana.*

Coryphantha pycnacantha (Mart.) Lem.
Flowers 4–5 cm broad, lemon-yellow. [K13/IP/K]
DISTRIBUTION: Mexico, Oaxaca State.

Coryphantha radians (DC) B. & R.
Fl lemon-yellow to over 7 cm broad. [K255/IP/K]
DISTRIBUTION: Central Mexico, Hidalgo State etc.
OTHER NAMES: *?C. pectinata, C. pseudoradians.*

Coryphantha ramillosa Cut.
Fl fairly large, more or less pink. [K231/IP/K]
DISTRIBUTION: Texas.

Coryphantha recurvata (Englm.) B. & R.

Fl lemon-yellow, notoriously reluctant to fl in cultivation. [K202/IP/K]

DISTRIBUTION: Arizona to N Sonora, Mexico.

Coryphantha reduncispina Boed.

Fl yellow with a red throat, 4–5 cm broad. The seedling illustrated is only just developing its 3 downwards pointing csp. [DHS]

DISTRIBUTION: Mexico, Tamaulipas.

Coryphantha retusa (Pfeiff.) B. & R.

[IP/K]

DISTRIBUTION: Mexico, Oaxaca State.

Coryphantha salm-dyckiana (Scheer) B. & R.

[K42/IP/K]

DISTRIBUTION: Mexico, Chihuahua State.

Coryphantha scheeri (Kuntze) Benson

Fl yellow, filaments pink. [K213/IP/K]

DISTRIBUTION: S Arizona to N Mexico.

OTHER NAMES: *Coryphantha muehlenpfordtii.*

Coryphantha scolymoides (Scheidw.) Berg.

Fl over 5 cm broad, yellow with a red throat. [K46/IP/K]

DISTRIBUTION: N Mexico.

Coryphantha speciosa Boed.

Flowers 6 cm across, golden yellow with a dark centre.
[K167/IP/K]

DISTRIBUTION: Mexico, Coahula State W of Monclova.

Coryphantha sulcata (Englm.) B. & R.

Clumping, heads to 12 cm across; rsp 12–14; csp 0 at first,
(as in the young plant illustrated) then several, one stouter,
curved outwards. Fl to over 5 cm wide, yellow with red
centre. [CS/PM]

DISTRIBUTION: S Texas.

Coryphantha sulcolanata (Lem.) Lem.
[K247/IP/K]

DISTRIBUTION: Mexico, Hidalgo, Mineral del Monte.

Coryphantha villarensis Bkbg.
Fl 5 cm across, light yellow. [CS/W]
DISTRIBUTION: Mexico, San Luis Potosi.

Coryphantha voghtherriana
Werd. & Boed.
[CS/PM]
DISTRIBUTION: Mexico, San Luis Potosi.

Coryphantha werdermannii Boed.
Fl with a red throat. [K230/IP/K]
DISTRIBUTION: Mexico, Sierra de la Paila.

Cumarinia odorata (Boed.) Buxb.
[CS]

DISTRIBUTION: Mexico, Tamaulipas and San Luis Potosi States.

OTHER NAMES: *Neolloydia odorata*

Denmoza rhodacantha
(Salm-Syck) B. & R.

Solitary, becoming slightly columnar to 30 cm across. Fl 7 cm long. [CS/PM]

DISTRIBUTION: Argentina, widespread in the mountains.

OTHER NAMES: *D. erythrocephala.*

Discocactus bahiensis B. & R.

Solitary, to 6 cm broad. Fl to 5 cm long, cream. [CS/GC]

DISTRIBUTION: Brazil, Bahia.

Discocactus hartmannii (Sch.) B. & R.

Broadly spherical, glossy. Fl white. [IP/DE Herdt Coll.]

DISTRIBUTION: Paraguay, Paraguari and Brazil, S Mato Grosso.

OTHER NAMES: *D. magnimammus, D. mamillosus, D. patulifolius.*

Discocactus heptacanthus
(Rodr.) B. & R.

Solitary, depressed spherical, to 16 cm across, exceedingly variable in spination and rib formation. Fl white. [CS/GC]

DISTRIBUTION: Brazil to Bolivia.

OTHER NAMES: *D. boliviensis, D. cangaensis, D. catingicola, D. cephaliaciculosus, D. diersianus, D. estevesii, D. flavispinus, D. goianus, D. lindaianus, D. melanochlorus, D. nigrisaetosus, D. paranaensis, D. rapirhizus, D. semi-campaniflorus, D. squamibaccatus, D. subterraneo-proliferans.*

Discocactus horstii Buin. & Bred.

Solitary, 4.5 cm across. Fl 6 cm wide, white. [EC]

DISTRIBUTION: Brazil, Grao Mogol.

OTHER NAMES: *D. woutersianus.*

Discocactus insignis Pfeiff.

Fl off-white. [CS/GC]

DISTRIBUTION: Brazil, Minas Geraes, Grao Mogol.

Discocactus placentiformis (Lem.) Sch.

Broadly flattened. Fl white [H]

DISTRIBUTION: Brazil, Minas Geraes and N Bahia.

OTHER NAMES: *D. alteolens, D. latispinus, D. linkii, D. multicolorispinus, D. pugionacanthus, D. pulvinicapitatus, D. subviridigriseus.*

Discocactus zehntneri B. & R.

Solitary or clustering, densely covered in spines. Fl only 3 cm long, white. [CS/GC]

DISTRIBUTION: Brazil, N Bahia,

OTHER NAMES: *D. albispinus, D. araneispinus, D. boomianus.*

Echinocactus grusonii Hildm.

A white-spined form of this species is now in cultivation. [CS/PM]

DISTRIBUTION: Mexico, San Luis Potosi to Hidalgo States.

Echinocactus horizonthalonius Lem.

An extremely variable plant in habitat, probably related to its enormous range with big variations in height of the plant, spine length and flexibility and spine count. Fl pink. **v. nicholii** L. Benson; columnar, to 50 cm high, spines fewer (Arizona Desert). [H]

DISTRIBUTION: Mexico State to S States of the USA, Chihuahuan Desert.

Echinocactus platyacanthus Link & Otto

Solitary, to 3 m high by 1 m. Fl yellow. Adult plants in the wild look quite unlike the seedling illustrated. [PM46/HS/PM]

DISTRIBUTION: Over a wide area of C and NC Mexico.

OTHER NAMES: *E. grandis, E. ingens, E. palmeri, E. visnaga.*

Echinocactus polycephalus Englm. & Big.

Spherical to cylindric, to 70 cm high, forming large groups of heads. Fl yellow. **v. xeranthemoides** Coulter (illus.); solitary or sparingly clumping, otherwise similar in appearance (Navajoan Desert). [H]

DISTRIBUTION: USA, Mojavian Desert.

OTHER NAMES: **v. xeranthemoides**: *E. xeranthemoides.*

Echinocactus texensis Hopff.

The plant shown is fairly typical, weaker or stronger-spined forms occur. Grows up to 15 cm high by 30 cm, flower 6 cm across. [HS/PM]

DISTRIBUTION: Texas and SE New Mexico to NE Mexico.

OTHER NAMES: *Homalocephala texensis.*

Echinocereus adustus Englm.

A few plants have a single, long, black central spine. [CS/PM]

DISTRIBUTION: Mexico, Chihuahua.

OTHER NAMES: *Echinocereus radians Englm.*

Echinocereus adustus v. schwarzii (Lau) N.P. Taylor

Csp vary from 1 to 5, flowers are generally larger than those of the type. [L1305/CS/PM]

DISTRIBUTION: Mexico, Durango.

OTHER NAMES: *E. schwarzii.*

Echinocereus barthelowanus B. & R.

A clumping plant with 8–10 ribs and a purple fl 5–7 cm across, though these are rarely seen in cultivation. [IP/ERC]

DISTRIBUTION: Mexico, Baja California, Santa Maria Bay.

Echinocereus berlandieri (Eng.) Hort. F.A. Haage

Stems creeping. 1.5–5 cm thick. Fl with a dark throat. [IP/ERC]

DISTRIBUTION: S Texas; NE Mexico, Nuevo Leon and Tamaulipas.

OTHER NAMES: *E. blanckii v. berlandieri.*

Echinocereus brandegeei (Coulter) Sch.

A plant very easily recognized by its sword-like central spines. Fl pink to pale purple with a bright crimson throat but seldom seen in cultivation. [CS/PM]

DISTRIBUTION: Mexico, Baja California and neighbouring islands.

Echinocereus bristolii W.T. Marsh

Solitary or sparingly branched, to 20 cm long by 5 cm; rsp c. 20. Fl to 11 cm long and 13 cm across, light magenta with darker midstripes. [IP/ERC]

DISTRIBUTION: Mexico, Sonora, Soyopa.

Echinocereus bristolii
v. pseudopectinatus N.P. Taylor

Update 1990: now a good species **E. pseudopectinatus** (N.P. Taylor) N.P. Taylor. Solitary, rsp 12–15. [L609/CS/PM]

DISTRIBUTION: Mexico, NE Sonora; SE Arizona.

OTHER NAMES: *E. pectinatus v. minor*. This variety was distributed for some years as the true **E. bristolii**.

Echinocereus chisoensis W.T. Marsh

Solitary. Fl 5 cm across, pinkish magenta, throat white. **v. fobeanus** (Oehme) N.P. Taylor (illus.); clumping, spines weaker. Fl 7–12 cm across. Plants become quickly deformed and ugly with age (Mexico, borders of SW Coahuila and E Durango). [HK303/CS/PM]

DISTRIBUTION: Texas, Chisos Mountains, Big Bend region.

OTHER NAMES: *E. reichenbachii v. chisoensis*. **v. fob.**: *E. fobeanus*.

Echinocereus chloranthus
(Englm.) Hort. F.A. Haage

Clumping, 20 cm high by 5–7.5 cm; csp 3–6. Fl never opens fully, unscented. **v. neocapillus** resembles **v. chloranthus** when mature. **v. cylindricus** (Englm.) N.P. Taylor (illus.); distinguished from **v. chloranthus** by csp. 0(–3). [HS/PM]

DISTRIBUTION: All three S New Mexico and W Texas.

OTHER NAMES: *E. viridiflorus v. chloranthus*. **v. cylindricus**: *E. viridiflorus v. cylindricus*.

Echinocereus chloranthus v. russanthus
(Wenig.) Lamb ex G. Rowley

A clumping variety more spiny than **v. chloranthus** and with a reddish fl. [L1076/CS/PM]

DISTRIBUTION: Mexico, Chihuahua and W Texas.

OTHER NAMES: '*E. finnii*', *E. russanthus*.

Echinocereus cinerascens (DC) Lem.

A very variable, clumping plant stems 4–10 cm broad, ribs 6–12, glassy spines; csp equal to or less than the stem diameter. Fl purple with a lighter throat, tends to be little seen in cultivation. **v. ehrenbergii** (Pfeiff.) H. Bravo-H. has fewer ribs and narrower stems whose diameter is exceeded by the csp. [H]

DISTRIBUTION: C Mexico.

OTHER NAMES: **v. ehrenbergii**: *E. ehrenbergii*.

Echinocereus engelmannii (illus. above) (Parry ex Englm.) Lem.

A very variable species split into a number of varieties; **v. acicularis, v. munzii, v. nicholii, v. armatus, v. chrysocentrus, v. howei, v. variegatus** (illus. above) **&. v. purpureus**. These differ mainly in details of spination. [H]

DISTRIBUTION: NW Mexico and SW USA.

Echinocereus engelmannii v. nicholii Benson

Update 1990: now a good species **E. nicholii** (Benson) Parfitt. The most distinctive segregate within the **engelmannii** complex, with its characteristic long, dense, straw-coloured spination and small, very pale-pink flower. [HS/PM]

DISTRIBUTION: Mexico, NW Sonora State to USA, SC Arizona.

Echinocereus enneacanthus Englm.

Stems to 15 cm broad, csp to 8 cm long. **v. brevispinus** has much slimmer stems to 5 cm, and shorter csp to 5 cm. [CS/PM]

DISTRIBUTION: N Mexico and adjacent areas of the USA.

OTHER NAMES: *E. dubius, E. enneacanthus, v. dubius, E. merkeri, E. sarissophorus.* **v. brevispinus**: *E. enneacanthus.*

Echinocereus fendleri (Englm.) Ruempler [HS/PM]

DISTRIBUTION: C and E Arizona, S Colorado, New Mexico, W Texas and Mexico in adjacent Chihuahua State.

Echinocereus fendleri v. bonkerae (Thornber & Bonker) Benson [H]

DISTRIBUTION: C and SE Arizona.

OTHER NAMES: *E. bonkerae* & *E. fasciculatus v. bonkerae.*

Echinocereus fendleri v. boyce-thompsonii (Orcutt) Benson

[H]

DISTRIBUTION: C Arizona

OTHER NAMES: *E. boyce-thompsonii, E. fasciculatus v. boyce-thompsonii.*

Echinocereus fendleri v. fasciculatus (Englm. ex B.D. Jackson) N.P. Taylor

[H]

DISTRIBUTION: W and C Arizona and SW New Mexico; Mexico, N and C Sonora State.

OTHER NAMES: *E. fasciculatus, E. fendleri v. robustus.*

Echinocereus fendleri v. kuenzleri (Castetter et al) Benson

Fl as in the species [HK1267/HS/PM]

DISTRIBUTION: S New Mexico.

OTHER NAMES: *E. hempelii, E. kuenzleri.*

Echinocereus fendleri v. ledingii (Peebles) N.P. Taylor

Easily recognized by its long, down-curved central spine, the small fl are not often seen in cultivation. Still considered by many to be a distinct species. [HS/PM]

DISTRIBUTION: Mountains, SE Arizona.

OTHER NAMES: *E. ledingii.*

Echinocereus fendleri v. rectispinus (Peebles) Benson

[H]

DISTRIBUTION: SE Arizona, SW New Mexico, W Texas and neighbouring parts of Sonora, Mexico.

OTHER NAMES: *E. rectispinus.*

Echinocereus ferreirianus H. Gates

Clustering, stems to 40 cm high by 8 cm; csp mostly 4. Fl with pale green to whitish stigmas. [CS/PM]

DISTRIBUTION: Mexico, N Baja California.

Echinocereus ferreirianus v. lindsayi (Meyran) N.P. Taylor

Solitary, to 13 cm high by 10 cm; much more strongly spined, csp 4−7. Stigma deep green. [ERC]

DISTRIBUTION: Mexico, Baja California, between Catavina and Laguna Chapala.

OTHER NAMES: *E. lindsayi.*

Echinocereus freudenbergeri Frank

A difficult species to fl in cultivation. Fl similar to that of **E. nivosus.** [CS/PM]

DISTRIBUTION: Mexico, S Coahuila.

OTHER NAMES: *E. delaetii v. freudenbergeri.*

Echinocereus grandis B. & R.

Fl can be white, pale yellow or pale pink. [CS/PM]

DISTRIBUTION: Islands in the Gulf of California.

Echinocereus knippelianus Liebner

Whereas the type is normally single-headed in habitat (but not always in cultivation), the **v. kruegeri** Glass & Foster is normally caespitose with whitish fl arising near the stem apex. [CS/PM]

DISTRIBUTION: Mexico, SE Coahuila and S Nuevo Leon.

OTHER NAMES: **v. kruegeri:** *E. knippelianus v. reyesii.*

Echinocereus lauii Frank

[L780/CS/PM]

DISTRIBUTION: Mexico, E Sonora near Yecora.

Echinocereus leucanthus N.P. Taylor

Stem 3−6 mm thick. Fl white, 4 cm broad. [SB435/CS/C]

DISTRIBUTION: Mexico, S Sonora and N Sinaloa, known from only a handful of localities.

OTHER NAMES: *Wilcoxia albiflora.*

E. poselgeri Lem. from S Texas, E. Coahuila, N Nuevo Leon and Tamaulipas is very similar but has thicker stems and a pink fl 7 cm across; *Wilcoxia poselg.*

Echinocereus longisetus (Englm.) Lem.

Fl purplish-pink with a white throat, 6 cm across. [IP/K]

DISTRIBUTION: Mexico, Coahuila State.

Echinocereus longisetus v. delaetii
(Guerke) N.P. Taylor

Easily recognized by its long, fine, hair-like spines. Its fl are usually only seen on fairly old plants in cultivation. [CS/PM]

DISTRIBUTION: Mexico, Coahuila.

OTHER NAMES: *E. delaetii.*

Echinocereus maritimus
(M.E. Jones) Sch.

Fl rarely produced in cultivation in the UK, 3–6 cm long, greenish-yellow in colour. **v. hancockii** (Dawson) N.P. Taylor is a more stoutly built plant with more and longer spines. [CS/PM]

DISTRIBUTION: Mexico, Baja California, W Coast and adjacent sand-dunes.

OTHER NAMES: **v. hancockii**; *E. hancockii.*

Echinocereus nivosus Glass & Foster

This species varies somewhat in the density of the spination depending upon which particular collection it comes from. It tends to be a shy flowerer in cultivation. [CS/P]

DISTRIBUTION: Mexico, SE Coahuila.

OTHER NAMES: *E. albatus, E. longisetus v. albatus.*

Echinocereus palmeri B. & R.

Develops a characteristic large taproot. [IP/P]

DISTRIBUTION: Mexico, Chihuahua State.

Echinocereus pamanesiorum Lau

Becomes quite large with stems up to 35 cm high by 8 cm. Small plants flower freely in cultivation. [L1247/CS/PM]

DISTRIBUTION: Mexico, W Zacatecas, W Rio Huaynamota Valley.

Echinocereus papillosus
A. Linke ex Ruempler

The **v. angusticeps** (Clover) W.T. Marsh (illus.) is more common in collections with stems up to 3 cm in diameter. The type has broader (3–5 cm) and longer stems and does not clump as readily. [CS/P]

DISTRIBUTION: Lowland areas of S Texas and adjacent Mexico.

OTHER NAMES: **v. angusticeps**: *E. angusticeps.*

Echinocereus parkeri N.P. Taylor

Clumping, stems to 6 cm across. Fl to 6 cm across, magenta to deep pink, throat white. **v. gonzalezii** N.P. Taylor (illus.); stems slimmer, more densely spiny (SE Nuevo Leon, SW Tamaulipas and N San Luis Potosi). [L1375/HS/PM]

DISTRIBUTION: Mexico, SE Nuevo Leon.

Echinocereus pectinatus
(Scheidw.) Englm.

Rsp 22–30, not interlaced. Fl are pinkish to lavender in colour with a maroon to white throat. **v. wenigeri** Benson, endemic to Texas, has fewer rsp (14–20). [HK1129/HS/GC]

DISTRIBUTION: N Mexico over a huge range northwards into S Texas.

Echinocereus pectinatus v. dasyacanthus
(Englm.) N.P. Taylor

Rsp 15–25, interlaced. Fl usually yellow but sometimes whitish, orange, pink or purplish. [HK1114/HS/GC]

DISTRIBUTION: N Mexico; Arizona, New Mexico and Texas.

OTHER NAMES: *E. dasyacanthus, E pectinatus v. neomexicanus* and *E. pectinatus v. ctenoides.*

Echinocereus pensilis
(K. Brandegee) Purpus

Stems slim, pendant, 1–4 m long, 2–5 cm broad; hangs from rocks. [IP/PM]

DISTRIBUTION: Mexico, Baja California, Cape region.

OTHER NAMES: *Morangaya pensilis.*

Echinocereus pentalophus (DC) Lem.

Ribs 4–5, spines 3–7; **v. leonensis** (Mathsson) N.P. Taylor from NE Mexico has 6–8 ribs and up to 9 spines per areole. Fl similar to the species. [PM32/HS/PM]

DISTRIBUTION: C to NE Mexico, S Texas.

OTHER NAMES: *E. procumbens, E. pentalophus v. procumbens, E. tulensis. E. berlandieri* sensu Weniger. **v. leonensis**: *E. leonensis.*

Echinocereus polyacanthus   Englm.

Stems 5–100. Fl 4–7 cm long, 3–4 cm across, free-flowering in cultivation. **v. pacificus** (Englm.) N.P. Taylor; up to 400 stems per clump. Fl 3–5 cm long, 2–3 cm wide (N Baja California). [CS/PM].

DISTRIBUTION: NW Mexico; SW USA.

OTHER NAMES: *E. durangensis.* **v. pacificus**: *E. pacificus.*

Echinocereus polyacanthus v. densus (Regel) N.P. Taylor

Characterized by its particularly large fl which is up to 8 cm in diameter and 14 cm in length, sometimes slightly zygomorphic. [HS/PM]

DISTRIBUTION: N, C and W Mexico.

OTHER NAMES: *E. acifer, E. leeanus.*

Echinocereus primolanatus F. Schwarz ex N.P. Taylor

Fl 10.5 cm in diameter, bright pink with a slightly darker mid-stripe. [Holotype/IP/ERC]

DISTRIBUTION: Mexico, S Coahuila, S edge of Sierra de la Paila.

Echinocereus pulchellus   (Mart.) Sch.

Stem 2.5–5 cm in diameter, spines usually short, around 4 mm in length. [CS/PM]

DISTRIBUTION: Mexico: N Oaxaca, Puebla, Hidalgo and SE Queretaro States.

Echinocereus pulchellus v. amoenus (Dietr.) Sch.

Stem 3–7.5 cm broad, spines usually around 6 mm long. [CS/PM]

DISTRIBUTION: Mexico: SW San Luis Potosi and S Nuevo Leon States.

OTHER NAMES: *E. amoenus.*

Echinocereus pulchellus v. weinbergii (Wgt.) N.P. Taylor

Stem 6–13 cm broad, spines obvious, up to 10 mm long. [CS/PM]

DISTRIBUTION: Mexico, W Zacatecas.

OTHER NAMES: *E. weinbergii.*

Echinocereus rayonesensis N.P. Taylor
[CS/PM]

DISTRIBUTION: Mexico, Nuevo Leon, Valley of Rayones.

OTHER NAMES: *E. longisetus* sensu Werd.

Echinocereus reichenbachii
(Terscheck ex Walp.) Hort. F.A. Haage

Csp always absent; rsp 18–30 or more up to 6 mm long, varying from brown to white. v. **armatus** (Poselger) N.P. Taylor (on right): rsp up to 23, to 8 mm in length, csp almost always present, to 20 mm long, usually black. Fl often large, pink with a green throat (Nuevo Leon, Huasteca Canyon). [HS/PM]

DISTRIBUTION: Texas, Oklahoma and NE Mexico.

OTHER NAMES: *E. caespitosus*, *E. purpureus*, *E. armatus*.

Echinocereus reichenbachii v. baileyi
(Rose) N.P. Taylor

Rsp up to 14, usually up to 12 mm (exceptionally 25 mm) long; csp 1–3, up to 3 mm long rather resembling the radials. Spines brown to white. [HK1148/HS/PM]

DISTRIBUTION: S Oklahoma and neighbouring areas of Texas.

OTHER NAMES: *E. baileyi*, *E. baileyi v. albispinus*, *E. reichenbachii v. albispinus*.

Echinocereus reichenbachii v. fitchii
(B. & R.) Benson

Rsp up to 22, up to 7.5 mm in length, csp 1–7 up to 9 mm long. The spectacular pink fl with its deep crimson throat is particularly attractive. [HK1277/HS/GC]

DISTRIBUTION: S Texas and adjacent NE Mexico.

OTHER NAMES: *E. fitchii*, *E. reichenbachii v. alberti*, *E. melanocentrus*.

Echinocereus reichenbachii v. perbellus
(B. & R.) Benson

Rsp up to 16 (occasionally 20), up to 6 mm in length. Csp not always present, only 1 mm long. Fl pinkish magenta with a crimson throat. [HS/PM]

DISTRIBUTION: S Colorado, E New Mexico, N and C Texas.

OTHER NAMES: *E. perbellus*.

Echinocereus rigidissimus
(Englm.) Hort. F.A. Haage

Stem to 11 cm in diameter, rsp 15–23, 6–10 mm in length. Fl brilliant pink with a white throat, 6–9 cm broad. [HK1283/HS/PM]

DISTRIBUTION: Mexico, N Sonora; SW New Mexico and SE Arizona.

OTHER NAMES: *E. pectinatus v. rigidissimus*.

Echinocereus rigidissimus v. rubispinus
(Frank) N.P. Taylor

Stem 4–6 cm broad, rsp 30–35 up to 5 mm long. Named for the deep pink of the young spines around the apex. [L088/CS/PM]

DISTRIBUTION: Mexico, W Chihuahua, Sierra Oscura.

OTHER NAMES: *E. pectinatus v. rubispinus*, 'E. rubispinus'.

Echinocereus scheeri (S-D) Scheer

There is probably no such thing as a typical **E. scheeri**. Fl vary through pink to scarlet and orange, ribs vary from 7–10, rsp from 9–13; usually 1 but as many as 4 csp. [L1082/CS/PM]

DISTRIBUTION: Mexico: Sonora, Chihuahua and Durango States.

OTHER NAMES: *E. salm-dyckianus, E. salmianus, E. ortegae.*

Echinocereus scheeri v. gentryi
(Clover) N.P. Taylor

Usually 4 or 5-ribbed but in cultivation may have up to 7. Spines absent or up to 2 mm long, [CS/PM]

DISTRIBUTION: Mexico: E Sonora and W Chihuahua States.

OTHER NAMES: *E cucumis, E. gentryi.*

Echinocereus schmollii
(Weingart.) N.P. Taylor

Shows little variation in cultivation where its swollen root can be susceptible to overwatering. [CS/PM]

DISTRIBUTION: Mexico, SE Queretaro.

OTHER NAMES: *Wilcoxia schmollii.*

Echinocereus sciurus
(K. Brandegee) Dams

A fairly constant species in cultivation, forming clumps; has the distressing habit of flowering from the apex of the stem and blinding itself. [CS/PM]

DISTRIBUTION: Southern end of Baja California Mexico.

Echinocereus sciurus v. floresii
(Bkbg.) N.P. Taylor

Differentiated from the type by the obvious central spines and the tendency to fl below the apex. [HK1036/HS/PM]

DISTRIBUTION: Mexico, Sinaloa.

OTHER NAMES: *E. floresii.*

Echinocereus scopulorum B. & R.

Normally solitary, 10–40 cm high by 10 cm. Fl funnelform and sweetly scented, 10 cm in diameter, pink with a white throat. Often flowers from the centre blinding itself. [CS/PM].

DISTRIBUTION: Mexico, Sonora State.

OTHER NAMES: *E. pectinatus v. minor.*

Echinocereus spinigemmatus Lau

This species flowers fairly readily in cultivation on mature stems when it is instantly recognized by the extremely spiny fl buds which later form equally spiny fruits. Clumping with stems up to 30 cm long. [L1246/CS/P]

DISTRIBUTION: Mexico: W Zacatecas and NW Jalisco States.

Echinocereus stoloniferus W.T. Marsh

Clumping solely via underground stolons; stems cylindrical up to 30 cm high by 5 cm. [CS/PM]

DISTRIBUTION: Mexico, SE Sonora.

Echinocereus stoloniferus v. tayopensis (W.T. Marsh) N.P. Taylor

Clumping from the stem base and sides; stems fatter than the type to 8 cm broad and 15 cm high. [L779/CS/PM]

DISTRIBUTION: Mexico: E Sonora and W Chihuahua.

OTHER NAMES: *E. tayopensis.*

Echinocereus stramineus (Englm.) Ruempler

Forms large handsome clumps of fiercely spined stems up to 45 cm long and 8 cm in diameter near the base. Fl large to 12.5 cm across. [PM56/HS/PM]

DISTRIBUTION: SW USA and N Mexico.

OTHER NAMES: *E. enneacanthus v. stramineus.*

Echinocereus subinermis S-D ex Scheer

Forms small compact clumps of fat heads. Csp 0–1; flowers up to 13 cm broad. [CS/PM]

DISTRIBUTION: Mexico: N Sinaloa, S Sonora and SW Chihuahua States.

OTHER NAMES: *E. luteus, E. subinermis v. luteus, E. subinermis v. aculeatus.*

Echinocereus subinermis v. ochoterenae (Ortega) Unger

Noticeably spinier than the type with more cylindrical heads; csp prominent, 1–4. Fl to 6.5 cm across. [L771/CS/PM]

DISTRIBUTION: Mexico, S Sinoloa.

OTHER NAMES: *E. ochoterenae.*

Echinocereus triglochidiatus   Englm.

Stems clumping up to 30 cm long by 7.5 cm; spines 3–4 to 2.5 cm long, triangular in section. Csp 0–1. **v. paucispinus** (Englm.) W.T. Marsh is similar but spines 4–6, 3–4 cm long, not angular, more closely applied to the body. [HK1442/HS/PM]

DISTRIBUTION: New Mexico, NE Arizona and S Colorado, **v. paucispinus**: S Texas.

Echinocereus triglochidiatus v. melanacanthus   (Englm.) Benson

Forming mounds, stems 7.5(–15) cm in length by 2.5–6 cm; spines 6–14 of which 1–3 are straight, smooth csp. **'fa. inermis'** is a spineless, usually dwarf form from mountains in Utah and Colorado. [HK 1258/HS/PM]

DISTRIBUTION: As for the species.

OTHER NAMES: *E. roemeri, E. coccineus.* **'fa. inermis'**: *E. 'inermis', E. hexaedrus, E. hexaedrus v. inermis.*

Echinocereus triglochidiatus v. mojavensis   (Englm. & Big.) Benson.

Forming clumps; spines 6–10 up to 7 cm long with 1–2 csp all curving and twisted. **v. gonacanthus** (Englm. & Big.) Boissev. & Davidson, spines 6–9, csp (0–) 1 (–2) to 4.4 cm long; fl as for species (New Mexico, NE Arizona, S Colorado). [H]

DISTRIBUTION: Mojave Desert region of USA and N Mexico.

OTHER NAMES: *E. mojavensis.* **v. gonacanthus**: *E. gonacanthus.*

Echinocereus triglochidiatus v. neomexicanus   (Standley) Benson

Clumping, spines 11–22 of which 4 are csp to 4 cm long. Fl scarlet, salmon-pink or white. **v. arizonicus** (Rose ex Orcutt) Benson similar with fewer, thicker spines (Arizona). **v. gurneyi** Benson stems few, spines 8–10 including 1–2 csp to 2 cm (SW USA, NW Mexico). [HS/PM]

DISTRIBUTION: SE Arizona, S and W New Mexico, W Texas; Mexico, N Chihuahua.

OTHER NAMES: *E. rosei, E. neomexicanus.* **v. arizonicus**: *E. arizonicus.*

Echinocereus viereckii   Werd.

Stems yellowish, ribs 6–9, tuberculate; spines very thin. Fl violet-pink to 11 cm broad. Illustrated is **v. morricalii** (Riha) N.P. Taylor. Usually seen as the slim-stemmed almost spineless plant illustrated but this grades into a larger, much thicker-stemmed and prominently spined plant. [HK376/HS/PM]

DISTRIBUTION: Mexico, SW Tamaulipas and adjacent Nuevo Leon.

OTHER NAMES: **v. mor.**: *E. morricalii.*

Echinocereus viridiflorus   Englm.

Spines red, brownish, pale grey or white, radials to 4.5 mm long. **v. correllii** Benson, from a small area in Texas, has yellowish-green and off-white spines in horizontal bands, the radials up to 9 mm long. Fl open widely, lemon scented. [SB931/CS/PM]

DISTRIBUTION: From S Dakota and SE Wyoming to Texas.

OTHER NAMES: **v. correllii**: *'E. correllii '*.

**Echinocereus viridiflorus
v. davisii**   (Houghton) W.T. Marsh

A tiny plant, in the wild only 1.2–2 cm high by 0.9–1.2 cm, growing larger and eventually clumping in cultivation. [CS/PM]

DISTRIBUTION: S of Marathon, Texas.

OTHER NAMES: *E. davisii.*

Echinocereus websterianus   Lindsay

Without experience not easily distinguished from **E. grandis** except when in flower, which in the present species is only 3–4 cm in diameter and of a deeper shade of pink. [CS/PM]

DISTRIBUTION: Mexico, Gulf of California, Isla San Pedro Nolasco.

Echinomastus durangensis   (Rge.) B. & R.

Globose to elongated, to 25 cm high by 10 cm. Fl small, brownish-red. [CS/W]

DISTRIBUTION: Mexico, Durango, Rio Nazas.

Echinomastus erectocentrus
(Coult.) B. & R.

Ovoid to short-cylindric, 20 cm high by 10 cm. Fl 3–4 cm wide, pink. [CS/W]

DISTRIBUTION: SE Arizona.

OTHER NAMES: *Neolloydia erectocentrus.*

Echinomastus intertextus
(Englm.) B. & R.

Stem to 12.5 cm high by 5–7 cm. Fl 2.5 cm long. [H]

DISTRIBUTION: Arizona, New Mexico, Texas.

OTHER NAMES: *Neolloydia intertexta* & *v. dasyacantha.*

Echinomastus mariposensis Hester

Stem solitary, 6–10 cm long by 4–6 cm. Fl to 4 cm across, pink. [CS/W]

DISTRIBUTION: Mexico, Coahuila and Texas, SW Brewster County.

OTHER NAMES: *Neolloydia mariposensis.*

Echinomastus unguispinus
(Englm.) B. & R.

Solitary, to 10 cm high by 7 cm. Fl 2.5 cm wide. [CS/GC]

DISTRIBUTION: Mexico: Chihuahua; Zacatecas.

OTHER NAMES: *E. mapimiensis, E. lauii.*

Echinomastus warnockii Glass & Foster

Solitary, to 11 cm high by 7.5 cm. Fl 2.5 cm wide. [SB417/CS/W]

DISTRIBUTION: Mexico, Chihuahua; Texas and New Mexico.

OTHER NAMES: *Neolloydia warnockii.*

Echinopsis ancistrophora Speg.

A small, flattened species up to 8 cm broad. Fl 12–16 cm long, unscented. [P231/CS/PM]

DISTRIBUTION: Argentina, Tucuman-Salta.

OTHER NAMES: *E. hamatacantha, E. kratochviliana, E. leucorhodantha, E. pelecyrhachis, E. polyancistra.*
E. ancistrophora and these other names have all been included in the genus *Pseudolobivia.*

Echinopsis arebaloi Card.

Freely offsetting to 10 cm high and broad, fl 16 cm long, white [KK469/IP/M]

DISTRIBUTION: Bolivia, Comarapa.

Echinopsis ayopayana Ritt. & Rausch.

Body at first globular, later strongly elongated. Fl 10–12 cm long, white. Fruit very large. **E. kladiwaiana** Rausch. would seem to be merely a taller-growing variety of this species with very long csp (up to 10 cm). [L973/IP/M]

DISTRIBUTION: Between Independencia and Tiquirpaya, Bolivia at 3000–3500 m altitude.

OTHER NAMES: *Lobivia megacarpa n.n.*

Echinopsis baldiana Speg.

Usually solitary, to 30 cm high by 15 cm. Fl very large and scented. The plant pictured seems to equate well with the original description of the species. [P166/M]

DISTRIBUTION: Argentina, Catamarca.

Echinopsis boyuibensis Ritt.

Ribs 10 to 12, rsp 2–6, 7–20 mm long, the longest usually with a hooked tip; csp usually lacking but when present often hooked, 2–4 cm long. Fl 20 cm long, white. [IP/M]

DISTRIBUTION: Bolivia, hills near Boyuibe.

OTHER NAMES: *Pseudolobivia boyuibensis.*

Echinopsis bridgesii S-D

Offsetting, stem to 10 cm broad, central spine long, fl 15–18 cm long. Similar but much more elongated, to 50 cm long, and with much shorter spines is **E. cochabambensis** Bkbg., from Cochabamba. [PM146/H]

DISTRIBUTION: Bolivia, highlands around La Paz.

OTHER NAMES: **E. cotacajesi** Card., **E. ibicuatensis** Card., **E. pojoensis** Card. and **E. vallegrandensis** Card. all appear to be forms of this variable species.

Echinopsis calochlora Sch.

Rather small, light green, 6–9 cm broad, ribs 13. Fl 16 cm long. [M]

DISTRIBUTION: Brazil, Corumba.

'Echinopsis cardenasiana'
published as *Lobivia cardenasiana* Rausch.

Simple, rather flattened to 10 cm broad. Fl from the side, 8–10 cm long, 6–7 cm broad, magenta or scarlet. [CS/PM]

DISTRIBUTION: Bolivia, E of Tarija.

OTHER NAMES: *E. ancistrophora subsp. cardenasiana.*

Echinopsis chacoana Schuetz

Becoming short-cylindric, light yellowish-green. Fl white. [P251/CS/PM]

DISTRIBUTION: Paraguayan Chaco.

Echinopsis dehrenbergii Fric

Solitary, spherical. Fl white. [CS/M]

DISTRIBUTION: Paraguay.

OTHER NAMES: *E. paraguayensis.*

Echinopsis eyriesii (Turp.) Zucc.

Solitary at first then freely offsetting, spines very short. Fl 17–25 cm long, white. [M]

DISTRIBUTION: S Brazil to Argentina, Entre Rios.

OTHER NAMES: *E. turbinata* and *E. gemmata* seem to equate with this species.

Echinopsis klingleriana Card.

Simple, 12–14 cm high by 13 cm. Fl funnelform, 12 cm long, white. [L362/IP/M]

DISTRIBUTION: Bolivia, Chiquitos.

Echinopsis leucantha (Gill.) Walp.

Spherical, never columnar to 15 cm across. Fl up to 17 cm long, white. [B29/IP/M]

DISTRIBUTION: Argentina, NW provinces.

OTHER NAMES: *E. intricatissima, E. campylacantha, E. cordobensis, E. spegazziniana.*

Echinopsis mamillosa Guerke

Solitary, to 12 cm high by 10 cm; rsp 5–10 mm long, csp to 10 mm. Fl 13–18 cm long by 8 cm, white. In **v. flexilis** Rausch the csp are very long (N Argentina). **v. hystrichoides** (Ritt.) Rausch also has pink fl (around Culpina). **v. kermesina** (Krainz) Fried. has huge, carmine fl. [KK769/CS/M]

DISTRIBUTION: Bolivia, around Tarija.

OTHER NAMES: *E. herbasii, E. orozasana, Pseudolobivia orozasana.* **v. hystrichoides**: *E. hystrichoides.* **v. kermesina**: *Pseudolobivia kermesina, 'E. kermesina'.*

Echinopsis melanopotamica Speg.

Becoming cylindrical to 50 cm high by 15 cm. Fl 22 cm long, whitish. [P98a/CS/M]

DISTRIBUTION: Argentina, Rio Negro and Rio Colorado.

Echinopsis minuana Speg.

Solitary, to 80 cm high by 15 cm. Fl unscented, 20 cm long, white. [P255/M]

DISTRIBUTION: Argentina, Entre Rios.

OTHER NAMES: *E. robinsoniana.*

Echinopsis molesta Speg.

Solitary, spherical up to 20 cm broad. Fl faintly perfumed, 20–24 cm long, white. [R134/CS/M]

DISTRIBUTION: Argentina, Cordoba.

Echinopsis obrepanda (S-D) Sch.

For a discussion of this complex group see Appendix 1. [CS/PM]

Echinopsis obrepanda v. calorubra (Card.) Rausch

Forms large, flattened clumps with individual heads up to 14 cm across and of a lighter shade of green than in other populations. Fl 15 cm long, pinkish-red. [CS/PM]

DISTRIBUTION: C Bolivia, e.g. Aiquile.

OTHER NAMES: *Pseudolobivia calorubra*, *Echinopsis calorubra.*

Echinopsis obrepanda v. mizquensis (Rausch) Rausch

Body only to 14 cm across. Fl smaller to 7.5 cm long, red. **v. aguilari** (Vasqu.) Rausch is similar but slightly larger and more densely covered in darker, longer spines (Bolivia, Molinero). [CS/PM]

DISTRIBUTION: Bolivia, between Vila Vila and Rio Caine.

OTHER NAMES: *Lobivia mizquensis.* **v. aguilari**: *Lobivia aguilari.*

Echinopsis oxygona (Link) Zucc.

Solitary or offsetting, up to 25 cm across, rsp to 1.5 cm, csp longer. Fl 22 cm long, pinkish red. **f. brevispina** Ritt. spines shorter. [Schl.IP/M]

DISTRIBUTION: S Brazil, Uruguay and NE Argentina.

OTHER NAMES: *E. brasiliensis* & *E. multiplex.* **f. brevispina**: *E. eyriesii v grandiflora* & *E. werdermannii.*

Echinopsis rauschii Fried.

Up to 9 cm across, fresh green in colour. Fl orange-red, 6 cm long. **v. grandiflora** Rausch (from Mizque); to 10 cm across with a brilliant red fl 10 cm long. **v. megalocephala** Rausch; to 13 cm across with the orange-red fl 12 cm long. [CS/PM]

DISTRIBUTION: Bolivia, Pojo.

OTHER NAMES: *Lobivia pojoensis* & *L. pojoensis v. grandiflora, Echinopsis ancistrophora subsp. pojoensis* & *vars. grandiflora* & *megalocephala.*

Echinopsis rhodotricha Sch.

Offsetting, becoming cylindric to 80 cm high by 9 cm. Fl 15 cm long, white. [HS/M]

DISTRIBUTION: Paraguay and NW Argentina.

Echinopsis semidenudata Card.

Becoming cylindrical, spines so short as almost to appear absent. Fl white with a long, narrow tube. [KK1273/IP/M]

DISTRIBUTION: Bolivia, Tarija, Villa Montes.

OTHER NAMES: *E. pamparuizii*, '*E. seminuda*'.

Echinopsis shaferi B. & R.

Solitary or occasionally offsetting, up to 1.5 m high by 18 cm. Fl 20 cm long, white. [M]

DISTRIBUTION: Argentina, Tucuman, Trancas.

Echinopsis silvestrii Speg.

At first globular then elongated to 10 cm high by 8 cm, spines all fairly short and stiff, to 1.2 cm long, pale yellow, becoming dirty grey. Fl 20 cm long, white, lacking perfume. [B36/IP/M]

DISTRIBUTION: Argentina, borders of Tucuman and Salta.

Echinopsis subdenudata Card.

Solitary up to 8 cm high by 12 cm. Fl to 20 cm long, white. [Lau IP/M]

DISTRIBUTION: Bolivia, Angosto de Villamontes.

Echinopsis sucrensis Card.

Spherical, later short cylindric forming large clumps. Fl 20 cm long, 10 cm across, white. Part of the **E. bridgesii** complex. [PM164/H]

DISTRIBUTION: Bolivia, Sucre and widespread in the district around.

Echinopsis tapecuana Ritt.

Body 5–12 cm broad. Fl 8 cm long, white. [FR777/CS/M]

DISTRIBUTION: Bolivia, Tapecua.

'Echinopsis tortispina'

Clumping, spines fairly long and twisted. Fl white. [L400/IP/M]

DISTRIBUTION: Argentina, Entre Rios.

Echinopsis tubiflora (Pfeiff.) Zucc.

Solitary or offsetting, up to 12 cm across, more or less spherical. Fl 20 cm long white. [Schl.IP/M]

DISTRIBUTION: Argentina: Tucuman; Salta and Catamarca.

Epithelantha bokei Benson

Simple or with a few offsets. [CS/PM]

DISTRIBUTION: W Texas.

OTHER NAMES: *E. micromeris v. bokei.*

Epithelantha micromeris (Englm.) Web.

Simple or offsetting, spines to 2 mm long. **v. densispina** (Bravo) Bkbg. spines to 1 cm in the crown **v. greggii** (Englm.) Borg longer, stouter csp (Coahuila). **v. unguispina** (Boed.) Bkbg. (lower) has curved, darker projecting spines (Nuevo Leon). [CS/W]

DISTRIBUTION: W Texas to N Mexico.

OTHER NAMES: *E. polycephala, E. rufispina.* **v. densispina**: *E. densispina.* **v. unguispina**: *E. spinosior.*

Epithelantha pachyrhiza   (Marsh.) Bkbg.

Elongated, sometimes forming cushions, with a taproot and a prominent tuft of spines in the crown. [CS/W]

DISTRIBUTION: Mexico, Coahuila.

Eriosyce megacarpa   Ritt.

Solitary, globular, 10–14 cm or more across. Fl 1.5–2 cm wide, purplish-red. [H]

DISTRIBUTION: Chile, Chanaral and to the N and S along the coast.

OTHER NAMES: *Rodentiophila megacarpa, E. rodentiophila = R. atacamensis.*

Eriosyce sandillon   (Remy) Phil.

Solitary, very variable in size and spination, usually to around 40 cm high and broad. Fl 2.5–3 cm across, purplish-red. [H]

DISTRIBUTION: Widespread in NC Chile.

OTHER NAMES: *E. aurata, E. algarrobensis, 'E. ausseliana', E. ceratistes* and *vars., E. ihotzkyanae, E. spinibarbis.*

Escobaria aguirreana
(Glass & Foster) N.P. Taylor
[CS/PM]

DISTRIBUTION: Mexico, Coahuila.

OTHER NAMES: *Gymnocactus aguirreanus.*

Escobaria chihuahuensis   B. & R.

Stems to 20 cm high by 7 cm. Fl 2 cm across, pale pink to purplish. [CS/PM]

DISTRIBUTION: Mexico, C Chihuahua.

Escobaria dasyacantha   (Englm.) B. & R.

To 7 cm across; fl to 2.5 cm long. [CS/PM]

DISTRIBUTION: S New Mexico, W Texas and Mexico, Coahuila and Chihuahua.

Escobaria dasyacantha v. chaffeyi (B. & R.) N.P. Taylor

Spines finer and more even in length than the species. Fl only to 1.5 cm long. **v. duncanii** (Hester) N.P. Taylor; stem to 3.5 cm broad. Fl to 3 cm long (S New Mexico and W Texas). [CS/PM]

DISTRIBUTION: Mexico, N Zacatecas.

OTHER NAMES: *E. chaffeyi.* **v. duncanii:** *Coryphantha duncanii, E. duncanii.*

Escobaria emskoetteriana (Quehl) Borg

Stems to 5 cm high by 4 cm, prolifically clustering. Fl to 3 cm long. [HK1321/HS/P]

DISTRIBUTION: NE Mexico and SW Texas.

OTHER NAMES: *E. muehlbaueriana, E. runyonii, Coryphantha pirtlei, C. robertii.*

Escobaria henricksonii Glass & Foster

Stems cylindric, to 3 cm across, clumping. Fl to 2.5 cm across, pinkish-purple. [CS/W]

DISTRIBUTION: Mexico, S Chihuahua and NE Durango.

Escobaria hesteri (Y. Wright) Buxb.

Stems to 4 cm high, globose. [CS/W]

DISTRIBUTION: Texas, Brewster County.

OTHER NAMES: *Coryphantha hesteri.*

Escobaria laredoi (Glass & Foster) N.P. Taylor

Stems globose or slightly elongated, to 4.5 cm across. Fl crimson, [CS/P]

DISTRIBUTION: Mexico, SE Coahuila.

OTHER NAMES: *Coryphantha laredoi, 'E. rigida'.*

Escobaria leei Boed.

Stem slimmer than in the related **E. sneedii** with which it occasionally occurs but apparently does not interbreed. Spines pointing inwards towards the stem. Fl dull brownish-pink [IP/DHS]

DISTRIBUTION: New Mexico, Guadalupe Mts.

OTHER NAMES: *Coryphantha sneedii v. leei, E. sneedii v. leei.*

Escobaria minima (Baird) D.R. Hunt

Stem to 4 cm high by 2 cm, clumping. [CS/GC]

DISTRIBUTION: Texas, near Marathon.

OTHER NAMES: *Coryphantha minima, C. nellieae, E. nellieae.*

Escobaria missouriensis
(Sweet) D.R. Hunt

Stems 5–10 cm across, clumping; rsp 8–20. Fl to 2.5 cm across, greenish-yellow to pink. **v. asperispina** (Boed.) N.P. Taylor; rsp 9–10 (NE Mexico). **v. marstonii** (Clover) D.R. Hunt; fl to 5 cm, yellow (Utah, Arizona). [IP/G]

DISTRIBUTION: Montana, N Dakota and W Minnesota south to N Colorado and Kansas.

OTHER NAMES: *Neobesseya miss., N. wissmannii, N. notesteini, N. asperispina, Coryphantha marstonii.*

Escobaria missouriensis v. similis
(Englm.) N.P. Taylor

Stem to 10 cm broad, clumping. Fl to 6 cm across, light yellow to pink. [HK1480/HS/GC]

DISTRIBUTION: SE Kansas, SW Arkansas, W Louisiana, E Oklahoma, E Texas.

OTHER NAMES: *Neobesseya similis, N. rosiflora, N. miss. v. caespitosa.*

Escobaria organensis
(Zimmerman) Castetter *et al.*

Stems to 12 cm high by 3 cm. Fl to 1.5 cm, pinkish. [CS/W]

DISTRIBUTION: New Mexico, Organ Mts.

OTHER NAMES: *Coryphantha organensis.*

Escobaria robbinsorum
(Earle) D.R. Hunt

Solitary, to 5 cm across and high. Fl pink to olive. [CS/DHS]

DISTRIBUTION: SE Arizona.

OTHER NAMES: *Cochiseia robb.*

Escobaria roseana
(Boed.) Schmoll ex Bux.

Stem to 5 cm across, clumping. Fl 2 cm across. A recently discovered form from Nuevo Leon resembles **Mammillaria elongata**. [CS/PM]

DISTRIBUTION: Mexico, SE Coahuila and adjacent Nuevo Leon.

OTHER NAMES: *Gymnocactus roseanus.*

Escobaria sneedii B. & R.

Stem to 7.5 cm high by 2.5 cm, densely clustering. Fl 12 mm across, pale pink to magenta. **E. guadalupensis** Brack & Heil is similar but usually solitary, to 10 cm high by 5 cm. Fl pale yellow, cream or pink, with pink midstripe (Texas, Guadalupe Mts.) [CS/E]

DISTRIBUTION: New Mexico, Dona Ana County and Texas, El Paso County.

OTHER NAMES: *Coryphantha sneedii.*

Escobaria strobiliformis Scheer ex Boed.

Extremely variable, 5–12 cm high by 2.5–7 cm. Fl 2.5–3.5 cm across, pale pink to whitish. [CS/PM]

DISTRIBUTION: New Mexico and W Texas; Mexico, Coahuila, Durango and Chihuahua States.

OTHER NAMES: *E. tuberculosa, E. varicolor, E. dasyacantha v. varicolor.*

Escobaria villardii Castetter *et al*

Clumping. Fl to 2.5 cm across, white with a light brown to pink midstripe. A member of the **E. orcuttii** group, including **E. sandbergii** and **E. albicolumnaria**, all of which are similar-looking plants (see Appendix 2). [CS/W]

DISTRIBUTION: New Mexico, W face of the Sacramento Mts.

Escobaria vivipara (Nutt.) F. Buxb.

Clustering, stem exposed. Fl to 6 cm wide. **v. kaibabensis** (P. Fisher) N.P. Taylor; usually solitary, spinier. Fl with pale throat (N Arizona). **v. radiosa** (Englm.) D.R. Hunt; tubercles longer; more, longer and paler spines, petals long and narrow (SW Oklahoma, NC Texas, SE New Mexico). [HS/PM]

DISTRIBUTION: S Canada and Kansas to Texas.

OTHER NAMES: *Coryphantha vivip.* **v. kaibab.**: *Cory vivip. v. kaibab.* **v. radiosa**: *C. columnaris.*

Escobaria vivipara v. arizonica (Englm.) D.R. Hunt

Clumping, stems to 9.5 cm high by 7 cm; csp 2–6. **v. neomexicana** (Englm.) Bux.; similar, csp 4–11, fl usually paler (New Mexico, W Texas, N Chihuahua). **v. rosea** (Clokey) D.R. Hunt; stem larger, rsp stouter (S Nevada, California). [H]

DISTRIBUTION: S Utah, SW Colorado, Arizona, NW New Mexico.

OTHER NAMES: *Coryphantha viv. v. arizonica & neomexicana.*

Escobaria vivipara v. bisbeeana (Orcutt) D.R. Hunt

Clumping, fl 5–7 cm wide, pink. **v. buoflama** (P. Fisher) N.P. Taylor; clumping, fl small, peach to light pink (Arizona, near Bagdad). **v. deserti** (Englm.) D.R. Hunt; similar to **v. buof.**, solitary, fl small, brownish (USA, Mojave Desert). [K238/IP]

DISTRIBUTION: SW USA and New Mexico.

OTHER NAMES: *Coryphantha aggregata, Escobaria agg.* (mis-applied names). *C. viv. v. bisb., C. viv. v. buof.* **v. deserti**: *C. chlorantha & v. deserti, Esc. chlorantha, Esc. deserti.*

Escobaria zilziana (Boed.) Bkbg.

Stem to 10 cm high by 3 cm, clumping. Fl 3 cm across, pale yellow, olive-green or whitish, petals with pink midstripe. [HK1326/HS/GC]

DISTRIBUTION: Mexico, Coahuila.

Ferocactus chrysacanthus (Orcutt) B. & R.

Solitary, spines usually yellow, sometimes red, stem to 1 m high by 30 cm. Fl yellow or orange. [CS/PM]

DISTRIBUTION: Mexico, Baja California, Cedros and San Benito Islands.

Ferocactus cylindraceus (Englm.) Orcutt

Usually solitary, to 3 m high by 50 cm. Fl green or yellow. **v. lecontei** (Englm.) H. Bravo-H., **v. eastwoodiae** (Benson) N.P. Taylor & **v. tortulispinus** (Gates) H. Bravo-H. differ mainly in spination. **F. johnstonianus** B. & R. is probably a dwarf island race. [HS/PM]

DISTRIBUTION: SW USA and NW Mexico.

OTHER NAMES: *F. acanthodes* & *vars.*, *F. rostii*. **v. tortulispinus**: *F. tortulospinus*.

Ferocactus echidne (DC) B. & R.

Very variable, 35–80 cm high by 20–30 cm. Fl occasionally red. Seed-raised plants flower well in cultivation. [CS/PM]

DISTRIBUTION: Widespread in EC Mexico.

OTHER NAMES: *F. rafaelensis*, *F. 'rhodanthus'*, *F. victoriensis*.

Ferocactus emoryi (Englm.) Orcutt

Solitary, to 2.5 m high by 1 m; csp 1, 4–10 cm long. Fl red or yellow. **v. rectispinus** (Englm.) N.P. Taylor; to 1.5 m high by 45 cm; csp to 25 cm; fl yellow (Baja California, San Ignacio to S of Loreto). [PF6853/HS/PM]

DISTRIBUTION: SW Arizona; Mexico, Sonora to N Sinaloa.

OTHER NAMES: *F. covillei*. **v. rect.**: *F. rectispinus*.

Ferocactus flavovirens (Scheidw.) B. & R.

Stems to 40 cm high by 20 cm, forming mounds 2 m broad. Fl red. [CS/PM]

DISTRIBUTION: Mexico, SE Puebla to N Oaxaca.

Ferocactus fordii (Orcutt) B. & R.

Solitary, spherical to short cylindric, to 12 cm across. Fl 4 cm long, purple. [H]

DISTRIBUTION: Mexico, W coast of Baja California.

Ferocactus glaucescens (DC) B. & R.

Stems solitary or clumping, to 45–70 cm high by 50 cm. Fl yellow, produced on very old plants in cultivation (see plate). [CS/P]

DISTRIBUTION: Mexico: Hidalgo; Queretaro and San Luis Potosi.

Ferocactus gracilis H. Gates

Solitary, to 3 m high by 30 cm. Fl red. **v. coloratus** (Gates) G. Lindsay (illus.) is shorter and thicker (S Baja California). *F. gatesii* G. Lindsay may be only an island form of **F. gracilis**. [H]

DISTRIBUTION: Mexico, Central N Baja California.

OTHER NAMES: **v. coloratus**: *F. color.*, *F. viscainensis*, *F. peninsulae v. visc.*

Ferocactus haematacanthus (S-D) H. Bravo-H.

Stem 30–120 cm high by 26–36 cm. Fl purplish-pink. [H]

DISTRIBUTION: Mexico, Puebla/Veracruz, Esperanza, Barrancas of Acultzingo and Maltrata.

Ferocactus hamatacanthus (Muehlpf.) B. & R.

Usually solitary, to 60 cm high by 30 cm, ribs rounded. Fl yellow, throat often red, to 7.5 cm wide. **v. sinuatus** (A. Dietr.) Benson; smaller, ribs more acute, lower csp twisted and flattened (SE Texas; NE Mexico). [PM45/HS/PM]

DISTRIBUTION: SE New Mexico, W and S Texas; CN Mexico, S to San Luis Potosi.

OTHER NAMES: *Hamatocactus ham.*, *'H. longihamatus'*, *F. ham. v. crassispinus.* **v. sinuatus**: *H. sinuatus*, *'F. sinuatus'*.

Ferocactus histrix (DC) G. Lindsay

Solitary, to 110 cm high by 80 cm. Fl yellow. [PM35/HS/PM]

DISTRIBUTION: Widespread in C Mexico.

OTHER NAMES: *'F. electracanthus'*.

Ferocactus latispinus (Haw.) B. & R.

Solitary, to 30 cm high by 40 cm. Fl 4 cm across, purplish or yellow. **v. spiralis** (Karw. ex Pfeiff.) N.P. Taylor; more cylindric, fl smaller, whitish with pinkish midstripes (Puebla to S Oaxaca). [H]

DISTRIBUTION: Very widespread in C Mexico.

OTHER NAMES: **v. spiralis**: *F. recurvus.*

Ferocactus lindsayi H. Bravo-H.

Solitary, to 60 cm high and 40 cm wide. Fl yellow. [H]

DISTRIBUTION: Mexico, Michoacan, of Rio Balsas basin, SE of Apatzingan.

Ferocactus macrodiscus (Mart.) B. & R.

Solitary, flattened, to 40 cm across, ribs 13–35. Fl 3–4 cm across, purplish-pink with white petal margins. A form with fewer, more pronounced ribs from Guanajuato is in trade and deserves a name. Flowers well in cultivation. [H, from Oaxaca]

DISTRIBUTION: Mexico, Oaxaca.

Ferocactus peninsulae (Weber) B. & R.

Solitary, to 2.5 m high by 50 cm. **v. townsendianus** (B. & R.) N.P. Taylor; smaller, rarely to 1 m (S Baja California). **v. santa-maria** (B. & R.) N.P. Taylor (see plate); globular, to 60 cm high, spines stout, free-flowering (Isla Magdalena & adjacent mainland). [CS/PM]

DISTRIBUTION: Mexico, C and E Baja California.

OTHER NAMES: **v. towns.**: *F. townsendianus.* **v. santa-maria**: *F. towns. v. santa-m.*

Ferocactus pilosus (Gal. ex S-D) Werd.

Stems clumping, to 3 m high by 50 cm. Fl small, orange.

DISTRIBUTION: Widespread in NC Mexico.

OTHER NAMES: *F. stainesii* & *v. pilosus.*

Ferocactus pottsii (S-D) Bkbg.

Solitary, to 1 m high by 50 cm, csp straight. Fl yellow. **v. alamosanus** (B. & R.) G. Unger; stems to 25 cm high by 30 cm, spination denser (Sonora, Alamos Mountain). [CS/PM]

DISTRIBUTION: Mexico, SW Chihuahua, SE Sonora and N Sinaloa.

OTHER NAMES: '*F. guirocobensis*'. **v. alamosanus**: *F. alamosanus.*

Ferocactus reppenhagenii Unger

Solitary, globose, then to 80 cm high by 24 cm. Seed-grown plants flower well in cultivation. [CS/PM]

DISTRIBUTION: Mexico: Colima; Michoacan and Oaxaca.

Ferocactus robustus (Pfeiff.) B. & R.

Stems 15–20 cm broad, forming clumps to 5 m across. Fl 3–4 cm wide, yellow. [PM16/HS/PM]

DISTRIBUTION: Mexico, Puebla.

Ferocactus schwarzii Lindsay

Solitary, to 80 cm high by 50 cm, flowering when around 10 cm across. [CS/P]

DISTRIBUTION: Mexico, Sinaloa.

Ferocactus viridescens
(Torrey & Gray) B. & R.

Solitary, to 30 cm high and broad, ribs 13–25; largest csps flattened. Fl 6 cm wide. **v. littoralis** G. Lindsay; stems to 30 cm by 18 cm across, ribs 21–34, spines not flattened. Fl 2.5 cm across (Baja, coast between Punta Salsipuedes and Mision Santo Domingo). [CS/PM]

DISTRIBUTION: California, SW corner; Mexico, NW Baja California.

OTHER NAMES: *F. orcuttii.*

Ferocactus wislizeni (Englm.) B. & R.

Solitary, to 1.6 m high by 80 cm. Fl orange to red. **v. herrerae** (J.G. Ortega) N.P. Taylor; to 2 m by 45 cm, less spiny (S Sonora, N Sinaloa, W Durango). **v. tiburonensis** Lindsay; fl yellow, from Tiburon Island. [H]

DISTRIBUTION: SW USA and NW Mexico.

OTHER NAMES: **vars:** *F. herrerae, F. tiburonensis.*

Frailea castanea Bkbg.

Solitary, fl 4 cm broad. [IP/RM]

DISTRIBUTION: S Brazil to N Uruguay.

OTHER NAMES: *F. asterioides.*

Frailea columbiana (Werd.) Bkbg.

Clumping, fl 2.5 cm long. [CS/PM]

DISTRIBUTION: Said to be from Colombia (Dagua) but never rediscovered despite considerable searching.

OTHER NAMES: ?*F. chrysacantha.*

Frailea grahliana (Haage jr.) B. & R.

Clumping, stems to 4 cm across. Fl 4 cm wide. [CS/PM]

DISTRIBUTION: Paraguay, Rio Paraguari and Argentina, Misiones, Santa Ana.

OTHER NAMES: ?*F. pseudograhliana,* ?*F. schilinzkyana.*

Frailea horstii Ritt.

Slender cylindric, to 10 cm and more high, 2.5 cm across. Fl 5 cm across. [CS/PM]

DISTRIBUTION: Brazil, Rio Grande do Sul, Cacapava.

Frailea phaeodisca Speg.

Solitary, flattened-globular, 1.5–3 cm broad. Fl 4 cm broad, yellow. [CS/P]

DISTRIBUTION: Uruguay, Tacuarembo.

OTHER NAMES: *F. perbella, F. pygmaea v. phaeodisca.*

Frailea pumila (Lem.) B. & R.

Clumping, spherical. Fl 2 cm. [Schl532/IP/RM]

DISTRIBUTION: Paraguay and adjacent Argentina.

OTHER NAMES: *F. albiareolata, F. carmenifilamentosa, F. friedrichii.*

Frailea pygmaea (Speg.) B. & R.

Solitary or offsetting, to 3 cm long and broad. Fl 3 cm across, yellow. [CS/R]

DISTRIBUTION: Uruguay and Argentina.

OTHER NAMES: *F. asperispina, F. aurea, F. aureinitens, F. aureispina, F. dadakii, F. fulviseta, F. pulcherrima.*

'Gymnocactus beguinii' nom. illeg. = Neolloydia smithii (Muehlpf.) Kladiwa & Fittkau
Solitary, to 10 cm high by 4.5 cm. Fl magenta with lighter petal margins. [CS/PM]
DISTRIBUTION: Mexico, Coahuila, near Saltillo and Nuevo Leon, e.g. near Ascension.
OTHER NAMES: *Gymnocactus beguinii* & *v. senilis* & *v. smithii.*

Gymnocactus gielsdorfianus (Werd.) Bkbg.
Solitary to clustering, 5–7 cm high by 4.5–5 cm. Fl 2 cm across. [CS/W]
DISTRIBUTION: Mexico, Tamaulipas, near Jaumave.
OTHER NAMES: *Neolloydia gielsd., Thelocactus gielsd., Turbinicarpus gielsd.*

Gymnocactus horripilus (Lem.) Bkbg.
Clustering, individual heads 10 cm high by 6.5 cm. Fl 2.5–3.5 cm across. [CS/PM]
DISTRIBUTION: Mexico, Hidalgo, Metztitlan.
OTHER NAMES: *Neolloydia horrip., Turbinicarpus horrip.*

Gymnocactus knuthianus (Boed.) Bkbg.
Usually solitary, to 6 cm high by 7 cm. Fl 2.5 cm across. [CS/PM]
DISTRIBUTION: Mexico, San Luis Potosi, near Guadalcazar.
OTHER NAMES: *Neolloydia knuth., Thelocactus knuth., Turbinicarpus knuth.*

Gymnocactus saueri (Boed.) Bkbg.
Solitary, to 5 cm high by 6 cm. Fl 2.5 cm across. [CS/W]
DISTRIBUTION: Mexico, Tamaulipas, near San Vicente.
OTHER NAMES: *Neolloydia saueri, Thelocactus saueri, Turbinicarpus saueri.*

Gymnocactus subterraneus (Bkbg.) Bkbg.
Stem solitary, to 7 cm high by 4 cm. Fl magenta.
v. zaragosae (Glass & Foster) from Dr. Arroyo has a brownish-yellow flower. [CS/J. Arnold]
DISTRIBUTION: Mexico, Nuevo Leon, Aramberri.
OTHER NAMES: *Neolloydia sub.* **v. zarag.**: *Neoll. sub. v. zar.*

Gymnocactus viereckii   (Werd.) Bkbg.

Heads to 5 cm across by 4 cm, clustering. Fl magenta.
v. major (Glass & Foster) Anderson; solitary, to 7 cm high
by 6.5 cm. Fl white (Nuevo Leon and San Luis Potosi).
[CS/PM]

DISTRIBUTION: Mexico, Tamaulipas, Jaumave Valley,
Los Ebanos.

OTHER NAMES: *Neolloydia viereckii, Turbinicarpus viereckii.*

Gymnocalycium achirasense
Till & Schatzl

Plant up to 6 cm high by 7 cm, more or less covered in
spines; fl funnel-shaped, 7 cm across, off-white flushed
with pink. Appears to be intermediate between
G. horridispinum and **G. monvillei**. [P104/HS/DHS]

DISTRIBUTION: Argentina, Province of San Luis at Achiras.

Gymnocalycium alboareolatum   Rausch

Flattened-globular. Fl pinkish-white. A member of the
G. mazanense complex. [P221/IP/DHS]

DISTRIBUTION: Argentina, La Rioja, near Sanagasta.

Gymnocalycium ambatoense   Piltz

Single, more or less globular, up to 15 cm across, 5–10 cm
high; fl up to 4.5 cm long, 3–4 cm across, white with
a pinkish midstripe or pink. Closely related to
G. mazanense. [P29/HS/DHS]

DISTRIBUTION: Argentina, Catamarca, Sierra Ambato
amongst grass and moss.

Gymnocalycium andreae   (Boed.) Bkbg.

One of the few yellow-flowered members of the genus;
offsetting with age. [Fechser IP/DHS]

DISTRIBUTION: Argentina, Cordoba.

OTHER NAMES: *G. andreae v. grandiflorum.*

Gymnocalycium anisitsii   (Sch.) B. & R.

Solitary, to over 10 cm long, leaf-green. Fl 4 cm long, white.
[GC]

DISTRIBUTION: Paraguay, Rio Tigatiyami.

Gymnocalycium baldianum (Speg.) Speg.

Usually solitary to 7 cm broad. Fl often bright red but can be pink or even white. [P127/CS/PM]

DISTRIBUTION: Argentina, Catamarca.

OTHER NAMES: *G. venturianum.*

Gymnocalycium bayrianum Till

Bluish-green, normally solitary. Fl 4 cm broad, creamy white with a pink throat. [L447/IP/DHS]

DISTRIBUTION: Argentina, Tucuman, near Medina.

Gymnocalycium bicolor Schuetz

Spherical, up to 15 cm across. Fl 4.5 cm broad, white. [B44/IP/DHS]

DISTRIBUTION: Argentina, Cordoba.

Gymnocalycium borthii Koop

Closely related to **G. gibbosum.** Body flattened becoming elongated-globular, up to 10 cm high by 9 cm. Fl 5 cm across, white with a pink throat. [OF19−80/HS/DHS]

DISTRIBUTION: Argentina, San Luis, at Quines.

Gymnocalycium bozsingianum Schuetz

Fl pink with a red throat, petals olive brown on the outside. [P205/IP/DHS]

DISTRIBUTION: Argentina, La Rioja, Chipes Viejo.

Gymnocalycium bruchii (Speg.) Hoss.

Forming large clumps of small, densely spined heads with white flowers flushed light to deep pink. v. **brigettii** Piltz has far fewer spines exposing the body beneath and bright pink flowers. [P200/IP/DHS]

DISTRIBUTION: Argentina, Cordoba.

OTHER NAMES: *G. albispinum, G. lafaldense.*

Gymnocalycium buenekeri Smales

Clumping, body not glossy, fl pink. [CS/PM]

DISTRIBUTION: Brazil, Rio Grande do Sul, Sao Francisco de Assis.

OTHER NAMES: *G. horstii v. buenekeri.*

Gymnocalycium calochlorum (Boed.) Ito

Forming mounds of rather small, flattened heads to 6 cm across. Fl 6 cm long, pale pink. **v. proliferum** Bkbg. has a darker body and a larger fl with brownish-white, pink or pure white petals. [P109b/IP/DHS].

DISTRIBUTION: N Argentina.

Gymnocalycium capillaense (Schick.) Bkbg.

To 9 cm high and broad, offsetting. Fl large up to 7 cm long and 6 cm across, delicate shell pink. Closely related to **G. sigelianum.** [B39/IP/DHS].

DISTRIBUTION: Argentina, Cordoba.

Gymnocalycium cardenasianum Ritt.

Noted for its long, strong spines. Fl pink to white, 5 cm long, up to 9 cm across, often failing to open properly because of the spines. [L929/IP/DHS]

DISTRIBUTION: Bolivia, Dept. of Tarija, Carrizal.

Gymnocalycium carminanthum Borth & Koop

Spines strong, curving back over the matt-green body, csp usually lacking. [P133/IP/DHS]

DISTRIBUTION: Argentina, Catamarca, Sierra de Ambato.

Gymnocalycium castellanosii Bkbg.

Body simple, matt bluish-green, up to 15 cm high and 10 cm broad, spines robust. Fl 4.5 cm broad, bell-shaped, white with a pinkish throat. [B73/IP/DHS].

DISTRIBUTION: Argentina, Cordoba.

OTHER NAMES: *G. acorrugatum.*

Gymnocalycium chiquitanum Card.

Flattened spherical, later offsetting round the base, 6–9 cm across, of a characteristic shade of greyish-green turning reddish in strong sunlight. Fl up to 6 cm long, lilac pink. [CS/PM].

DISTRIBUTION: Bolivia, San Jose.

OTHER NAMES: 'G. hammerschmidii'.

Gymnocalycium damsii (Sch.) B. & R.

Simple, light, shiny green often flushed red. Fl up to 5 cm long and 5 cm across, white with a red centre.
v. tucavocense Bkbg. differs in its prolific branching habit while Backeberg's other varieties *v. centrispinum*, *v. rotundulum* & *v. torulosum* differ in no significant way from the species. [KK497/CS/PM]

DISTRIBUTION: N Paraguay. **v. tucavocense**, Bolivia, San Jose.

Gymnocalycium denudatum (Link & Otto) Pfeiff.

Body flattened-globose, up to 8 cm broad, spines usually 5. Fl up to 7 cm across, white. [Pazout IP/GC]

DISTRIBUTION: Over a wide area of NE Argentina and SW Brazil.

OTHER NAMES: *G. paraguayense*.

Gymnocalycium erinaceum Lambert

Solitary, globose to 5 cm high by 5.5 cm. Fl to 5.5 cm in diameter, white. [JL40/HS/DHS]

DISTRIBUTION: Argentina, Cordoba, Sierra de Tulumba, Sauce Punco.

Gymnocalycium eurypleurum Ritt.

Simple, up to 7 cm across. Fl 4.5–5 cm broad. [CS/GC]

DISTRIBUTION: Paraguay, Cerro Leon.

Gymnocalycium ferrarii Rausch

Single, flattened-globular, 3–4 cm high by 9 cm greenish-grey. Fl 4.5 cm long and 3.5 cm across, whitish-pink with pink midstripe, throat pink. [IP/DHS]

DISTRIBUTION: Argentina, Catamarca, near Santa Theresa.

Gymnocalycium fleischerianum Bkbg.

Spherical to elongated, occasionally offsetting. Fl up to 4 cm long, white with a pink throat. [CS/GC]

DISTRIBUTION: Paraguay.

Gymnocalycium friedrichii Pazout

Body reddish brown with sharply angled ribs, marked with distinctive horizontal banding. Flowers pink. [CS/GC]

DISTRIBUTION: Paraguayan Chaco.

Gymnocalycium gibbosum (Haw.) Pfeiff.

A very variable species, body spherical to elongated, up to 6 cm high by 15 cm, varying from green to black, spines thin. Fl up to 6.5 cm long, whitish. [P101/IP/DHS]

DISTRIBUTION: S Argentina, widespread.

OTHER NAMES: *G. brachypetalum*, *G. chubutense*, '*G. gerardii*'.

Gymnocalycium glaucum Ritt.

Slow-growing, up to 12 cm across. Fl up to 4.5 cm across, white with darker midstripe. [P36/IP/DHS]

DISTRIBUTION: N Argentina, SE of Tinogasta.

'Gymnocalycium griseopallidum' Bkbg.

Body pale greyish-green up to 6.5 cm across and 3 cm high, later forming offsets. Fl off-white, similar to those of **G. damsii**. [CS/GC]

DISTRIBUTION: Bolivia, salt dunes near San Jose.

Gymnocalycium hamatum Ritt.

Body sub-spherical, coppery brown; spines often but not always hooked. Fl 5 cm long, white. [CS/GC]

DISTRIBUTION: Bolivia, Province of Gran Chaco, Palos Blancos.

Gymnocalycium horridispinum Frank

To 20 cm or more high by 8 cm, epidermis dark green. Fl white with pinkish edging to the petals or wholly pink, 6 cm across. [CS/PM]

DISTRIBUTION: N Argentina, Cordoba, SW of Salsacate.

Gymnocalycium horstii Buin.

Up to 7 cm high by 11 cm, glossy, bright green. Fl up to 11 cm long and broad, white. [IP/R]

DISTRIBUTION: Brazil, Rio Grande do Sul, near Cacapava.

Gymnocalycium hybopleurum (Sch.) Bkbg.

Body broadly spherical, spination very variable with some plants being extremely strongly spined. Fl 4 cm long, white. The seven varieties erected by Backeberg have little or no botanical significance in such a variable plant. [L491/IP/GC]

DISTRIBUTION: Argentina, Cordoba.

OTHER NAMES: *G. euchlorum* nom. prov. '*G. eluhilton*', *G. pugionacanthum.*

'Gymnocalycium intertextum' Bkbg.

Depressed spherical to 11 cm across. Fl white. [CS/DHS]

DISTRIBUTION: Given as N Argentina, not positively recollected in view of Backeberg's typically inadequate habitat information.

Gymnocalycium kieslingii Ferrari

Stems globose, depressed, grey-green, solitary, 6–9 cm broad and 2 cm high. Fl 5–6 cm broad, white. [B63/IP/GC]

DISTRIBUTION: Argentina, La Rioja.

Gymnocalycium leeanum (Hook.) B. & R.

Usually clumping. [CS/PM]

DISTRIBUTION: Uruguay and adjacent areas of Argentina.

Gymnocalycium mazanense Bkbg.

A large, spherical species, dull green and strongly spined. Fl short and stout, whitish to pink. Probably conspecific with **G. nidulans** & **G. weissianum**, also described by Backeberg from the same general area. [L510/IP/DHS]

DISTRIBUTION: Argentina, Mazan.

OTHER NAMES: *G. mucidum, G. guanchinense.*

Gymnocalycium mesopotamicum Kiesling

Stem solitary (seems to clump in cultivation) up to 4 cm broad, dark, fairly glossy green. Fl 7 cm long by 6.5 cm petals long and thin, white with a pinkish-green midstripe. [P241/CS/PM]

DISTRIBUTION: Argentina, Province of Corrientes, Mercedes.

Gymnocalycium mihanovichii (Fric & Guerke) B. & R.

Broadly spherical, becoming elongated and up to 6 cm broad; generally a very variable plant in both spination and flower colour, which varies from yellowish white to pink. In view of the broad distribution and innate variability, the many named varieties probably have little botanical significance. [FR1181/GC]

DISTRIBUTION: Paraguayan Chaco.

OTHER NAMES: *v. friedrichii* Werd. = **G. friedrichii** Pazout.

Gymnocalycium monvillei (Lem.) B. & R.

Body simple, spherical, up to 22 cm across, of a characteristic glossy shade of light green. Fl up to 8 cm long and broad, white, often flushed with pink. [IP/DHS]

DISTRIBUTION: Paraguay.

OTHER NAMES: *G. brachyanthum.*

Gymnocalycium moserianum Schuetz

Depressed spherical, up to 15 cm across and 10 cm high. Fl white with a red centre. [Fechser IP/DHS]

DISTRIBUTION: Argentina, N Cordoba near Serrazuela.

Gymnocalycium mostii (Guerke) B. & R.

Simple, bluish-green, up to 13 cm high and across. Fl large, up to 8 cm across, pink. In **v. kurtzianum** (Guerke) Bkbg. the fl is white with a red throat. [B9/IP/DHS]

DISTRIBUTION: Both from Argentina, Cordoba.

OTHER NAMES: **v. kurtzianum:** *G. kurtzianum.*

Gymnocalycium multiflorum
(Hook.) B. & R.

Eventually forming clumps, single heads up to 9 cm high
and more, by 12 cm, fresh green; spines very variable in
length. Fl up to 4 cm long, pink to almost white. The named
varieties fall within the species. [B17/IP/DHS]

DISTRIBUTION: Argentina, Cordoba and San Luis.

OTHER NAMES: *G. ourselianum.*

Gymnocalycium nidulans   Bkbg.

Solitary later clumping, up to 30 cm high by 18 cm
spination very variable. Probably conspecific with
G. mazanense & **G. weissianum** from the same general
area. [CS/PM]

DISTRIBUTION: Argentina, Mazan.

Gymnocalycium nigriareolatum   Bkbg.

Broadly spherical, simple, up to 15 cm across. Fl
shimmering porcelain-white. Despite the name, the areoles
are not black in young, cultivated plants. [IP/GC]

DISTRIBUTION: Argentina, Catamarca.

Gymnocalycium occultum
Fric ex Schuetz

Solitary, flattened. Fl 3 cm long by 2−2.5 cm off-white.
[B131/IP/DHS]

DISTRIBUTION: Argentina, N Cordoba and S La Rioja.

Gymnocalycium paediophilum
Ritt. ex Schuetz

Plant normally solitary. Fl 5.5 cm broad, creamy yellowish at
first, later white. [ISI1593/M]

DISTRIBUTION: Paraguay, Cerro Leon.

Gymnocalycium pflanzii   (Vpl.) Werd.

Body very large, to 50 cm across, matt green. Fl only 5 cm
long and broad, white to salmon-pink. **vars. millaresii**, &
riograndense (Card.) Don. show only superficial
differences from the species. [L.938/IP/DHS]

DISTRIBUTION: N Argentina and S Bolivia.

OTHER NAMES: The above varieties as species, *G.
chuquisacanum, G. comarapense n.n., G. marquezii.*

Gymnocalycium pflanzii v. lagunillasense
(Card.) Don.

This is the most easily recognizable member of the group
(upper illus.) [KK492/IP/DHS]. **v. zegarrae** (Card.) Don.
(lower illus.) has the strongest spination. [L946/IP/DHS]
(Bolivia, Perez-Mairano road)

DISTRIBUTION: Bolivia, Lagunillas.

OTHER NAMES: *G. lagunillasense.* **v. zegarrae**: *G. zegarrae.*

Gymnocalycium piltziorum   Shuetz

Single, flattened globular, 10 cm high and 16 cm broad. Fl
7 cm long and 6 cm broad, pinkish. [P38/IP/DHS]

DISTRIBUTION: Argentina, La Rioja, Sierra Velasco.

Gymnocalycium quehlianum
(Haage jr.) Berg.

A very variable species, plants from each of the widely
scattered populations often differing in numerous details.
Body usually to 7 cm broad, greenish grey to reddish. Fl
with a slender tube, up to 6 cm long, white with a reddish
throat. [CS/P160/DHS]

DISTRIBUTION: Argentina, Cordoba.

OTHER NAMES: *v. albispinum, v. flavispinum, v. rolfianum &
v. zantnerianum* fall within the species.

Gymnocalycium ragonesii   Castellanos

Small, noticeably flattened, greyish-brown. Fl up to 4 cm
long, creamy-white with a dull red throat. [CS/EC]

DISTRIBUTION: Argentina, Catamarca.

Gymnocalycium ritterianum   Rausch

Simple or forming small groups, later developing offsets on
the upper part of the body. Fl 6.5 cm long by 7.5 cm, glossy
white with a pale violet-pink throat. [Kiesling IP/DHS]

DISTRIBUTION: Argentina, La Rioja, near Famatina.

Gymnocalycium saglione   (Cels) B. & R.

Simple, up to 30 cm broad. Fl only 3.5 cm long, white
tinged with pink. [IP/DHS]

DISTRIBUTION: Argentina: Salta; Catamarca and
Tucuman.

OTHER NAMES: *Brachycalycium tilcarense.*

Gymnocalycium schatzlianum
Strigl & W. Till

Body flattened-globular, dark bright green. Fl 7−8 cm broad, funnel-shaped, white with a greenish-white throat. [P93/CS/GC]

DISTRIBUTION: Argentina, Province of Buenos Aires, Sierra de Tandil.

Gymnocalycium schickendantzii
(Web.) B. & R.

Simple, to 10 cm across, in habitat becoming columnar with age, spination very variable. Fl up to 5 cm long, whitish or pinkish. **v. delaetii** (K. Sch.) Bkbg. is a distinctive plant with more rounded tubercles and shorter spines. [L473/CS/PM]

DISTRIBUTION: NW Argentina, Cordoba to Tucuman.

OTHER NAMES: *G. pungens*. **v. delaetii**: *G. delaetii*.

Gymnocalycium schroederianum
van Osten

Body simple, depressed, up to 15 cm broad and 5 cm high, ribs 15−18. Fl up to 7 cm long and 5.5 cm broad, whitish. **v. bayense** Kiesling has smaller stems, mostly up to 7 cm broad and fl only 4−5 cm long. **v. paucicostatum** Kiesling has only 9−11 very angulate ribs and only 3 spines as against 5−7 for the other varieties. [CS/PM]

DISTRIBUTION: Uruguay (species only) and Argentina (species and vars.)

Gymnocalycium schuetzianum
Till & Schatzl

Flattened-globular, 9−11 cm broad, old plants up to 15 cm high and 17 cm broad, offsetting with age. Fl 6−8 cm broad. Related to **G. monvillei**. [FR430/offset from type plant/DHS]

DISTRIBUTION: Argentina, Cordoba, near Cruz del Eje. (Found by Ritter).

Gymnocalycium sigelianum
(Schick) Berg.

Flattened to over 7 cm broad. Fl pink. Closely related to **G. capillaense**. [IP/DHS]

DISTRIBUTION: Argentina, Cordoba.

Gymnocalycium spegazzinii   B. & R.

Simple, depressed-globose, up to 20 cm high and 18 cm broad. Spination very variable in length, sometimes clasping the body, sometimes not. Fl up to 7 cm long and 5 cm across, white, sometimes with a pink tinge. [L530/IP/DHS]

DISTRIBUTION: Argentina: Salta; Catamarca and Tucuman.

Gymnocalycium stellatum   (Speg.) Speg.

One of the most variable species in the genus. Body flattened to 10 cm broad, greyish, brownish or blackish-green, spines brown or black, variable in number and length. Fl 6 cm long, white, *v. paucispinum* fits within the species. [L.479/IP/DHS]

DISTRIBUTION: Argentina, Cordoba.

OTHER NAMES: *G. asterium* and its vars. *G. ochoterenai* and 4 vars., *G. bodenbenderianum*, *G. kozelskyanum*, *G. riojense*, *G. triacanthum*.

Gymnocalycium striglianum   Jeggle

Body simple, bluish-grey to brown, up to 5 cm high and 8 cm across. Fl 4 cm broad, 5 cm long, creamy-white, suffused with pink. [WR548/IP/DHS]

DISTRIBUTION: Argentina, Mendoza.

Gymnocalycium sutterianum (Schick) Berg.

Solitary, flattened-spherical. Fl large, whitish-pink. [B93/IP/DHS]

DISTRIBUTION: Argentina, Cordoba.

'Gymnocalycium taningaense'

Characteristically dark bodied. [P212/IP/DHS]

DISTRIBUTION: Argentina, E Cordoba.

Gymnocalycium tillianum   Rausch

Simple, up to 10 cm high and 15 cm across, greyish-green. Fl 3 cm long, 2.5 cm broad, red. [CS/PM]

DISTRIBUTION: Argentina, Sierra Ambato.

Gymnocalycium tudae   Ito

Flattened-spherical, up to 6 cm high and 17 cm across, greyish-green, rsp to 7, csp absent. Fl 4 cm long and broad, white. [CS/DHS]

DISTRIBUTION: Paraguay to Brazil.

OTHER NAMES: *G. fricianum*, *G. karwinskyanum*, *G. marsoneri*, *G. matoense*, *G. megatae*, *G. onychacanthum*, *G. rotundicarpum*, *G. seminudum*, *G. tortuga*.

'Gymnocalycium tudae v. izozogsii'

Smaller than the species, with more rsp and one central spine. [CS/GC]

DISTRIBUTION: Bolivia, Santa Cruz, Izozog basin.

OTHER NAMES: *G. izozogsii, G. pflanzii v. izozogsii.*

'Gymnocalycium tudae v. pseudomalacocarpus' (Bkbg.) Don.

Flattened-globular, 7 cm broad and 3 cm high, offsetting, usually reddish-green, spines 3–5. [CS/GC]

DISTRIBUTION: Bolivia, salt dunes near San Jose.

OTHER NAMES: *G. pseudomalacocarpus.*

Gymnocalycium uebelmannianum Rausch

Simple, flattened-globular, 1 cm high and up to 7 cm across, with a huge taproot, green with a waxy bloom. Fl 3.5 cm long and broad, white with a pink throat. [WR141/IP/DHS]

DISTRIBUTION: Argentina, Sierra de Velasco.

Gymnocalycium uruguayense (Arech.) B. & R.

Clumping to form many headed mounds in cultivation of dark green, flattened-globular heads. Fl 4 cm long, yellow, white or pink. [WR350/IP/DHS]

DISTRIBUTION: Uruguay.

OTHER NAMES: *G. artigas, G. guerkeanum, G. melanocarpum.*

Gymnocalycium valnicekianum Jajo

Broadly spherical, becoming elongated up to 30 cm high by 18 cm, bright grassy-green. Fl 5 cm broad, white with a reddish throat. [B165/IP/GC]

DISTRIBUTION: Argentina, Cordoba.

OTHER NAMES: *G. immemoratum.*

Gymnocalycium vatteri Buin.

Flattened, 4 cm high, 9 cm broad, matt olive-green, spines mostly only 1–3. Fl 5 cm long and 4 cm broad, white with a reddish throat. [CS/GC]

DISTRIBUTION: Argentina, Cordoba, Sierra Grande, near Nono.

Gymnocalycium weissianum Bkbg.

Broadly globular, up to 9 cm high and 14 cm across, matt greyish-green. Fl more or less bell-shaped, brownish or whitish-pink with a darker throat. Probably conspecific with **G. mazanense** and **G. nidulans**. [L485/IP/GC]

DISTRIBUTION: Argentina, Mazan.

Leuchtenbergia principis Hook.

Simple or offsetting with age, up to 70 cm high. Fl up to 8 cm long, yellow to pink. [CS/PM]

DISTRIBUTION: C to N Mexico.

Lobivia acanthoplegma (Bkbg.) Bkbg.

Holotype Das Kakteen Lexikon 1965 p195 Ill 190. Single, flattened-globular, up to 15 cm across, csp 0. Fl 5 cm across, red, often with a purple sheen. [CS/PM]

DISTRIBUTION: Bolivia, near Ansaldo on the road to the Rio Caine.

OTHER NAMES: *Pseudolobivia acanthoplegma*, *Lobivia taratensis*, *L. cinnabarina subsp. acanthoplegma*, *Cinnabarinea acanthoplegma*.

Lobivia acanthoplegma v. oligotricha (Card.) Rausch

Single, globular to somewhat elongated, up to 10 cm across, spination variable in density according to the population from which the plants are derived. Fl 3–3.5 cm broad, red, sometimes with a paler throat. [WB5108–3/IP/DHS]

DISTRIBUTION: Bolivia around Tiraque.

OTHER NAMES: *Lobivia oligotricha*, *L. neocinnabarina*, *L. pseudocinnabarina*, *Cinnabarinea pseudocinnabarina*, *L. cinnabarina subsp. acanthoplegma, v. oligotricha* & *v. neocinnabarina*.

Lobivia acanthoplegma v. patula Rausch

Single, flattened-globular, bright grassy-green, up to 15 cm across. Fl 3–5 cm across, blood-red to orange, without purple tints. [PM190/H]

DISTRIBUTION: Bolivia, Cliza, in an unusual habitat for a lobivia on flat alluvial land where farming and building have rendered this beautiful variety virtually extinct.

Lobivia acanthoplegma v. roseiflora Rausch

Noticeably more flattened than the previous three, spination white. Fl smaller to 3 cm, always pink, sometimes with a white throat. [CS/PM]

DISTRIBUTION: Bolivia, Angostura.

OTHER NAMES: *Lobivia cinnabarina subsp. acanthoplegma v. roseiflora*

Lobivia arachnacantha Buin. & Ritt.

Offsetting, heads to 4 cm broad. Fl to 4 cm long.
v. torrecillasensis (Card.) Bkbg. (from Comarapa, Bolivia) spination denser, flowers red. **v. sulphurea** Vasqu. (from Pasorapa, Bolivia) brighter green, lemon-yellow flower. [KK499/IP/GC]

DISTRIBUTION: Bolivia, Samaipata.

OTHER NAMES: *Echinopsis arachnacantha, E. ancistrophora subsp. arachnacantha.*

Lobivia arachnacantha v. densiseta
Rausch

Distinguished by its dense covering of brownish-red spines up to 20 mm long and its red flowers 7.5 cm long. [CS/GC]

DISTRIBUTION: Bolivia, Valle Grande.

OTHER NAMES: *Echinopsis arachnacantha v. vallegrandensis, E. ancistrophora subsp. arachnacantha v. densiseta & v. vallegrandensis.*

Lobivia aurea (B. & R.) Bkbg.

Single-headed, body spherical to elongated up to 10 cm high, with 14–15 acute ribs. Rsp whitish, usually 10 around 1 cm long, csp darker, usually 1 sometimes up to 4, thicker, up to 3 cm long. Fl 9 cm long, 8 cm broad, lemon-yellow. [P185/IP/DHS]

DISTRIBUTION: Argentina, Cordoba.

OTHER NAMES: *Echinopsis aurea, Lobivia cylindrica, Pseudolobivia aurea, P. luteiflora, Hymenorebutia aurea.* For varieties of **L. aurea** other than those below see Appendix 3.

Lobivia aurea v. fallax (Oehme) Rausch

Single or forming small groups, up to 40 cm high by 8 cm, strongly spined. [P137/CS/PM]

DISTRIBUTION: Argentina, Sierra de Malanzan.

OTHER NAMES: *Lobivia fallax, Pseudolobivia aurea v. fallax, Hymenorebutia aurea v. lariojensis.*

Lobivia aurea v. quinesensis
(Rausch) Rausch

Single, short-cylindrical, up to 12 cm high by 6 cm, densely spined, csp up to 6 cm long. Fl pale yellow. [WR112/IP/DHS]

DISTRIBUTION: Argentina, San Luis, between Quines and San Martin.

OTHER NAMES: *Echinopsis aurea v. quinesensis.*

Lobivia aurea v. shaferi (B. & R.) Rausch

Stem to 25 cm high by 4 cm; csp 5 cm long. **v. leucomalla** (Wessn.) Rausch from San Luis; solitary, to 12 cm high by 6 cm, densely covered with whitish bristly spines. [IP/GC]

DISTRIBUTION: Argentina, Andalgala.

OTHER NAMES: *Lobivia cylindracea, L. shaferi.*
v. leucomalla: *L. leucomalla, 'L. densispina v. leucomalla', L. famatimensis v. leucomalla.*

Lobivia backebergii (Werd.) Bkbg.

Solitary or offsetting, flattened-globular in habitat, much more cylindrical in cultivation, when the stem is also much brighter green. Fl red to carmine with a white throat. [PM141/H]

DISTRIBUTION: Bolivia, highlands around La Paz.

Lobivia bruchii B. & R.

Large, globular, to 20 cm or more across. FL 5 cm across, deep red. [RM]

DISTRIBUTION: N Argentina, Tafi del Valle.

OTHER NAMES: *Soehrensia bruchii, L. formosa v. bruchii, Trichocereus bruchii.*

Lobivia caineana Card.

Solitary, up to 20 cm high and 9 cm thick. Fl 7 cm long. [IP/DHS]

DISTRIBUTION: Bolivia, Rio Caine, e.g. at Capinota.

Lobivia chrysantha (Werd.) Bkbg.

Single, up to 7 cm across, with a tap-root. Fl 5.5 cm long, yellow with a red throat. **v. hypocyrta** Rausch has a yellow fl striped red. [CS/PM]

DISTRIBUTION: Argentina, Salta, around Puerta Tastil.

OTHER NAMES: *Lobivia janseniana, L. staffenii, L. klusacekii, L. dragai, L. polaskiana.*

Lobivia chrysochete Werd.

Body flattened-globular, to 20 cm across, spines 30, to 10 cm. Fl 4 cm wide, orange-red to red. [IP/M]
v. markusii (Rausch) Rausch (lower illus.); spines 50, to 5 cm, much thinner, golden yellow (Volcan). [CS/PM]
v. tenuispina (Ritt.) Rausch; spines to 20, to 9 cm, brown to black. Fl yellow to orange (Bolivia, San Antonio to Iscayache).

DISTRIBUTION: Argentina, Santa Victoria.

OTHER NAMES: **v. markusii**: *L. markusii.* **v. tenuispina**: *L. tenuispina.*

Lobivia cinnabarina (Hook.) B. & R.

Mainly solitary, flattened-globular, up to 15 cm across. Fl 6–8 cm across. [KK228/CS/PM]

DISTRIBUTION: Bolivia, widespread around Sucre, variable hence the following synonyms.

OTHER NAMES: *Lobivia charcasina, Cinnabarinea cinnabarina, L. cinnabarina v. walterspielii, C. walterspielii v. sanguiniflora, L. zudanensis, L. cinn. v. zudanensis, L. prestoana, L. cinn. v. grandiflora.*

Lobivia cinnabarina v. draxleriana (Rausch) Rausch

Solitary, up to 15 cm across. Fl 7 cm across. [CS/PM]

DISTRIBUTION: Bolivia, Aiquile.

OTHER NAMES: *L. draxleriana.*

Lobivia famatimensis (Speg.) B. & R.

Solitary, up to 3.5 cm across with a fleshy tap-root. Fl 3–5 cm across. **v. sanjuanensis** Rausch; up to 20 cm high and 5 cm across. Fl up to 9 cm across (from San Juan). **v. jachalensis** Rausch; areoles more woolly, fl smaller (near Jachal). [WR127/IP/DHS]

DISTRIBUTION: Argentina, La Rioja, in the Famatina Mountains.

OTHER NAMES: *Reicheocactus pseudoreicheanus.*

Lobivia ferox B. & R.

Solitary, 30–70 cm high by 30 cm, csp up to 18 cm long. Fl 9–11 cm long, 6–8 cm broad, white to whitish-pink. [CS/PM]

DISTRIBUTION: Very widespread, from Oruro in N Bolivia to Purmamarca in Argentina.

OTHER NAMES: *Lobivia ferox v. camargensis, L. ferox v potosina, L. ducis pauli, L. potosina, Echinopsis ferox, E. lecoriensis, E. potosina, E. cerdana, Pseudolobivia ferox, P. lecoriensis & P. potosina.*

Lobivia ferox v. longispina (B. & R.) Rausch

Always smaller, sometimes even flattened. Fl white, yellow, pink or red, often scarcely opening because of wild spination. [PM184/H]

DISTRIBUTION: N Argentina to S Bolivia.

OTHER NAMES: *Lobivia longispina, L. aureolilacina, L. claeysiana, L. ducis pauli v. rubriflora, L. hastifera, L. horrida, L. pictiflorea, L. variispina, Pseudolobivia longispina, P. wilkeae.*

Lobivia grandiflora B. & R.

Short-cylindric, individual stems to 20 cm high by 10 cm, clumping. Fl 8–10 cm long. [CS/PM]

DISTRIBUTION: Argentina, Catamarca, between Andalgala and Conception.

OTHER NAMES: *Echinopsis rowleyi, Trichocereus rowleyi, Helianthocereus grandiflorus, Hymenolobivia purpureomineata, Lobivia grand. v. lobivioides.*

Lobivia grandiflora v. crassicaulis (Bkbg.) Rausch

Stems 15 cm high and 11.5 cm across, offsetting. Fl 6–8 cm long. [CS/PM]

DISTRIBUTION: Argentina, Catamarca, La Estancia.

OTHER NAMES: *Helianthocereus crassicaulis, Lobivia andalgalensis B. & R. non Web., L. crassicaulis, Trichocereus catamarcensis.*

Lobivia haematantha (Speg.) B. & R.

Solitary, 5–10 cm high by 6–7 cm. Fl 5–7 cm long and broad, red with a white throat. [WR157/CS/PM]

DISTRIBUTION: Argentina, Salta, W of Cachi to Angostaco.

v. chorrillosensis (Rausch) Rausch (illus.); body 4 cm across, solitary or sometimes with one or two offsets. Fl orange-red to red, 4–5 cm across.

DISTRIBUTION: Argentina, Quebrada del Toro.

OTHER NAMES: **v. chorril.**: *Lobivia chorrillosensis.*

Lobivia haematantha v. amblayensis (Rausch) Rausch

Normally solitary 2 cm high by 3 cm (often clumping in cultivation and becoming much more lax and elongated). Fl 6–10 cm across, yellow to orange. [L569/CS/PM]

DISTRIBUTION: Argentina, Amblaya.

OTHER NAMES: *Lobivia amblayensis* & *v. albispina, L. haem. subsp. kuehnrichii v. Ambl.*

Lobivia haematantha v. densispina (Werd.) Rausch

Solitary, 8 cm high and 7 cm across. Fl 6–8 cm broad. [CS/PM]

DISTRIBUTION: Argentina, Jujuy, near Tumbaya.

OTHER NAMES: *Lobivia densispina, 'L. famatimensis' hort.*

Lobivia haematantha v. elongata (Bkbg.) Rausch

Solitary, to 20 cm high by 6 cm. Fl 5–6 cm across. [WR25/CS/PM]

DISTRIBUTION: Argentina, S of Cachi.

OTHER NAMES: *L. elongata.*

Lobivia haematantha v. hualfinensis (Rausch) Rausch

Solitary, 7 cm across with csp up to 8 cm long. Fl 5.5 cm across, orange-red to red with a white throat. [WR146/IP/M]

DISTRIBUTION: Argentina, Catamarca, near Hualfin.

OTHER NAMES: *Lobivia hualfinensis* & *v. fechseri.*

Lobivia haematantha v. kuehnrichii (Fric) Rausch

Solitary (clumping in cultivation) 4–6 cm across. Fl yellow, orange or red, 5 cm across. [WR238/CS/PM]

DISTRIBUTION: Argentina, Salta, from La Poma to Piedra de Molino.

OTHER NAMES: *Lobivia kuehnrichii, L. drijveriana* & *vars, L. nigrispina, L. penca poma.*

Lobivia haematantha v. rebutioides
(Bkbg.) Rausch

In habitat solitary but clumping in cultivation; heads 3–5 cm across. Fl 6–8 cm broad, white, yellow, orange, red, pink to violet. [OF91–80/IP/DHS]

DISTRIBUTION: Argentina, Jujuy, Quebrada de Humahuaca.

OTHER NAMES: *Lobivia rebutioides* & *vars*, *L. sublimiflora*, *L. pectinifera*, *L. chlorogona*, *L. wessneriana*, '*L. famatimensis*', *L. napina*.

Lobivia hertrichiana Bkbg.

Forming many-headed clumps, individual heads up to 8 cm across; spination very variable, from sparse and short to dense and long (to 6 cm in *L. echinata*). Fl bright red to carmine often with a white throat. [PM68/HS/PM]

DISTRIBUTION: Peru, Urubamba Valley.

OTHER NAMES: *Lobivia allegraiana*, *L. backebergi subsp. hert.* & *v. laui*, *L. binghamiana*, *L. incaica*, *L. huilcanota*, *L. minuta*, *L. planiceps*, *L. wegneriana*, *L. echinata*, *L. lauii*, *L. hert. v. lauii*, *Neolobivia divaricata*, *N. prolifera*.

Lobivia hertrichiana v. simplex
(Rausch) Rausch

Solitary, 20 cm high by 10 cm; csp can be up to 8 cm long. Fl 5 cm across, red with a white throat. [WR423/CS/PM]

DISTRIBUTION: Peru, Huambutio.

OTHER NAMES: *Lobivia simplex*, *L. backebergii subsp. hert. v. simplex*.

Lobivia jajoiana Bkbg.

Solitary, globular, up to 6 cm across; csp up to 3 cm long, somewhat hooked. Fl up to 6.5 cm broad, tomato red with a glossy black/violet hymen, scented. [CS/PM]

DISTRIBUTION: Argentina, Volcan.

OTHER NAMES: *L. buiningiana*, *Hymenolobivia buiningiana*.

Lobivia jajoiana v. nigristoma
(Buin.) Bkbg.

Solitary, somewhat elongated up to 7 cm across; csp up to 6 cm long, brown to black. Fl to 8 cm across, yellow, orange or red with a black/violet hymen. [FR401/CS/PM]

DISTRIBUTION: Argentina, Quebrada de Humahuaca.

OTHER NAMES: *Lobivia nigristoma*, *L. vatteri*, *L. chrysantha subsp. jajoiana v. vatteri*.

Lobivia jajoiana v. paucicostata
(Rausch) Rausch

Single (usually sparingly offsetting in cultivation), of a characteristic shade of matt greyish-green. Fl 5 cm across, red with a black hymen. [CS/PM]

DISTRIBUTION: Argentina, S of Purmamarca.

OTHER NAMES: *Lobivia glauca* & *v. paucicostata*, *Hymenolobivia miniatinigra*, *L. chrysantha subsp. jajoiana v. pauc.*

Lobivia kieslingii Rausch

Solitary, globular up to 25 cm across. Fl 9 cm across, orange-red to carmine. [CS/PM]

DISTRIBUTION: Argentina, Tucuman, in the Sierra de Quilmes.

OTHER NAMES: *Lobivia formosa v. kieslingii.*

Lobivia larae Card.

Solitary, up to 10 cm or more high and across; spines up to 4.5 cm long (central to 6 cm at times). Fl 6 cm long. [IP/DHS]

DISTRIBUTION: Bolivia, Tarata-Rio Caine.

OTHER NAMES: *Lobivia pentlandii v. larae, L. backebergii v. larae.*

Lobivia lateritia (Guerke) B. & R.

Solitary, to 50 cm high by 10 cm, spines pale. Fl 5 cm long, amazingly variable in colour even within a single population: white, pink, yellow, orange, red and crimson and every possible intermediate or even combinations, e.g. yellow with a pink centre. [PM173/H]

DISTRIBUTION: Bolivia, widespread across the mts from El Puente to Impora and Cotagaite.

OTHER NAMES: *Lobivia cintiensis, L. scopulina, L. camataquiensis, Hymenorebutia cintiensis, L. imporana n.n.*

Lobivia lateritia v. kupperiana (Bkbg.) Rausch

Solitary, up to 10 cm high by 8 cm, spines dark, up to 4 cm long. Fl 5 cm across, ochre-yellow. **v. rubriflora** (Bkbg.) Rausch has dark spines to 5 cm long and a brilliant red flower (Bolivia, Mal Paso). [CS/PM]

DISTRIBUTION: Bolivia, Tupiza.

OTHER NAMES: *Lobivia kupperiana.* **v. rubriflora:** *L. kupperiana v. rubriflora, Hymenorebutia torataensis, H. torreana, 'L. horrida v. sanguiniflora'.*

Lobivia marsoneri (Werd.) Bkbg.

Solitary, up to 8 cm across with a short taproot; csp up to 7 cm long. Fl up to 6 cm broad, yellow to red with a red throat, scented. In **v. iridescens** (Bkbg.) Rausch spines are only to 10 mm long. Fl 4.5 cm broad (Tres Cruzes, Azul Pampa etc.). [L470/CS/PM]

DISTRIBUTION: Argentina, Jujuy, Quebrada de Humahuaca.

OTHER NAMES: *Lobivia rubescens, L. haageana & vars., L. chrysantha subsp. mars. & v. rubescens.* **v. iridescens:** *L. iridescens, L. uitewaaleana, L. muhriae.*

Lobivia maximiliana (Heyder) Bkbg.

Mound-forming with individual heads up to 10 cm across. Fl 5 cm long and 4 cm across, orange. **v. violacea** (Rausch) Rausch from Altamachai has a beautiful violet fl and longer spines. [L252/CS/PM]

DISTRIBUTION: Bolivia, around Lake Titicaca.

OTHER NAMES: *Lobivia corbula, L. pentlandii v. maximiliana, L. cariquinensis, L. pseudocariquinensis.* **v. violacea:** *L. caespitosa v. violacea.*

Lobivia maximiliana v. caespitosa
(Purp.) Rausch

Clumping, heads up to 20 cm high by 6 cm; csp to 7 cm long. Fl 7−9 cm long, 5−6 cm across, orange.
v. miniatiflora (Ritt.) Rausch; stem to 6 cm high by 4 cm; csp to 5 cm. Fl 6 cm long, 4 cm wide, cinnabar (Inquisivi-Quime). [WR57/IP/DHS]

DISTRIBUTION: Bolivia, from Cocapata and Challa to Copachuncho.

OTHER NAMES: *Lobivia caespitosa, L. longiflora.*
v. miniatiflora: *L. miniatiflora.*

Lobivia maximiliana v. charazanensis
(Card.) Rausch

Clumping, heads in cultivation becoming rather long and cylindrical; spination yellowish. Fl yellow. v. hermanniana (Bkbg.) Rausch, from N of La Paz, forms large clumps with much longer spines and a 7 cm long and 6 cm broad orange-coloured fl. [CS/PM]

DISTRIBUTION: Bolivia, Charazani.

OTHER NAMES: *Lobivia charazanensis, L. max. subsp. caespitosa v. chara.,* v. hermanniana: *L. hermanniana, L. caespitosa v. rinconadensis, L. max. subsp. caesp. v. herm.*

Lobivia maximiliana v. corbula
(Herrera) Rausch

Sparingly offsetting, heads up to 8 cm across, spines brown, csp 0. Fl 5−6 cm long and 4 cm across, golden yellow, red or violet. v. sicuaniensis (Rausch) Rausch from Sicuani, is mainly differentiated by its 3−4 cm long fl. [L154/CS/PM]

DISTRIBUTION: Bolivia, around Cuzco.

OTHER NAMES: *Lobivia lauramarca.* v. sicuaniensis: *L. sicuaniensis.*

Lobivia maximiliana v. westii
(Hutch.) Rausch

Sparingly offsetting, heads up to 20 cm high by 7 cm, csp may attain 10 cm. Fl 7−9 cm long, 4−6 cm across, orange. v. intermedia (Rausch) Rausch (illus.), from Chalhuanca, is mainly distinguished by its red fl, 7.5 cm long by 4 cm broad. [CS/PM]

DISTRIBUTION: Bolivia, Andahuaylas.

OTHER NAMES: *Lobivia westii, L. cruciaureispina.*
v. intermedia: *L. intermedia, L. max. subsp. westii v. intermedia.*

Lobivia oxyalabastra   Card. & Rausch

Offsetting with heads up to 6 cm across. Fl 5 cm long. [WR200/CS/PM]

DISTRIBUTION: Bolivia, Tapacari.

OTHER NAMES: *L. backebergii v. oxyalabastra.*

Lobivia pampana   B. & R.

Single or very sparingly clumping, globular, 10 cm across; spines up to 7 cm long but usually shorter. Fl 7 cm across. [CS/PM]

DISTRIBUTION: Bolivia, Pampa de Arrieros, Volcan Misti, Moquegua etc.

OTHER NAMES: *Lobivia mistiensis* & *vars., L. aureosenilis, L. glaucescens.*

Lobivia pentlandii (Hook.) B. & R.

Extremely variable, clumping, heads to 12 cm across; spines short or up to 10 cm. Fl 5 cm across, yellow, orange, pink, violet or red, all with a white throat. [PM143/H]

DISTRIBUTION: Bolivia, S of Titicaca to Potosi.

OTHER NAMES: *Lobivia aculeata, L. argentea, L. aurantiaca, L. boliviensis, L. brunneo-rosea, L. carminantha, L. capinotensis, L. hardeniana, L. higginsiana, L. johnsoniana, L. leucorhodon, L. leucoviolacea, L. omasuyana, L. raphidacantha, L. schneideriana, L. titicacensis, L. varians & L. wegheiana.*

Lobivia pugionacantha (Rose & Boed.) Bkbg.

Single, up to 7 cm across; spines dagger-like with broad bases, radials 5–7 to 2 cm long and lying horizontal on the body. Fl 5 cm broad, yellow to yellowish-orange. **v. cornuta** (Rausch) Rausch from S of Tarija has broader, flatter ribs and a more upstanding spination. [CS/PM]

DISTRIBUTION: Bolivia/Argentina border region, e.g. Villazon and La Quiaca.

OTHER NAMES: *Lobivia pugionacantha v. flaviflora.* **v. cornuta**: *L. adpressispina, L. cornuta.*

Lobivia pugionacantha v. culpinensis (Ritt.) Rausch

Single, body 5–15 cm across; csp 2–6 cm long. Fl 6 cm across, yellow, orange or red. [PM180/H]

DISTRIBUTION: Bolivia, around Culpina.

OTHER NAMES: *Lobivia culpinensis, L. campicola, L. pug. v. haemantha.*

Lobivia pugionacantha v. salitrensis (Rausch) Rausch

Sparingly clumping, heads 4–6 cm across. [WR636/CS/PM]

DISTRIBUTION: Bolivia, Salitre and Yuquina.

OTHER NAMES: *Lobivia salitrensis & v. flexuosa.*

Lobivia rauschii Zecher

Offsetting to form many-headed mounds, body up to 15 cm high by 5 cm. Fl 4 cm across, red. [WR635/IP/GC]

DISTRIBUTION: Bolivia, Yuquina near Culpina.

Lobivia rosarioana Rausch

Solitary, globular up to 10 cm across. Fl 6.5 cm long by 5 cm. [WR129/DHS]

DISTRIBUTION: Argentina, Sierra Famatina.

OTHER NAMES: *Lobivia formosa v. rosarioana, 'L. grandis v. aureiflora'.*

Lobivia rossii Boed.

Single (but sparingly offsetting in cultivation), up to 7 cm across; spines up to 6 cm long, awl-shaped, brownish-yellow. Fl 5−6 cm across, shades of yellow or yellow-orange. [CS/PM]

DISTRIBUTION: Bolivia, Potosi, near Huari Huari.

OTHER NAMES: *Cinnabarinea boedekeriana*, *L. pugionacantha v. rossii*.

Lobivia saltensis (Speg.) B. & R.

Single, to 5 cm across; spines thin. Fl to 5 cm across.
v. pseudocachensis (Bkbg.) Rausch; bodies small, clumping, more densely spined than the species, fl similar (Argentina, Escoype). [WR177/DHS]

DISTRIBUTION: Argentina, between Salta and Tucuman.

OTHER NAMES: **v. pseudocachensis**: *L. pseudocach.* & *vars.*, *L. emmae*.

Lobivia sanguiniflora Bkbg.

Solitary, flattened up to 8 cm across, csp sometimes hooked. Fl 5 cm broad, red with a white throat. [CS/PM]

DISTRIBUTION: Argentina, around Santa Victoria.

OTHER NAMES: *Lobivia sanguiniflora v. pseudolateritia, v. breviflora & v. duursmaiana, L. breviflora, L. duursmaiana & L. polycephala.*

Lobivia schieliana Bkbg.

Multiheaded, heads to 5 cm across, dark green; spines to 3 cm long, bent towards the body. Fl 5 cm across, red or yellow. **v. quiabayensis** (Rausch) Rausch; heads 6 cm across, grass-green, spines wavy to 5 cm; fl orange/red, red to carmine. [L1004/IP/DHS]

DISTRIBUTION: Bolivia, valley of the Rio Consato.

OTHER NAMES: *Lobivia backebergii subsp. schieliana.*
v. quiabayensis: *L. quiabayensis* & *L. maximiliana subsp. quiab.*

Lobivia schieliana v. leptacantha
(Rausch) Rausch

Cylindrical, 15 cm high by 7 cm, sparingly offsetting; spines 3−7 cm long, thin, elastic. Fl 5.5 cm across, yellow, red to violet. [WR422/IP/DHS]

DISTRIBUTION: Peru, at Paucartambo.

OTHER NAMES: *Lobivia leptacantha, L. maximiliana subsp. quiabayensis v. lept.*

Lobivia schreiteri Castell

Body 2−4 cm across, clumping. Fl 3 cm across, orange to dark red with a black throat. [CS/PM]

DISTRIBUTION: Argentina, Tucuman, Tafi del Valle.

OTHER NAMES: *Lobivia saltensis v. schreiteri.*

Lobivia schreiteri v. stilowiana (Bkbg.) Rausch

Heads up to 7 cm across, sparingly offsetting. Fl 4 cm broad, orange or carmine without the black throat. **v. riolarensis** Rausch is solitary, up to 12 cm across with an orange fl (Argentina, Catamarca, Rio Lara). [CS/PM]

DISTRIBUTION: Argentina, Tucuman, Abra de Infernillo.

OTHER NAMES: *Lobivia stilowiana, L. saltensis v. stilowiana.*

Lobivia silvestrii (Speg.) Rowley

Forming dense masses of finger-like stems. Fl 4 cm across, orange-red to red. [IP/DHS]

DISTRIBUTION: Argentina, between Tucuman and Salta.

OTHER NAMES: *Chamaecereus silvestrii.*

Lobivia tegeleriana Bkbg.

Usually solitary, up to 10 cm across. Fl 4 cm long and 1.5 cm across, yellow, orange or red. **v. incuiensis** (Rauh & Bkbg.) Rausch is bigger. Fl 2 cm broad, red. **v. akersii** (Rausch) Rausch is up to 70 cm across. Fl 2 cm across, orange. [CS/DHS]

DISTRIBUTION: C Peru.

OTHER NAMES: *Acantholobivia tegeleriana, Lob. ayacuchoensis.* **v. incuiensis:** *L. incui, Acanth. incui.* **v. akersii:**, *L. akersii, L. oyonica, L. churinensis.*

Lobivia tiegeliana Wessn.

Single, up to 7 cm across, flattened-globular. Fl 5.5 cm across, purple to violet-red. **v. ruberrima** Rausch, the plant illustrated, differs mainly by its pure red fl and slightly less dense spination. [CS/PM]

DISTRIBUTION: Bolivia, near Tarija.

OTHER NAMES: *Lobivia peclardiana.*

Lobivia tiegeliana v. cinnabarina (Fric) Rowley

Body normally single (clumping in cultivation), up to 7 cm across. Fl 3.5 cm across, red with violet tints. [WR513/CS/PM]

DISTRIBUTION: Argentina, Salta, Rodeo to Nazareno.

OTHER NAMES: *Lobivia graulichii v. cinnabarina, L. fricii & L. tieg. v. fricii.*

Lobivia tiegeliana v. pusilla (Ritt.) Rausch

Heads up to 4 cm across forming multi-headed clumps. Fl 4 cm across. **v. flaviflora** (Ritt.) Rausch differs mainly by its lemon-yellow fl. [CS/PM]

DISTRIBUTION: Bolivia, S of Tarija.

OTHER NAMES: *Lobivia pusilla, Mediolobivia hirsutissima, L. tieg. v. uriondoensis.* **v. flaviflora:** *L. pusilla f. flaviflora.*

Lobivia versicolor Rausch

Solitary, globular to short-cylindric, 5–7 cm across, csp 6 cm long. Fl yellow, 3–4 cm across. [PM168/H]

DISTRIBUTION: Bolivia, Cuchu Ingenio.

OTHER NAMES: *Lobivia pugionacantha v. versicolor.*

Lobivia wrightiana Bkbg.

Single (often forming large clumps in cultivation), csp 1, to 7 cm long, twisted. Fl 5 cm across. [CS/PM]

DISTRIBUTION: Peru, around Huancavelica.

OTHER NAMES: *Lobivia chilensis* & *L. backebergii subsp. wrightiana.*

Lobivia wrightiana v. winteriana
(Ritt.) Rausch

Solitary, 7 cm thick, becoming quite elongated in cultivation. Fl 8 cm across, brilliant pink and orange-pink. [CS/DHS]

DISTRIBUTION: Peru, Villa Azul.

OTHER NAMES: *Lobivia winteriana* & *L. backebergii subsp. wrightiana v. winteriana.*

Lobivia zecheri Rausch

Solitary or sparingly offsetting, becoming somewhat cylindrical, 6–7 cm thick; csp 0–1, to 8 cm long. Fl 4 cm broad. [KK1546/IP/M]

DISTRIBUTION: Peru, between Ayacucho and Huanta.

OTHER NAMES: *Lobivia zecheri v. fungiflora, L. backebergii subsp. zecheri.*

Lophophora diffusa (Croiz.) Bravo
[CS/PM]

DISTRIBUTION: Mexico, Queretaro.

OTHER NAMES: *L. echinata v. diffusa.*

Lophophora williamsii
(Lem. ex S–D) Coulter

Fl can be deep violet-pink in '**f. jordanniana**'. [CS/PM]

DISTRIBUTION: Texas to C Mexico.

OTHER NAMES: *Lophophora fricii, L. williamsii v. decipiens.*

Mammillaria alamensis Craig

Although included here as a separate species its closeness to
M. sheldonii is very obvious. [Repp. 569a/CS/W]

DISTRIBUTION: Mexico, Sonora, Alamos.

Mammillaria albata Repp.

Forms beautiful white clumps of heads 4–8 cm high and
5–8 cm across. **v. longispina** Repp. (illus.) is always
single-headed, 10 cm or more high (Buenavista, SLP).
v. sanciro Repp. forms small clumps, csp brown or black
(San Ciro, SLP). [K260/IP/K]

DISTRIBUTION: Mexico, San Luis Potosi, Arroyo Carrizal.

Mammillaria albicans (B. & R.) Berg.

Plant clumping, stems 20 cm long and 6 cm broad.
[K305/IP/K]

DISTRIBUTION: Mexico, islands of Santa Cruz and San
Diego, Baja California.

OTHER NAMES: *Mammillaria slevinii.*

Mammillaria albicoma Boed.

Clumping, heads 5 cm across. [CS/PM]

DISTRIBUTION: Mexico, Tamaulipas, near Jaumauve and
Miquihuana.

Mammillaria albiflora (Werd.) Bkbg.

Eventually clumping from the base. Fl white, 3 cm across.
[W]

DISTRIBUTION: Mexico, Queretaro.

OTHER NAMES: *M. herrerae v. albiflora.*

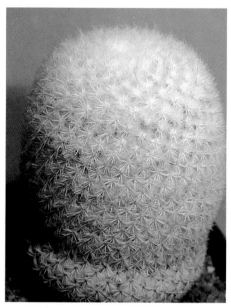

Mammillaria albilanata Bkbg.

Stem up to 15 cm high by 8 cm; fl 7 mm long, deep carmine
but a rather shy flowerer in cultivation. [IP/K]

DISTRIBUTION: Mexico, Guerrero, Chilpancingo.

Mammillaria angelensis Craig

There has been some confusion over the identity of this species but illustrated is a plant collected from the original type locality by H. Klein. [K307/IP/K]

DISTRIBUTION: Mexico, Baja California, Angel de la Guarda Is.

Mammillaria angelensis v. estebanensis (Lindsay) Repp.

The plant illustrated is from the type locality of the Isla San Esteban in the Gulf of California. Csp brown. Fl 2 cm across, yellow. [K309/IP/K]

DISTRIBUTION: Mexico, Baja California, Isla San Esteban.

OTHER NAMES: *M. estebanensis.*

Mammillaria anniana Glass & Foster

Offsetting, heads up to 3 cm diameter; fl only 6 mm across. [CS/PM]

DISTRIBUTION: Mexico, Tamaulipas, E of Ciudad Mante, Cerro Bernal.

Mammillaria apamensis Repp.

Solitary, to 9 cm high by 12 cm; rsp 13–16, 3–5 mm long; csp 1–2, 7–10 mm long. Fl 14–16 mm across, carmine. Closely related to **M. discolor**. [Repp910/IP/Repp]

DISTRIBUTION: Mexico, Hidalgo, San Lorenzo Apam.

Mammillaria apozolensis Repp.

Forming large clumps with heads up to 12 cm high and 8 cm across, spines fox-red. **v. saltensis** Repp. is always single-headed up to 12 cm high and broad, spines yellow (Monte Escobado, Zac.) [L1045/IP/K]

DISTRIBUTION: Mexico, Zacatecas, along Rio Juchipila, near Apozol.

Mammillaria arida Rose ex Quehl

Solitary, flattened-globular, to 6 cm across; closely related to **M. baxteriana** but with more csp and a different ecology. [K192–1/IP/K]

DISTRIBUTION: Mexico, Baja California, near La Paz.

Mammillaria armillata K. Brandegee

Sparingly clumping, up to 30 cm high, 5 cm across. Fl 2 cm long and broad, white to pink. [K245−1/IP/K]

DISTRIBUTION: Mexico, Baja California, San Jose del Cabo.

Mammillaria aureilanata Bkbg.

Solitary, up to 7.5 cm high, young spines white turning pale yellow with age, the **v. alba** Bkbg. maintains a white spination. [CS/PM]

DISTRIBUTION: Mexico, San Luis Potosi.

Mammillaria aurihamata Boed.

Solitary or clumping, stems to 4 cm across; fl 1.2 cm across. [CS/W]

DISTRIBUTION: First recorded from Monte Gordo, Guanajuato, Mexico, but apparently not recently recollected from this locality.

Mammillaria aurispina (Lau) Repp.

Cylindrical up to 12 cm high by 5 cm; fl carmine. [L1055/CS/PM]

DISTRIBUTION: Mexico, Oaxaca, Quiotepec and Yolox.

OTHER NAMES: *Mammillaria rekoi v. aurispina.*

Mammillaria backebergiana Buchenau

Becoming elongated, 5−6 cm broad, soon offsetting, faded green. [CS/PM]

DISTRIBUTION: Mexico, border areas of Guerrero, Michoacan and Mexico DF, e.g. near Ixtapan.

OTHER NAMES: *Mammillaria fertilis.*

Mammillaria backebergiana v. ernestii (Fitt.) Glass & Foster

Differs from the species by its darker green body and fewer, thicker spines. [CS/PM]

DISTRIBUTION: Mexico, Tonatico.

OTHER NAMES: *Mammillaria ernestii.*

Mammillaria bambusiphila Repp.

Cylindrical up to 20 cm high by 8 cm, rsp 16–20, 3–6 mm long, csp 4, to 11 mm long. [Repp. 748/CS/W]

DISTRIBUTION: Mexico, Michoacan, near Huascana.

Mammillaria barbata Englm.

Solitary or clumping, heads up to 5 cm broad; fl 2 cm across. [K237/IP/K]

DISTRIBUTION: Mexico, Chihuahua, Cosihuiriachi and other localities.

OTHER NAMES: *Mammillaria garessii, M. morricalii, M. santaclarensis.*

Mammillaria baumii Boed.

Forming compact, low clumps, individual heads up to 6 cm across; fl to 3 cm across, highly perfumed. [CS/PM]

DISTRIBUTION: Mexico, Tamaulipas, near San Vicente and Jaumave.

OTHER NAMES: *Dolichothele baumii, ?Mammillaria radiaissima.*

Mammillaria baxteriana (Gates) Boed.

Solitary, flattened-globose, up to 10 cm across.
M. marshalliana (Gates) Boed., (lower illus.) [CS/PM]), from near San Bartolo is distinctive but probably conspecific. [CS/W]

DISTRIBUTION: Mexico, Baja California, SE of La Paz.

Mammillaria beiselii Diers

Clumping, heads up to 40 cm high and 12 cm across. [IP/K]

DISTRIBUTION: Mexico, borders of Colima and Michoacan near the coast.

Mammillaria bella Bkbg.

Solitary later offsetting, stems 15 cm high and 9 cm across; fl bright carmine. [CS/W]

DISTRIBUTION: Mexico, Guerrero, near Taxco.

OTHER NAMES: *M. deliusiana.*

Mammillaria beneckei Ehrenb.

Clumping, stems up to 10 cm high and 7 cm broad; seldom flowers in cultivation, winter tender. [CS/GC]

DISTRIBUTION: Mexico, widely distributed from Sinaloa to Oaxaca.

OTHER NAMES: *Dolichothele balsasoides, D. beneckei, D. nelsonii, M. balsasoides, M. aylostera, M. balsasensis, M. barkeri, M. colonensis, M. guiengolensis, M. nelsonii.*

Mammillaria berkiana Lau

Forming clumps of up to 40 heads, each 4–6 cm broad. Rsp 35–38, 6 mm long, white; csp 5–8, with 2–4 hooked, 10 mm long, brown. Fl 10 mm across. [CS/PM]

DISTRIBUTION: Mexico, Jalisco, San Andres Cohamiata.

Mammillaria bernalensis Repp.

Stems to 20 cm long by 8 cm, clumping; rsp 1–3, 1–3 mm long, white or brown; csp 3–5, 5–50 mm long, the lowest the longest, grey tipped brown. Fl 1.5–2 cm broad, pink to carmine. Closely related to **M. compressa**. [Repp790/IP/Repp]

DISTRIBUTION: Mexico, Queretaro, San Pablo/Bernal.

Mammillaria blossfeldiana Boed.

Single in habitat, clumping in cultivation, up to 4 cm across, short-cylindric. **v. shurliana** (Gates) Wiggins (illus.) is solitary, more cylindric and has pinker flowers. [CS/PM]

DISTRIBUTION: Mexico, Baja California.

OTHER NAMES: *M. shurliana.*

Mammillaria bocasana Poselger

Clumping, heads 4–8 cm across; various cultivars exist, mainly selected for their dense, white wool. [PM36/HS/PM]

DISTRIBUTION: Mexico, San Luis Potosi, near the state capital.

Mammillaria bocensis Craig

Clumping, heads flattened-globular, to 8.5 cm broad and 9 cm high. [L76/IP/K]

DISTRIBUTION: Mexico, Sonora, Las Bocas.

OTHER NAMES: *?M. neoschwarzeana.*

Mammillaria bocensis v. rubida Repp.

Usually solitary, stems to 9 cm high by 13 cm.
[K184/IP/K]

DISTRIBUTION: Mexico, Sinaloa, Sierra Madre near
Bacuribito.

OTHER NAMES: *M. rubida.*

Mammillaria bombycina Quehl

Solitary or strongly clumping, heads up to 20 cm high by
6 cm. [CS/PM]

DISTRIBUTION: Mexico, only recently re-discovered in the
wild.

Mammillaria boolii Lindsay

Sparingly clumping, heads up to 4 cm high by 3 cm; fl
2.5 cm wide. [CS/PM]

DISTRIBUTION: Mexico, Sonora, San Pedro and San Carlos
Bays.

Mammillaria brandegeei
(Coulter) K. Brandegee

Globose to cylindric, later clumping sparingly, heads to
9 cm across; fl greenish-yellow. **v. gabbii** (Coulter) Craig
has a smaller, reddish yellow fl (Baja California, San
Ignacio). [K201/IP/K]

DISTRIBUTION: Mexico, Baja California, San Jorge.

Mammillaria brauneana Boed.

Solitary, flattened-globular, up to 8 cm across, greyish-
green. [CS/PM]

DISTRIBUTION: Mexico, Tamaulipas, Jaumave.

Mammillaria brevicrinita Repp.

Forming small clumps, heads up to 4 cm high and broad.
[Repp1483/CS/PM]

DISTRIBUTION: Mexico, San Luis Potosi, Labor Vieja.

Mammillaria bucareliensis Craig

Usually clumping, to 5 cm high by 9 cm. **v. multiflora** Repp. (lower illus., [Repp355a/CS/PM]); always solitary, smaller, the crown woollier (Ciudad Maiz, San Luis Potosi). **v. tamaulipa** Repp.; noted for its long, twisted, black spines (Ocampo Pass, Tamaulipas). [CS/PM]

DISTRIBUTION: Mexico, Guanajuato, Bucarel.

OTHER NAMES: *M. bicornuta.*

Mammillaria buxbaumeriana Repp.

To 12 cm high by 5 cm, usually clumping; rsp 15–20, 7–11 mm long, white tipped black, csp 1–4, 5–8 mm long, brown to black. Closely related to **M. densispina**. [Repp2037/IP/Repp]

DISTRIBUTION: Mexico, Guanajuato, Tierra Blanca.

Mammillaria cadereytensis Craig

Solitary, branching dichotomously; the plant pictured comes close to the original description and some (but not all) plants in cultivation under this name are very similar. [IP/K]

DISTRIBUTION: Mexico, Queretaro, Cadereyta.

Mammillaria calacantha Tiegel

Solitary, stoutly cylindric. Closely related to **M. rhodantha**. [CS/PM]

DISTRIBUTION: Mexico, Queretaro, Angostura de Charcos.

Mammillaria camptotricha Dams

Clumping, single heads up to 7 cm broad. [CS/PM]

DISTRIBUTION: Mexico, Queretaro between Higuerillas and San Pablo.

OTHER NAMES: *Dolichothele camptotricha, D. albescens, M. albescens.*

Mammillaria candida Scheid.

Solitary to clumping, spines white but sometimes with a pink flush in the crown (*v. rosea*), up to 14 cm across. [PM2S/HS/PM]

DISTRIBUTION: Mexico, widely distributed in Coahuila, Nuevo Leon, San Luis Potosi and Tamaulipas.

OTHER NAMES: *M. estanzuelensis, M. ortizrubiana, M. 'ortizrubiona'.*

Mammillaria canelensis Craig

Solitary, globose, csp 2–4, 3 cm long orange-yellow, rsp 22–25, 5–15 mm long, white. Fl greenish-yellow. No plants now available exactly fit this description. The above plant, perhaps an imposter, is in trade as this species. [CS/E]

DISTRIBUTION: Mexico, Chihuahua, Sierra Canelo.

OTHER NAMES: *M. auricantha, M. auritricha, M. bellacantha, M. floresii, M. laneusumma, M. mayensis, ?M. montensis.*

Mammillaria capensis (Gates) Craig

Clustering, stems cylindric, up to 25 cm high by 3.5 cm, csp hooked or straight; fl pinkish or whitish. This name is often wrongly applied to other similar species. [CS/W]

DISTRIBUTION: Mexico, Baja California, inland from Puerto de Bahia de los Muertos, Cabo San Lucas.

Mammillaria carmenae Casteneda

Clumping with heads 5–8 cm long and 3–4 cm in diameter; fl white, tinged pink, or cream. [CS/W]

DISTRIBUTION: Mexico, Tamaulipas, between Ciudad Victoria and Jaumave on the ranch 'La Reja'.

Mammillaria carnea Zucc. ex Pfeiff.

Solitary or forming small clumps, stems to 10 cm high, 4–5 cm across; spine length very variable, forms with very long spines occur. [K91–2/IP/K]

DISTRIBUTION: Mexico: Puebla; Oaxaca and Guerrero.

Mammillaria carretti Rebut ex Sch.

Forming clusters of flattened-globular heads 5–7 cm in diameter. [CS/PM]

DISTRIBUTION: Mexico, Nuevo Leon, scattered.

OTHER NAMES: *M. saffordii.*

Mammillaria casoi Bravo

Spherical, dividing dichotomously. Closely related to *M. mystax.* [K146–1/IP/K]

DISTRIBUTION: Mexico, Oaxaca, between Suchixtlahuaca and Tejupan in oak woodland.

OTHER NAMES: *M. mixtecensis.*

Mammillaria centralifera   Repp.

Stem to 8 cm high and 9 cm across, sometimes clumping; rsp 4–5, 2–12 mm long; csp (1–)2, 1–6 cm long; spines glassy-yellow or glassy-white tipped black. Fl 2 cm wide, carmine. Closely related to **M. compressa.** [Repp1140/IP/Repp]

DISTRIBUTION: Mexico. Queretaro, Arroyo Seco.

Mammillaria centraliplumosa   Fittkau

Stems cylindric up to 15 cm high by 5 cm, eventually clumping. A member of the **M. spinosissima** complex. [CS/PM]

DISTRIBUTION: Mexico, Mexico DF, near Calderon.

Mammillaria cerralboa   (B. & R.) Orcutt

Stem elongated to 40 cm or more high by 6 cm, usually solitary. Possibly an island form of **M. armillata.** [CS/PM]

DISTRIBUTION: Mexico, Baja California, Cerralbo Is.

Mammillaria chica   Repp.

Solitary, in cultivation becoming cylindric up to 8 cm high and 4 cm across. [CS/E]

DISTRIBUTION: Mexico, Coahuila, Viesca.

OTHER NAMES: *M. viescensis n.n.*

Mammillaria chionocephala   Purpus

Solitary up to 20 cm high by 12 cm. [K101/IP/K]

DISTRIBUTION: Mexico, Coahuila, Sierra de Parras.

OTHER NAMES: *M. caerulea.*

Mammillaria claviformis   Repp.

Stems to 20 cm high by 7 cm, clumping; rsp 20–28, 2–6 mm long, glassy; csp 4–6, 4–15 mm long, brown, lowest longest and often hooked. Fl 1.5 cm across, carmine. [Repp1462/IP/Repp]

DISTRIBUTION: Mexico, Puebla, Tecocoyuca.

Mammillaria coahuilensis (Boed.) Moran

Usually solitary, to 4 cm across with a huge, carrot-like root. Fl 3 cm broad, white with a pinkish midstripe. [CS/PM]

DISTRIBUTION: Mexico, Coahuila, near San Pedro.

OTHER NAMES: *M. albiarmata, Porfiria schwartzii, M. schwartzii.*

Mammillaria columbiana S–D

Stems up to 15 cm or more tall, columnar, later offsetting around the base. Fl small, hardly protruding through the wool, pinkish-red. [CS/W]

DISTRIBUTION: Colombia and Venezuela.

OTHER NAMES: *M. bogotensis, M. hennisii, M. tamayonis, M. soehlemanni.*

Mammillaria compacticaulis Repp.

Body usually solitary, up to 10 cm high by 7.5 cm. [Repp1047/CS/PM]

DISTRIBUTION: Mexico, Michoacan, Uruapan.

Mammillaria compressa DC

Forming huge, many-headed clumps, individual stems to 20 cm long, 8 cm across; flowers sparingly in cultivation. [PM2/HS/PM]

DISTRIBUTION: Mexico, widespread in Hidalgo and Queretaro.

OTHER NAMES: *M. angularis, M. cirrhifera.*

Mammillaria conspicua Purpus

Always solitary, to 40 cm and more high by 10 cm. A close but distinctively large relative of *M. haageana.* [K148/IP/K]

DISTRIBUTION: Mexico, Puebla, Zapotitlan.

Mammillaria craigii Lindsay

Solitary, flattened-globular up to 10 cm across. [CS/W]

DISTRIBUTION: Mexico, SW Chihuahua, Sierra Tarahumare, in the Barranca del Rio Urinque.

Mammillaria crassa Repp.

Solitary, to 8 cm high by 9 cm; rsp 7−9, 4−9 mm long, fox-red or brown tipped dark; csp 1−3, 7−15 mm long, brown, fox-red or black. Fl 2.5 cm wide, whitish-pink. Closely related to **M. pettersonii**. [Repp980/IP/Repp]

DISTRIBUTION: Mexico, Aguascalientes, Colomos.

Mammillaria crassimammillis Repp.

Body 4 cm high by 7 cm, clumping to form large mounds; spines 4−6, 2−8 mm long, yellowish to brownish, tipped dark. Fl 3−3.5 cm across, brownish-yellow. Closely related to **M. winterae**. [Repp1620/IP/Repp]

DISTRIBUTION: Mexico, Nuevo Leon, Aramberri.

Mammillaria crassior Repp.

Stems to 50 cm long by 9 cm, clumping; rsp 10−15, 4−18 mm long, pale yellowish; csp 2−6, 6−30 mm long, glassy-yellow often tipped brown. Fl 2−2.5 cm across, carmine. Closely related to **M. spinosissima**. [Repp761/H]

DISTRIBUTION: Mexico, Morelos, Tlayacapan.

Mammillaria crinita DC.

Spherical, up to 4 cm across, sometimes clumping; fl 1.6 cm long, white to yellowish or pinkish-cream. The plant illustrated seems firmly attached to this name within the trade but may not be the plant originally described. [CS/W]

DISTRIBUTION: Mexico, Hidalgo, Zimapan.

OTHER NAMES: ?M. criniformis.

Mammillaria crucigera Mart.

Clumping by splitting dichotomously, heads to 4 cm across; fl small, deep pinkish-purple. New and distinctive forms of this species are constantly being collected from new localities. [K11/IP/K]

DISTRIBUTION: Mexico, seemingly fairly widespread in the border area between Puebla and Oaxaca.

OTHER NAMES: M. buchenauii.

Mammillaria decipiens Scheidw.

Clumping, individual heads 4−7 cm across. [CS/PM]

DISTRIBUTION: Mexico: San Luis Potosi and Queretaro.

OTHER NAMES: Dolichothele decipiens.

Mammillaria deherdtiana   Farwig

Clumping in cultivation, heads up to 4.5 cm across; csp 0–6, 3–7 mm long. Fl 5 cm across. **v. dodsonii** (Bravo) Glass & Foster (illus.) csp 3–5, 1–2 cm long (N of Oaxaca City). [P345/IP/DHS]

DISTRIBUTION: Mexico, Oaxaca, around Nejapa.

OTHER NAMES: **v. dodsonii:** *M. dodsonii.*

Mammillaria densispina   (Coulter) Orcutt

Solitary, up to 10 cm high and broad; fl small, pale yellow. [CS/W]

DISTRIBUTION: Widely distributed in C Mexico.

OTHER NAMES: *M. esaussieri.*

Mammillaria dioica   K. Brandegee

Offsetting from the base to form small clumps, stems to 33 cm high by 10 cm. [K244/IP/K]

DISTRIBUTION: S California to Mexico, mainland Baja California and several islands.

Mammillaria discolor   Haw.

Clumping, heads up to 18 cm high by 13 cm; fl 1.6 cm wide; rsp 22–28, csp 4–6. [DH8525/HS/E]

DISTRIBUTION: Mexico: Puebla; Hidalgo; Oaxaca and Mexico DF.

OTHER NAMES: *M. amoena, M. esperanzaensis, M. ginsaumae, M. ochoterenae, M. pachyrhiza, M. schmollii.*

Mammillaria discolor v. multispina Repp.

Generally smaller than the species, body to only 8 cm across, rsp 30–38, csp 6–8 (upper illus. [K315/IP/K]). **v. longispina** Repp. (lower illus. [K316/IP/K]) is characterized by its golden csp up to 4 cm long.

DISTRIBUTION: **v. multispina** Zimapan/Sierra Juarez, Hidalgo & **v. longispina** San Alejo, Hidalgo, Mexico.

Mammillaria dixanthocentron Bkbg. ex Mottram

Solitary, to 20 cm high and 7 cm across. [K140/IP/K]

DISTRIBUTION: Mexico: Puebla and Oaxaca.

**Mammillaria dixanthocentron
v. flavicentra** (Bkbg.) Repp.

Solitary, to 18 cm or more high by 9–10 cm. [K143/IP/K]

DISTRIBUTION: Mexico, Puebla/Oaxaca border.

OTHER NAMES: *M. flavicentra.*

Mammillaria droegeana
Hild. emend. Repp.

Cylindrical, solitary or offsetting, heads up to 20 cm long by 6 cm; rsp 24–32, 6–8 mm long, csp 8–11, 7–12 mm long. Fl 1.5 cm across, pink. [K279–1/IP/K]

DISTRIBUTION: Mexico, Queretaro, Sierra de San Moran.

Mammillaria dumetorum Purpus

Clumping, heads up to 2.5 cm across, spines stiff, a spring flowering species. [CS/GC]

DISTRIBUTION: Mexico, San Luis Potosi, near Minas de San Rafael.

Mammillaria duoformis Craig & Dawson

Stems up to 9 cm high by 3.5 cm, later clumping, csp straight or hooked. [Repp850/CS/W]

DISTRIBUTION: Mexico, Puebla, near Tehuitzingo.

Mammillaria durangicola Repp.

Solitary, 4–8 cm high by 5–8 cm; rsp 10–16, 4–15 mm long, csp 1–3, 10–17 mm long. Fl 2.5–3 cm broad. Closely related to **M. pachycylindrica.** [K35/IP/K]

DISTRIBUTION: Mexico, Durango, Cuencame.

Mammillaria durispina Boed.

Solitary, up to 20 cm high by 11 cm. Closely related to **M. polythele.** [K149/IP/K]

DISTRIBUTION: Mexico: Guanajuato; Queretaro, Sierra Zamorano W of Bernal.

Mammillaria duwei Rogozinski & Braun
Later clumping in cultivation, heads up to 5 cm across; csp 0–2. [P301/IP/GC]

DISTRIBUTION: Mexico, Guanajuato, near San Luis de la Paz.

Mammillaria elongata DC.
Stems narrow, elongated, spination very variable from pale cream to dark reddish-brown, csp 0–4. **v. echinaria** (DC) Bkbg. is a stouter plant which always has fairly long csp. [FO-045/CS/PM]

DISTRIBUTION: Mexico, Hidalgo.

OTHER NAMES: *M. echinaria.*

Mammillaria erectacantha C.F. Foerster
Becoming squatly columnar, with a large fleshy root. [CS/PM]

DISTRIBUTION: Mexico, Sierra de Guadalupe and Tlalnepantla, NE of Mexico City.

Mammillaria eriacantha
Link & Otto ex Pfeiff.
Stems elongated to 30 cm and more, 5 cm across, eventually offsetting at the base; fl minute, not protruding beyond the spines. [PM19/HS/PM]

DISTRIBUTION: Mexico, Vera Cruz, Jalapa district.

Mammillaria erythra Repp.
Solitary, to 9 cm high by 20 cm; rsp 0–4, 2–3 mm long; csp 2, 4–30 mm long. Fl 10–12 mm broad, carmine. Closely related to **M. mystax**. [Repp1350/H]

DISTRIBUTION: Mexico, Puebla/Veracruz border, Puerto del Aire.

Mammillaria erythrocalix Buchenau
Clumping, individual heads up to 15 cm high. Possibly only a form of **M. duoformis**. [Repp838/CS/PM]

DISTRIBUTION: Mexico, Puebla, S of Chiautla.

Mammillaria erythrosperma Boed.

Forms clumps of small heads up to 5 cm high by 4 cm, spination variable in both length and density. [ISI1172/IP/DHS]

DISTRIBUTION: Mexico, San Luis Potosi, Alvarez.

OTHER NAMES: *M. multiformis.*

Mammillaria evermanniana (B. & R.) Orcutt

Usually solitary, spherical to oblong, 5–7 cm across; flower 1.5 cm long, yellowish-cream with a pinkish-brown midstripe. [CS/W]

DISTRIBUTION: Mexico, Baja California, Cerralbo Island.

Mammillaria felipensis Repp.

Always solitary, up to 6 cm high and 4 cm across. [Repp636/CS/W]

DISTRIBUTION: Mexico, Guanajuato, San Felipe.

Mammillaria fera-rubra Schmoll ex Craig

Solitary, up to 10 cm high by 9 cm; fl purplish-red, 1.5 cm long. Closely related to **M. rhodantha.** [CS/P]

DISTRIBUTION: Mexico, Queretaro, San Lazara.

Mammillaria fittkaui Glass & Foster

Clumping, stems 10 cm high by 4–5 cm. [CS/PM]

DISTRIBUTION: Mexico, Jalisco, Lake Chapala.

Mammillaria formosa Gal. ex Scheidw.

A very variable plant, usually solitary, depressed-globose up to 10 cm or more across; spines can be light or dark, also longer than pictured. Body colour from dark green to lighter blue-green. [PM33/HS/PM]

DISTRIBUTION: Mexico, San Luis Potosi.

Mammillaria fraileana (B. & R.) Boed.

Stems cylindric up to 15 cm high, later clumping; fl 3 cm across. [CS/PM]

DISTRIBUTION: Mexico, Baja California, Pichilingue Island and on the mainland opposite.

Mammillaria freudenbergeri Repp.

Solitary, globose, to 20 cm across; rsp 4–6, 6–15 mm long; csp 0. A member of the **M. heyderi** group. [IP/Repp]

DISTRIBUTION: Mexico, Coahuila, Muralla.

'Mammillaria fuscohamata' Bkbg.

Spherical, up to 6 cm high and broad. [Repp717/CS/PM]

DISTRIBUTION: Mexico, Jalisco.

Mammillaria gasseriana Boed.

Globular, 3–4 cm broad. [CS/W]

DISTRIBUTION: Mexico, Coahuila, Torreon; the plant pictured is from the adjacent Rio Nazas area of Durango.

Mammillaria gasterantha Repp.

At first solitary but soon offsetting at the base to form mounds. Heads at first globular, later to 14 cm high and 5.5 cm across. Fl small, not opening widely. [Repp934/CS/PM]

DISTRIBUTION: Mexico, N Guerrero, W of Iguala.

Mammillaria gatesii M.E. Jones

Mostly solitary, up to 20 cm high by 15 cm. Closely related to **M. baxteriana** and **M. petrophila**. [K195–2/IP/K]

DISTRIBUTION: Mexico, Baja California, between Cabo San Lucas and San Jose del Cabo.

Mammillaria gaumeri (B. & R.) Orcutt

Forming small clumps, individual heads up to 15 cm across; . fl 10–14 mm long. [CS/P]

DISTRIBUTION: Mexico, Yucatan, on sand dunes near Progreso.

Mammillaria geminispina Haw.

Forming magnificent mounds up to 2 m broad in habitat. Heads up to 18 cm long, 8 cm across; csp 1–8 cm long. Fl sparingly produced, small, cream with a carmine centre. [K250/IP/K]

DISTRIBUTION: Mexico, Hidalgo, widespread S of Zimapan but at its best in the Barranca de Metztitlan.

OTHER NAMES: *M. geminispina v. nobilis.*

Mammillaria gigantea Hildm. ex Sch.

Solitary, depressed-spherical, up to 10 cm high and 17 cm across; spines brown, to black in *'ocotillensis'*. Fl 1.5 cm broad, reddish bordered green. [K313/IP/K]

DISTRIBUTION: Mexico, Guanajuato.

OTHER NAMES: *M. armatissima, M. hamiltonoytea, M. hastifera, M. ocotillensis.*

Mammillaria gilensis Boed.

Globose to short cylindrical, up to 4 cm across, sparingly offsetting. Spines originally described as brownish-yellow but in the form pictured, from Ojo Caliente, they are blackish-red. [CS/W]

DISTRIBUTION: Mexico, Aguascalientes, San Gil.

Mammillaria glareosa Boed.

Flattened, usually solitary, up to 4cm across. Closely related to **M. brandegeei.** [K203–2/IP/K]

DISTRIBUTION: Mexico, Baja California.

OTHER NAMES: *M. dawsonii.*

Mammillaria glassii R.A. Foster

Clustering, heads to 3 cm across; fl tiny, pink. **v. ascensionis** (Repp.) Glass & Foster (illus.); fl 1.8–2.2 cm broad (Nuevo Leon, Ascension). **v. nominis-dulcis** Lau; heads to 5 cm broad; fl to 1.8 cm across (N.L., Dulces Nombres). **v. siberiensis** Lau to 10 cm across (N.L., Siberia). [CS/PM]

DISTRIBUTION: Mexico, Nuevo Leon, near Dieciocho de Marzo.

OTHER NAMES: **v. ascen.**: *M. ascensionis.*

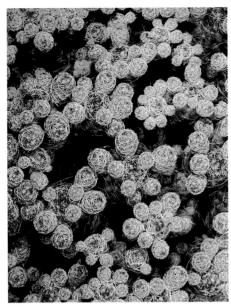

Mammillaria gracilis Pfeiff.

Cylindric, up to 10 cm high by 4.5 cm, prolifically offsetting; csp described as light to dark brown. Fl 1.3 cm across, yellowish-white. The densely white-spined form normally seen is a cultivar 'Pulchella'. [F]

DISTRIBUTION: Mexico: Hidalgo around Meztitlan and Zimapan; Queretaro, San Joaquin.

OTHER NAMES: *M. fragilis.*

Mammillaria grahamii Englm.

Stems up to 11 cm high and 8 cm across, csp 1–3, the longest hooked; fl 3.5–4 cm across. **v. oliviae** (Orcutt) Benson has shorter, unhooked csp. [CS/W]

DISTRIBUTION: Arizona, New Mexico and E Texas.

OTHER NAMES: *M. microcarpa v. grahamii.* **v. oliviae**: *M. marneriana, M. oliviae, M. pseudoalamensis.*

Mammillaria grusonii Runge

Usually solitary, spherical to elongated, up to 25 cm across. [HS/PM]

DISTRIBUTION: Mexico, Coahuila, Sierra Bola.

Mammillaria guelzowiana Werd.

Simple or clustering, heads up to 7 cm across; fl 6 cm wide. [CS/PM]

DISTRIBUTION: Mexico, Durango, mountainsides N of Rio Nazas.

OTHER NAMES: *Krainzia guelzowiana.*

Mammillaria guerreronis
(Bravo) [attrib. to Boed. by] Bkbg. & Knuth

Body cylindric up to 60 cm long, 6 cm broad, eventually clumping; csp hooked or straight. Fl small, red. [IP/K]

DISTRIBUTION: Mexico, Guerrero, Canyon del Zapolite.

OTHER NAMES: *M. zapilotensis.*

Mammillaria gummifera Englm.

Solitary, up to 12 cm across and 11 cm high. [HS/PM]

DISTRIBUTION: Mexico, Chihuahua, Cosihuiriachi.

Mammillaria haageana Pfeiff.

Usually solitary, to 15 cm tall by 10 cm. [PM6/HS/PM]

DISTRIBUTION: Mexico, widespread in Puebla and Oaxaca.

OTHER NAMES: *M. acanthophlegma, M. albidula, M. collina, M. dealbata, M. donatii, M. dyckiana, M. kunthii, M. sanangelensis, M. vaupelii.*

Mammillaria hahniana Werd.

Clustering, heads up to 9 cm high by 10 cm; some plants are far more hairy than others. [CS/PM]

DISTRIBUTION: Mexico, Queretaro, Sierra de Jalapa.

OTHER NAMES: *M. bravoae, M. mendeliana, 'M. quevedoi', M.woodsii.*

Mammillaria halei T.S. Brandegee

Clustering, stems up to 50 cm high by 7.5 cm; fl 2.5–5 cm long, scarlet, long tubed. [CS/PM]

DISTRIBUTION: Mexico, Baja California, Magdalena and Santa Margareta Islands and the adjacent mainland.

OTHER NAMES: *Cochemiea halei.*

Mammillaria hamata Lehm. ex Pfeiff.

Identity somewhat suspect. The name is currently attached to the plant pictured, which fits the rather brief original description quite well. [Repp957/CS/W]

DISTRIBUTION: Mexico, NW Puebla.

Mammillaria heidiae Krainz

Simple or clustering, stem to 6 cm across, rather flattened. [CS/P]

DISTRIBUTION: Mexico, Puebla, N of Acatlan, near El Papayo.

Mammillaria hernandezii Glass & Foster

Solitary, depressed globose, 2.5–4.5 cm across; fl 2 cm across. [Hernandez IP/W]

DISTRIBUTION: Mexico, Oaxaca, near Telixtlahuaca.

Mammillaria herrerae Werd.

Solitary or clustering from the base, globular but elongating with age, up to 3.5 cm across; fl 2.5 cm across. [DHS]

DISTRIBUTION: Mexico, Queretaro near Cadereyta and in adjacent San Luis Potosi.

Mammillaria hertrichiana Craig

Heads flattened-globular, up to 13 cm across, clustering to form clumps nearly 1 m wide. [CS/PM]

DISTRIBUTION: Mexico, Sonora on the Rancho El Agriminsor E of Tesopaco.

Mammillaria heyderi Muehlpf.

Becoming fairly globular, to about 12 cm across; fl 2–2.5 cm long, brownish-pink.

DISTRIBUTION: New Mexico and widespread in Texas and N Mexico.

OTHER NAMES: *M. applanata, M. heyderi v. applanata, M. heyderi v. bullingtoniana.*

Mammillaria heyderi v. hemisphaerica Englm.

Flattened, 8–12 cm across, spines usually shorter than in the plant pictured, which is from a local population in N Mexico. [K166–1/IP/K]

DISTRIBUTION: S Texas and N Mexico.

OTHER NAMES: *M. hemisphaerica.*

Mammillaria huajuapensis Bravo

Solitary, 10–12 cm in diameter; fl small, purple. Probably a variety of **M. mystax**. [NPT540/H]

DISTRIBUTION: Mexico, Oaxaca, hills E of Huajuapan de Leon.

Mammillaria hubertmulleri Repp.

Always solitary, at first globular, later columnar up to 30 cm high and 10 cm across; rsp 14–22 to 7 mm long, white, csp 2–4, 5–15 mm long, the lower one longest and hooked, brown to black. [FO-2/CS/PM]

DISTRIBUTION: Mexico, Morelos, wooded gorge near Chinameca, El Cajon.

Mammillaria huiguerensis Repp.

Solitary, to 20 cm high by 15 cm. Rsp 7–9, 3–15 mm long.
Csp 2, 11–30 mm long. Fl 25–30 mm long bright pink.
Closely related to **M. wagneriana.** [Repp 975/CS/W]

DISTRIBUTION: Mexico, Zacatecas, La Huiguera.

Mammillaria huitzilopochtli D.R. Hunt

Solitary, eventually branching, up to 13 cm high by 9 cm.
Csp 0–1, 4 mm long; an additional curving, dark csp is
sometimes produced later in older plants. Fl not opening
widely, small, carmine. [LAU/IP/GC]

DISTRIBUTION: Mexico, Oaxaca, Tomellin Valley.

Mammillaria ?huitzilopochtli v. L1495.

A distinctive plant with its frizzy spination. [L1495/CS/W]

DISTRIBUTION: Mexico, Oaxaca, Rio Grande-Rio Santo
Domingo.

Mammillaria humboldtii Ehrenb.

Solitary or clumping, individual heads globose, up to 7 cm
across. [IP/EC]

DISTRIBUTION: Mexico, Hidalgo, hills between
Ixmiquilpan and Metztitlan.

Mammillaria hutchisoniana
(Gates) Boed.

Usually clumping, stems up to 20 cm tall by 4–6 cm; fl
3 cm across, cream, outer petals striped maroon. [CS/W]

DISTRIBUTION: Mexico, C and S Baja California.

OTHER NAMES: *M. bullardiana.*

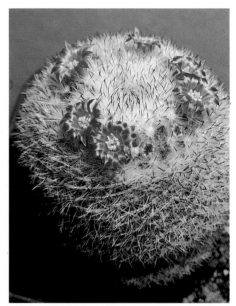

Mammillaria ignota Repp.

Solitary or clumping, heads up to 7 cm high and thick. Rsp
20–22, 2–4 mm long, white; csp 2–4, 4–7 mm long,
white with brown tip. Fl 1.8 cm long. [L1108/IP/K]

DISTRIBUTION: Mexico, Oaxaca, Tomellin Canyon.

Mammillaria igualensis Repp.

Stems to 10 cm high and 6 cm across, clumping to form large mounds; rsp 20–25, 3–5 mm long; csp 2–4, 5–12 mm long. Fl 8–10 mm broad, dark carmine. Closely related to the solitary-growing **M. albilanata**. [Repp932/IP/Repp]

DISTRIBUTION: Mexico, Guerrero, Iguala.

Mammillaria insularis Gates

Usually solitary, cultivated plants shortly columnar, old plants sparingly offsetting around the base. Fl 2.5 cm across. [CS/W]

DISTRIBUTION: Mexico, outermost islet of Smith Island group, Los Angeles Bay, Baja California.

Mammillaria isotensis Repp.

Stems to 25 cm high by 5.5 cm, clumping; rsp 10–13, 3–7 mm long; csp 2, 6–17 mm long, lowest longest and hooked, brown to black. Fl 16–18 mm across, carmine. [CS/PM]

DISTRIBUTION: Mexico, Mexico DF, El Isote.

Mammillaria jaliscana (B. & R.) Boed.

Solitary, becoming oblong, up to 5 cm broad. [L1044/CS/PM]

DISTRIBUTION: Mexico, various localities in Jalisco and in bordering areas of Aguascalientes, Queretaro and Guanajuato.

OTHER NAMES: *M. flavihamata.*

Mammillaria johnstonii (B. & R.) Orcutt

Solitary, up to 20 cm high by 10 cm; spination very variable, from short and straight to long and twisted, this being linked, incorrectly, to varietal names. [K181–1/IP/K]

DISTRIBUTION: Mexico, Sonora, San Carlos Bay.

OTHER NAMES: *M. johnstonii* v. *guaymensis* & v. *sancarlensis.*

Mammillaria karwinskiana Mart.

Offsetting or branching dichotomously, stems up to 10 cm across. Spine length and axillary wool amounts very variable. [PM7/HS/PM]

DISTRIBUTION: Mexico, around the city of Oaxaca.

OTHER NAMES: *M. confusa, M. multiseta, M. conzattii, M. ebenacantha, M. fischeri, M. neomystax, M. pyrrhocephala.*

Mammillaria kleiniorum Appenzeller

Solitary, stem up to 13 cm across; fl 2 cm across. Related to *M. jaliscana* & *M. zacatecasensis*. [K190–7/IP/K]

DISTRIBUTION: Mexico, Michoacan, Iquilpan.

Mammillaria klissingiana Boed.

At first globular then elongating to 16 cm high and 9 cm across; eventually offsetting. Fl shyly produced, 8 mm across, pale pink. [SB270/CS/PM]

DISTRIBUTION: Mexico, Tamaulipas, Jaumave Valley.

Mammillaria knebeliana Boed.

Stem offsetting, to 6 cm high, 4.5 cm across; csp at first 4, later 5–7, the lowest 15 mm long, hooked, reddish-brown. Rsp 20–25, very fine, white. Fl 15 mm broad, yellow. Plant pictured, SB29, appears to fit the original description. [SB29/CS/PM]

DISTRIBUTION: Mexico, Sierra de San Luis Potosi.

OTHER NAMES: *M. haehneliana*.

Mammillaria knippeliana Quehl

Stems up to 8 cm high by 6 cm, strongly offsetting; fl 10 mm broad, straw yellow with red tips to the petals. [CS/W]

DISTRIBUTION: Mexico, Morelos, near Cuernavaca.

Mammillaria kraehenbuehlii
(Krainz) Krainz

Densely clumping, individual stems up to 3.5 cm across. [CS/W]

DISTRIBUTION: Mexico, Oaxaca, near Tamazulapan.

OTHER NAMES: 'M. alpina'.

Mammillaria krasuckae Repp.

Solitary, to 8 cm high by 6 cm; rsp 26–32, 2–4 mm long, white; csp 4–6, 6–25 mm long, yellowish, dark-brown or black, lowest longest and usually hooked. Fl 2 cm broad, carmine. Closely related to **M. rekoi**. [Repp1647/IP/Repp]

DISTRIBUTION: Mexico, Oaxaca, near Reforma.

Mammillaria lanigera Repp.

Solitary, up to 12 cm high by 8 cm across.
[Repp944/CS/W]

DISTRIBUTION: Mexico, Oaxaca, San Miguel
Maninaltepec.

Mammillaria lasiacantha Englm.

Stem small, usually solitary but eventually clustering in
cultivation. Fl white, striped brownish-red. [H]

DISTRIBUTION: W Texas, New Mexico and a large area of
NW Mexico.

OTHER NAMES: *M.denudata, M. lasiacantha v. denudata,
'M. egregia'.*

Mammillaria laui D.R. Hunt

Strongly clumping, individual heads up to 4.5 cm across;
spines stiff. [L1171/IP/DHS]

DISTRIBUTION: Mexico, Tamaulipas, between Ciudad
Victoria and Jaumave, La Reja.

Mammillaria lenta K. Brandegee

Forming small clumps of flattened heads to 5 cm across.
[IP/EC]

DISTRIBUTION: Mexico, Coahuila, Viesca and Cuatro
Cienegas.

Mammillaria leptacantha (Lau) Repp.

Cylindrical, offsetting, 8–10 cm high by 5–6 cm.
[L1314/IP/GC]

DISTRIBUTION: Mexico, Oaxaca, near Las Animas.
OTHER NAMES: *M. rekoi v. leptacantha.*

Mammillaria leucantha Boed.

Solitary or clustering, up to 3.5 cm across the stems.
[CS/PM]

DISTRIBUTION: Mexico, San Luis Potosi, near Soledad
Diez Gutierrez.

Mammillaria lewisiana Lindsay

Solitary, flattened to globular, up to 11 cm across. [CS/PM]

DISTRIBUTION: Mexico, Baja California, N Viscaino Desert, 7 miles NW of Mesquital Ranch.

Mammillaria limonensis Repp.

Body 12 cm high by 5 cm, clumping; rsp 14−20, 4−7 mm long, white; csp 4−7, 7−18 mm long, lowest longest and hooked, all brown to black. Fl 14 mm across, pink. Closely related to **M. fittkaui**. [Repp1620/H]

DISTRIBUTION: Mexico, Jalisco, El Limon.

Mammillaria lindsayi Craig

Clumping, heads up to 30 cm high by 15 cm. The plant pictured is the one usually traded as this species but differs from the original description in a number of ways. [CS/PM]

DISTRIBUTION: Mexico, Chihuahua, Molinas to Sierra Colorado.

Mammillaria lloydii (B. & R.) Orcutt

At first flattened but later becoming elongated up to 10 cm high by 7 cm. Perhaps a straight-spined form of **M. uncinata**. [K68−1/IP/K]

DISTRIBUTION: Mexico, Zacatecas and San Luis Potosi.

Mammillaria longiflora (B. & R.) Berg.

Usually solitary, up to 10 cm across. **fa. stampferi** (Repp.) D.R. Hunt, from El Salto, Durango is pictured above the species, although it would seem to us to be more deserving of the rank of variety rather than mere form [CS/PM]

DISTRIBUTION: Mexico, Durango, near Santiago Papasquiaro.

OTHER NAMES: *Krainzia longiflora.* **fa. stampferi:** *M. stampferi.*

Mammillaria longimamma DC.

Solitary or clumping, individual heads to 12 cm across; fl 6 cm wide. [CS/PM]

DISTRIBUTION: C Mexico, Hidalgo, e.g. near Venados.

OTHER NAMES: *Dolichothele longimamma, D. uberiformis, M. long. v. uber., M. uber.*

Mammillaria louisiae Lindsay

Usually solitary, becoming rather cylindrical in cultivation, which usually encourages clumping. Stem up to 6 cm tall and half as broad. A close relative of **M. hutchisoniana.** [CS/PM]

DISTRIBUTION: Mexico, Baja California, S of Socorro.

Mammillaria macdougalii Rose

Plants flattened-globular up to 12.5 cm broad. [HS/PM]

DISTRIBUTION: SE Arizona and adjacent Sonora, Mexico.

OTHER NAMES: *M. heyderi v. macdougalii, M. gummifera v. macdoug.*

Mammillaria magallanii Schmoll ex Craig

Sparingly clumping, stems to 6 cm high by 4.5 cm; csp 0–1 usually straight, may be hooked. Probably only a form of **M. lasiacantha.** [CS/E]

DISTRIBUTION: Mexico, Coahuila, near Parras.

OTHER NAMES: *M. roseocentra, M. mag. v. hamatispina, M. neobertrandiana.*

Mammillaria magnifica Buchenau

Clumping, individual stems to 40 cm high and 9 cm across. **v. minor** Buch. from a separate population is smaller and more weakly spined. [CS/P]

DISTRIBUTION: Mexico, Morelos, El Penon de Amayuca, between Cuautla and Izucar de Matamoros.

Mammillaria magnimamma Haw.

Very variable, clustering with heads up to 12 cm across. Csp short and fairly straight through to long and curved or even twisted. Fl deep pink to pale yellow. [K254/IP/K]

DISTRIBUTION: Mexico, Hidalgo; S San Luis Potosi and near Mexico City.

OTHER NAMES: *M. centricirrha, M. flavovirens, M. gladiata, M. macracantha, M. trohartii, M. vagaspina.*

Mammillaria mainiae K. Brandegee

Clustering, stems 12 cm broad by 10–15 cm. [HS/PM]

DISTRIBUTION: S Arizona and Mexico, Sonora, near Nogales.

Mammillaria mammillaris (L.) Karsten

Usually solitary, up to 8 cm high by 5 cm. Fl minute.
[CS/PM]

DISTRIBUTION: Lesser Antilles, some islands of the
Netherlands Antilles and widespread in Venezuela.

OTHER NAMES: ?M. ekmanii, M. pseudosimplex, M. simplex.

Mammillaria maritima
(Lindsay) D.R. Hunt

Forming clumps 1 m in diameter, stems to 50 cm high by
3–7 cm broad. Fl 3 cm long, scarlet. [IP/W]

DISTRIBUTION: Mexico, Baja California, Punta Blanca.

OTHER NAMES: Cochemiea maritima.

Mammillaria marksiana Krainz

Body bright green, up to 5 cm tall by 8 cm, later clumping.
[CS/PM]

DISTRIBUTION: Mexico, Sinaloa, W Sierra Madre and in
Durango in the Quebrada de Topia.

Mammillaria mathildae
Kraehenbuehl & Krainz

Clustering, stems 5–6 cm tall and 5 cm across. [CS/PM]

DISTRIBUTION: Mexico, Queretaro, near La Canada.

Mammillaria matudae H. Bravo

Solitary or clustering from the base, stems to 30 cm or more
high to 5 cm broad. **v. serpentiformis** Fittkau has stems up
to 1.55 m long (Guerrero, La Laguna). [CS/PM]

DISTRIBUTION: Mexico, La Junta.

Mammillaria mazatlanensis
Sch. ex Guerke

Clumping, stems cylindric up to 12 cm high by 4 cm.
[Repp680/CS/W]

DISTRIBUTION: Mexico, Sinaloa, Mazatlan.

OTHER NAMES: M. patonii, M. sinaloensis.

Mammillaria meiacantha Englm.

Solitary, flattened-globular, up to 11 cm across. [HS/PM]

DISTRIBUTION: SE Arizona, New Mexico, Texas and in Mexico southwards to Zacatecas.

OTHER NAMES: *M. gummifera v. meiacantha, M. heyderi v. meiacan.*

Mammillaria meissneri Ehrenb.

Stems cylindric, up to 12.5 cm high by 2.5 cm, offsetting from the sides. The plant pictured, L679, is one of a number of contenders for this name, some of which are wider-bodied, less freely-clumping plants with less wool. [L679/IP/K]

DISTRIBUTION: Originally given as just Mexico, L679 is from between San Antonio and Calapa, Oaxaca.

OTHER NAMES: *M. elegans v. schmollii.*

Mammillaria melaleuca Karw.

Usually solitary, globular, glossy green. [CS/E]

DISTRIBUTION: Mexico, Tamaulipas, near Jaumave.

OTHER NAMES: *Dolichothele melaleuca.*

Mammillaria melanocentra Poselger

Solitary, up to 16 cm high by 11 cm, bluish-green; csp up to 5.5 cm long. Fl 2.5 cm broad, pink. [K165–1/HS/PM]

DISTRIBUTION: Mexico, Nuevo Leon, Huasteca Canyon and elsewhere near Monterrey.

OTHER NAMES: *M. euthele, M. runyonii.*

Mammillaria mercadensis Patoni

Globular, up to 5 cm across, forming small clusters; fruit red. **v. guillauminiana** (Bkbg.) Repp.; heads slightly broader, fruit white (El Salto, Durango). [CS/PM]

DISTRIBUTION: Mexico, Durango, Cerro Mercado.

OTHER NAMES: *M. ocamponis.* **v. guillaum.**: *M. guillaum.*

Mammillaria meyranii Bravo

Stem columnar up to 55 cm long by 5 cm, clustering from the base. [Repp968/CS/PM]

DISTRIBUTION: Mexico, valley of the Rio Tilostoc and Michoacan, barranca of San Jose Purna.

OTHER NAMES: *M. meyranii v. michoacana*, possibly '*M. michoacanensis*'.

Mammillaria microhelia Werd.

Stems up to 15 cm long by 3.5–4.5 cm, clustering from the base with age. Fl white to yellowish-green, sometimes pink. [CS/PM]

DISTRIBUTION: Mexico, Queretaro, Sierra de Zamorano.

OTHER NAMES: *M. microheliopsis.*

Mammillaria microthele Muehlenpfordt

Heads flattened, up to 8 cm across, eventually clustering; fl white. [K116/IP/K]

DISTRIBUTION: Mexico, Tamaulipas and San Luis Potosi, E of Huizache.

OTHER NAMES: *M. microthele v. superfina n.n.*

Mammillaria miegiana Earle

Solitary, up to 16 cm high by 10 cm. [K207/IP/K]

DISTRIBUTION: Mexico, Sonora, between the Rio Sonora and Rio Moctezuma, N of Ures.

Mammillaria mieheana Tiegel

Clustering, stems up to 15 cm long by 5 cm; fl 15 mm long, pale yellow. Intermediate between **M. elongata** and **M. densispina**. [W]

DISTRIBUTION: Mexico, Queretaro.

Mammillaria milleri (B. & R.) Boed.

Clustering, heads up to 15 cm high by 5 cm; fl 2.5 cm broad. [PM79/HS/PM]

DISTRIBUTION: Arizona, E California and N Sonora, Mexico.

OTHER NAMES: *M. microcarpa* & *vars.*

Mammillaria moelleriana Boed.

Solitary, globose to short-cylindric, up to 11 cm high and 10 cm broad; fl pale pink or white with yellowish midstripe. [CS/PM]

DISTRIBUTION: Mexico, Durango and near Jerez, Zacatecas.

OTHER NAMES: *M. cowperae.*

Mammillaria mollendorffiana Shurly

Solitary, up to 35 cm high by 10 cm. [K253/IP/K]

DISTRIBUTION: Mexico, Hidalgo between Cardonal and Sanctuario.

Mammillaria monticola Repp.

Usually solitary, to 8 cm high by 6 cm; rsp 20–27, 2–5 mm long, white; csp 1–2, 2–3 mm long, brown or whitish tipped brown. Fl 18 mm broad, dark carmine. Closely related to **M. conspicua**. [Repp844/IP/Repp]

DISTRIBUTION: Mexico, Puebla, Puente Marques.

Mammillaria morganiana Tiegel

Stem 8 cm broad, dichotomizing to produce clumps, csp 4–5, 10 mm, white tipped brown; rsp 40–50, hairlike, white. The plant illustrated, K112, seems to fit the original description fairly closely. [K112/IP/K]

DISTRIBUTION: Mexico, Guanajuato.

Mammillaria muehlenpfordtii Foerst.

Globular, to 15 cm broad. [K149–1/IP/K]

DISTRIBUTION: Mexico: Queretaro; Guanajuato and S San Luis Potosi.

OTHER NAMES: *M. celsiana, M. neopotosina.*

Mammillaria multidigitata
[Radley] ex Lindsay

Heads cylindric, 20 cm long by 5 cm, forming large clumps. [CS/PM]

DISTRIBUTION: Mexico, Baja California, San Pedro Nolasco Is.

Mammillaria multiseta Ehrenb.

Globular, up to 12 cm high by 8 cm, sometimes dichotomizing. The plant illustrated, Repp 940, appears to fit the original description reasonably well. [Repp940/CS/PM]

DISTRIBUTION: Mexico, original description without locality, reported by Bravo & Reppenhagen from Puebla, between Petlalzingo and Acatlan.

Mammillaria mundtii Sch.

Spherical to elongated, up to 7 cm broad. The plant illustrated has become widely distributed as this species but does not exactly fit the original brief description and illustration. [CS/PM]

DISTRIBUTION: Mexico, originally without locality. Present plants originally came from Nevado de Toluca, Mexico DF.

Mammillaria mystax Mart.

Solitary, to 30 cm high by 15 cm. [K226/IP/K]

DISTRIBUTION: Mexico: Puebla and Oaxaca.

OTHER NAMES: *M. atroflorens*, *M. crispiseta*, *M. mutabilis*, *M. neomystax*.

Mammillaria nagliana Repp.

To 9 cm high by 8 cm, clumping; rsp 5–7, 4–11 mm long, glassy tipped dark; csp 1, 4–20 mm long, glassy brown tipped black. Fl 18 mm across, bright yellow. [Repp1045/IP/Repp]

DISTRIBUTION: Mexico, Michoacan, Aguililla.

Mammillaria nana Bkbg. ex R. Mottram

Solitary or clustering, heads to 4 cm across. [CS/W]

DISTRIBUTION: Mexico, San Luis Potosi, road to Balnearios de Lourdes.

OTHER NAMES: 'M. monancistracantha', 'M. rawlii'.

Mammillaria napina Purpus

Usually solitary, 4–6 cm broad. Fl 4 cm across. [CS/E]

DISTRIBUTION: Mexico, Puebla, near Tehuacan.

Mammillaria nazasensis
(Glass & Foster) Repp.

Freely clustering, heads 2–4 cm across. [CS/PM]

DISTRIBUTION: Mexico, Durango, near the Rio Nazas.

OTHER NAMES: *M. pennispinosa v. nazasensis*.

Mammillaria nejapensis   Craig & Dawson
Body to 15 cm high by 7.5 cm, offsetting or branching dichotomously. Apparently just a distinctive form of **M. karwinskiana**. [CS/PM]
DISTRIBUTION: Mexico, Oaxaca, Nejapa.

Mammillaria neopalmeri   Craig
Heads up to 9 cm high by 5 cm, strongly clumping. [CS/PM]
DISTRIBUTION: Mexico, Baja California, San Benito Island.

Mammillaria nivosa   Link ex Pfeiff.
Solitary or clustering, globular, to 7 cm broad. Fl. 1.5 cm long, cream. [CS/EC]
DISTRIBUTION: Numerous islands in the West Indies.
OTHER NAMES: *M. flavescens v. nivosa.*

Mammillaria noureddineana   Repp.
Solitary, up to 15 cm high by 8 cm. Rsp 15–20, 2–4 mm, white; csp 4–6, 4–5 mm, white with a brown tip. Fl 10 mm broad, carmine. Fruit red. [K223/IP/K]
DISTRIBUTION: Mexico, Oaxaca, San Lazaro.

Mammillaria nunezii   (B. & R.) Orcutt
Usually solitary, to 15 cm or more high, 8 cm across. Csp straight or occasionally hooked. [K281/IP/K]
DISTRIBUTION: Mexico, Guerrero, Cerro de Buenavista de Cuellar and Taxco.
OTHER NAMES: *M. solisii, M. wuthenauiana.*

Mammillaria obconella   Scheidw.
Solitary, up to 30 cm or more high, 12 cm across. [K314/IP/K]
DISTRIBUTION: Mexico: Hidalgo, Metztitlan and Venados; S San Luis Potosi; Queretaro Toliman; Guanajuato, W of Xichu.
OTHER NAMES: *M. dolichocentra, M. tetracantha.*

Mammillaria occidentalis   (B. & R.) Boed.

Stem cylindric to 15 cm high by 3 cm, strongly clumping. Csp 4–5, the lowest hooked or straight. [ISI1235/IP/GC]

DISTRIBUTION: Mexico, Colima, near Manzanillo.

Mammillaria orcuttii   Boed.

Solitary, globose to short-cylindric to 20 cm tall by 12 cm. The plant pictured, PM30, from hills W of Santa Catarina, San Luis Potosi corresponds well to the original illustration. [PM30/HS/PM]

DISTRIBUTION: Mexico, originally reported from Puebla, probably in error, present collections are from San Luis Potosi.

Mammillaria oteroi   Glass & Foster

Profusely clustering, heads to 4 cm across. [CS/PM]

DISTRIBUTION: Mexico, Oaxaca, Alta Mixtcca, near Buenavista de la Concepcion.

Mammillaria pachycylindrica   Bkbg.

Solitary, up to 26 cm high by 11 cm. [K185/IP/K]

DISTRIBUTION: Mexico, originally without locality, recent collections from Nazas, Durango.

Mammillaria pacifica
(Gates) Boed. ex Bkbg. & Knuth

Flattened-globular, up to 15 cm across, often clumping. Closely related to **M. petrophila**. [K194–1/IP/K]

DISTRIBUTION: Mexico, Baja California, just N of Todos Santos.

Mammillaria papasquiarensis
(Bravo) Repp.

Globular to 30 cm and more across. [K294/IP/K]

DISTRIBUTION: Mexico, Monte Blanco, S of Nazas.

OTHER NAMES: *M. tesopacensis. v. pap.*

Mammillaria parkinsonii Ehrenb.

Heads 15 cm high and 8 cm broad branching dichotomously to form large groups. [K85/IP/K]

DISTRIBUTION: Mexico, Hidalgo, near San Onofre in the Mineral del Doctor.

OTHER NAMES: *M. auriareolis, M. avila-camachoi, M. infernillensis, M. queretarica, M. rosensis, M. tiegeliana, M. vonwyssiana.*

Mammillaria parrasensis Repp.

Body to 6 cm high by 10 cm, branching when old; rsp 5–7, 2–10 mm long; csp 1, 5–7 mm long. Fl 3 cm wide, whitish-pink. Closely related to **M. grusonii**. [Repp1083/IP/Repp]

DISTRIBUTION: Mexico, Coahuila, Parras.

Mammillaria pectinifera
(Ruempler) Web.

Solitary, to 7 cm high by 4 cm. [CS/PM]

DISTRIBUTION: Mexico, Puebla, near Tehuacan.

OTHER NAMES: *Solisia pectinata.*

Mammillaria peninsularis
(B. & R.) Orcutt

Flattened-globular, to 5 cm across. [DHS]

DISTRIBUTION: Mexico, Baja California, Cabo San Lucas.

Mammillaria pennispinosa Krainz

Body 4 cm across, eventually clustering. [CS/PM]

DISTRIBUTION: Mexico, SW Coahuila and N Durango between Bermejillo and Mapimi.

OTHER NAMES: *M. penn. v. nazasensis* = **M. nazasensis**.

Mammillaria perbella Hildm. ex Sch.

Heads to 6 cm across, branching dichotomously to form small clumps. [E]

DISTRIBUTION: Mexico; Hidalgo, Toliman and Queretaro, San Pablo.

OTHER NAMES: Probably *M. aljibensis.*

Mammillaria perezdelarosae
Bravo & Scheinvar
Solitary or clustering, heads to 7.5 cm high by 4.5 cm.
[HS/R]

DISTRIBUTION: Mexico, Jalisco.

Mammillaria petrophila K. Brandegee
Bodies 15 cm high and broad, axils very woolly.
[L052/CS/W]

DISTRIBUTION: Mexico, Baja California, Sierra de la
Laguna and San Francisquito.

Mammillaria petterssonii Hildm.
Globular, to 30 cm across, usually solitary, spine length and
colour variable. [HS ex Lau/GC]

DISTRIBUTION: Mexico. Recent collections from near the
city of Guanajuato; original locality not given.

OTHER NAMES: Probably *M. obscura*; *M. pilensis.*

Mammillaria phitauiana (Baxter) Werd.
Stems cylindrical to 25 cm high, eventually clumping.
[K311-1/IP/K]

DISTRIBUTION: Mexico, in the less arid parts of the central
part of the Cape region of Baja California.

Mammillaria picta Meinshausen
Heads becoming elongated to 4 cm across, eventually
clumping. [CS/E]

DISTRIBUTION: Mexico, Tamaulipas, Rio Blanco.

OTHER NAMES: *M. aurisaeta*, *M. schieliana.*

Mammillaria pilcayensis Bravo
Stems to 50 cm high by 5 cm, spines whitish-yellow,
sometimes tipped red. A member of the **M. spinosissima**
complex. [CS/PM]

DISTRIBUTION: Mexico. In the Barranca de
Pilcaya, Guerrero and Barranca de
Malinaltenango, Mexico DF.

OTHER NAMES: *M. pitcayensis.*

Mammillaria pilispina Purpus

Heads to 4.5 cm across forming small clumps. [CS/W]

DISTRIBUTION: Mexico, San Luis Potosi, Minas de San Rafael.

OTHER NAMES: *M. sanluisensis, M. subtilis.*

Mammillaria plumosa Web.

Forming large mounds, heads to 7 cm across. Fl sparingly produced. [IP/P]

DISTRIBUTION: Mexico: Coahuila, Mariposa and in Nuevo Leon, Huasteca Canyon.

Mammillaria polyedra Mart.

Stems 10 cm high and broad, eventually clumping. Rsp 2–4, uppers 3–4 mm long, lower 6–25 mm long. [CS/W]

DISTRIBUTION: Mexico, Oaxaca, e.g. Tonala and Huajuapan.

Mammillaria polythele Mart.

Solitary, cylindric to 60 cm tall by 10 cm. A very variable species. [FO-059/CS/W]

DISTRIBUTION: Mexico, Hidalgo, between Zimapan and Actopan.

OTHER NAMES: *M. affinis, M. neophaeacantha, M. hoffmanniana, M. kelleriana, M. kewensis, M. subdurispina, M. hidalgensis, M. ingens.*

Mammillaria pondii Greene

Stems cylindric to 30 cm high by 4 cm, branching sparingly. Fl nearly 5 cm long, scarlet. [F]

DISTRIBUTION: Mexico, Baja California, Cedros Island.

OTHER NAMES: *Cochemiea pondii.*

Mammillaria poselgeri Hildm.

Stems long and slender to 2 m long by 4–5 cm, branching from the base and soon sprawling. [CS/PM]

DISTRIBUTION: Mexico, lower elevations of Cape region of Baja California.

OTHER NAMES: *Cochemiea poselgeri.*

Mammillaria pottsii Scheer ex S-D

Stems cylindric, to 15 cm high by 4 cm, clumping.
v. multicaulis Repp.; very strongly clumping, stems slimmer (Lerdo, Durango). **v. gigas** Repp.; stouter, to 25 cm long and 7 cm broad (La Cardona, Zacatecas). [CS/W]

DISTRIBUTION: S Texas through N Mexico S to Zacatecas.

OTHER NAMES: *M. leona.*

Mammillaria priessnitzii Repp.

Solitary, flattened-globular, 3−9 cm high by 5−11 cm. Rsp 4−5, 2−7 mm long, white tipped brown. Csp 1−2, 4−15 mm long, thicker, grey or brown with black tip. Fl 16 mm across. [K258/IP/K]

DISTRIBUTION: Mexico, Queretaro, Jalpan.

Mammillaria pringlei (Coulter) K. Brandegee

Stems to 20 cm high by 15 cm, solitary or branching dichotomously. Fl purple 10 mm across. [CS/W]

DISTRIBUTION: Mexico, San Luis Potosi, e.g. Toltenango and Jilotopec.

OTHER NAMES: *M. parensis.*

Mammillaria prolifera (Miller) Haw.

Heads 4.5 cm broad, clumping. **v. arachnoidea** D.R. Hunt from Tamaulipas & Hidalgo, **v. haitensis** (K. Schum.) Borg from Haiti and **v. texana** (Poselger) Borg from Texas differ mainly in details of spination and stem size. [SB713/CS/PM]

DISTRIBUTION: Cuba.

OTHER NAMES: *M. multiceps, M. pusilla.*

Mammillaria pseudocrucigera Craig

Solitary or clustering, heads to 9 cm across. [K86/IP/K]

DISTRIBUTION: Mexico, Queretaro, Bernal.

Mammillaria pseudoperbella Quehl

Usually solitary, to 10 cm high by 8 cm. [IP/K]

DISTRIBUTION: Mexico, originally without locality, recently reported from Queretaro, Higuerillas.

Mammillaria puberula Repp.

Solitary or rarely sprouting from the base to form small clumps. Stems 1–5 cm high by 2–6 cm; rsp 14–19, 4–6 mm long; csp 3–4, 7–11 mm long, thicker than the rsp, the lowest hooked. Fl 15–18 mm across, white to yellowish. [CS/PM]

DISTRIBUTION: Mexico, San Luis Potosi, Solis.

Mammillaria pullihamata Repp.

Body solitary, to 6 cm high by 5 cm. [IP/K]

DISTRIBUTION: Mexico, Oaxaca, Nejapa, near Portillo.

Mammillaria pygmaea (B. & R.) Berg.

Usually clustering, stems to 10 cm high by 5.5 cm. [CS/PM]

DISTRIBUTION: Mexico, S Queretaro.

OTHER NAMES: *M. mollihamata, M. cadereytana, ?M. painteri, M. pubispina.*

Mammillaria rectispina (Dawson) Repp.

Heads 6 cm high by 5 cm, often later clumping. [CS/K]

DISTRIBUTION: Mexico, Baja California, Cedros Island.

OTHER NAMES: *M. goodrichii v. rectispina.*

Mammillaria rekoi (B. & R.) Vaupel

Solitary, to 12 cm high by 5–6 cm. Lower csp hooked or straight. [FO-022/CS/PM]

DISTRIBUTION: Mexico, Oaxaca, Mitla.

OTHER NAMES: *M. mitlensis, M. pseudorekoi, 'M. rekoiana'.*

Mammillaria reppenhagenii D.R. Hunt

Usually solitary, to 15 cm high by 6 cm. [CS/P]

DISTRIBUTION: Mexico, Colima, Rancho Tecuan, Cerro Barrigon and nearby on Cerro de Carrizal.

Mammillaria rettigiana   Boed.

Solitary, globular, about 4 cm across. Fl pale pink, 1.5 cm across. [CS/W]

DISTRIBUTION: Mexico, original locality not cited, plants fitting the description have been collected recently between the city of Guanajuato and Dolores Hidalgo.

OTHER NAMES: *M. posseltiana.*

Mammillaria rhodantha   Link & Otto

Usually solitary, stems to 40 cm high by 12 cm. Rsp 17–24, 4–9 mm, glassy-white to pale yellow; csp 4–9, to 25 mm, yellowish to reddish-brown. [K248/IP/K]

DISTRIBUTION: Mountains to the E and N of the Valley of Mexico.

OTHER NAMES: *M. aureiceps, M. fuscata.*

Mammillaria ritteriana   Boed.

Solitary, globular, 6 cm across. Closely related to **M. chionocephala** but much smaller and with longer and finer spines. [K286-1/IP/K]

DISTRIBUTION: Higueras, between Monterrey and Saltillo, in Coahuila, Mexico.

Mammillaria roseoalba   Boed.

Solitary, depressed-globose, to 18 cm across, 6 cm high. [SB285/CS/PM]

DISTRIBUTION: Mexico, Tamaulipas, Progreso, near Victoria.

Mammillaria rubrograndis   Repp. & Lau

Solitary, 4–10 cm high by 10–18 cm. Fl rarely produced, (at least in the British Isles), 4.5 cm across, bright carmine. [CS/PM]

DISTRIBUTION: Mexico: Tamaulipas, between Jaumave and Ciudad Victoria; Nuevo Leon, Dulces Nombres.

Mammillaria ruestii   Quehl

Solitary, to 40 cm high by 7 cm. [CS/W]

DISTRIBUTION: Guatemala, Honduras.

Mammillaria saboae Glass

Clumping, stems 1–2 cm tall and broad. Fl 4 cm across.
v. goldii (G. & F.) Glass & Foster, (illus.); sparingly
offsetting, stem to 3 cm by 3 cm. Fl 3.5 cm wide (Nacozari,
Son.) **fa. haudeana** (Lau & Wagner) D. Hunt; clumping,
stem to 4 cm tall. Fl 6.5 cm wide (Yecora, Son.) [IP/P]

DISTRIBUTION: Mexico, SW Chihuahua, near Terrero.

OTHER NAMES: **v. goldii**: *M. goldii.* **fa. haudeana**:
M. haudeana.

Mammillaria saetigera Boed. & Tieg.

Solitary, globose, to 7 cm high. Fl 2 cm wide, white with
pink midstripe. A plant of uncertain status but the
illustration shows a habitat specimen of the plant commonly
in circulation as this species. [H]

DISTRIBUTION: Mexico: Queretaro and San Luis Potosi.

Mammillaria sartorii Purpus

Stems to 12 cm tall by 10 cm, clumping. [CS/P]

DISTRIBUTION: Mexico, Vera Cruz, Barranca de Tenampa.

Mammillaria saxicola Repp.

Heads to 10 cm high by 8 cm, later offsetting to form small
clumps. Rsp 6–8, 2–5 mm, glassy-yellow, brown tipped;
csp 1–2, 7–40 mm long, lowest longest, glassy-yellow or
brown, dark tip. Fl 20 mm long. [Repp1139/CS/PM]

DISTRIBUTION: Mexico, Queretaro, Jalpan.

Mammillaria schiedeana Ehrenb.

Heads to 10 cm high by 4 cm, clustering, spines soft; fl in
autumn. [CS/W]

DISTRIBUTION: Mexico, Hidalgo, Puente de Dios and
Barrancas around Metztitlan.

Mammillaria schumannii Hildm.

Heads to 13 cm long by 4.5 cm, strongly clumping. Fl 4 cm
across. **v. globosa** Wolf is solitary, globose, 4–5 cm across,
with shorter spination (Cabo San Lucas). [CS/W]

DISTRIBUTION: Mexico, Baja California, near San Jose del
Cabo and between Bahia de las Palmas and Cabo San
Lucas.

OTHER NAMES: *Bartschella schumannii.*

Mammillaria schwarzii   Shurly

Heads 2–3 cm across, clumping. Spines glassy-white, often tipped reddish-brown. [CS/DHS]

DISTRIBUTION: Mexico, N Guanajuato.

Mammillaria scrippsiana   (B. & R.) Orcutt

Solitary or clumping, to 29 cm high by 8.5 cm, rsp 6–10, csp 1–2. Fl pink. **v. pseudoscrippsiana** (Bkbg.) Repp. has cream fl with reddish-brown midstripe (Ahuacatlan, Nayarit). [K91/IP/K]

DISTRIBUTION: Mexico. Numerous localities in Jalisco and Nayarit and from Santa Rosa in Zacatecas.

OTHER NAMES: *M. ortegae, M. scrip. v. autlanensis.* **v. pseudoscrip.:** *M. pseudoscrippsiana.*

Mammillaria sempervivi   DC.

Solitary later clumping, heads to over 7 cm broad, spherical to elongated. Csp 2–4. Fl dirty white with pink midstripe. [CS/E]

DISTRIBUTION: Mexico, Hidalgo, Zimapan to Venados.

OTHER NAMES: *M. semp. v. tetracantha, M. caput-medusae, M. semp. v. caput-med.*

Mammillaria senilis
[attrib. to Lodd. by] S-D

Heads globular to cylindric, up to 15 cm high by 10 cm forming large mounds. [CS/PM]

DISTRIBUTION: Mexico, from Chihuahua through the high Sierra Madre S to Jalisco.

OTHER NAMES: *Mamillopsis senilis.* Probably *M. diguetii* originally *Mamillopsis diguetii.*

Mammillaria setispina
(Coulter) K. Brandegee

Heads up to 30 cm high by 6 cm, strongly clustering. Fl red, 5 cm long. [CS/PM]

DISTRIBUTION: Mexico, Baja California, San Julio Canyon, near San Borgia.

OTHER NAMES: *Cochemiea setispina.*

Mammillaria sheldonii   (B. & R.) Boed.

Stems to 10 cm high by 3 cm, clumping. [SB545/CS/PM]

DISTRIBUTION: Mexico, Sonora, Hermasillo to N Sinaloa.

OTHER NAMES: *?M. gueldemanniana, ?M. guirocobensis.*

Mammillaria silvatica Repp.

Body to 9 cm high by 6 cm, solitary or clumping; rsp 19–24, 3–8 mm long, glassy white; csp 2–5, 6–20 mm long, brown. Fl 10–12 mm broad, carmine. A member of the **M. spinosissima** complex. [Repp1603/IP/Repp]

DISTRIBUTION: Mexico, Jalisco, Los Cerritos.

Mammillaria sinistrohamata Boed.

Solitary, (clumping in cultivation), heads to 4.5 cm across, globose. Closely related to **M. mercadensis**. [CS/W]

DISTRIBUTION: Mexico, NE Zacatecas.

Mammillaria solisioides Bkbg.

Solitary in habitat, clustering in cultivation, stems to 6 cm high and 5 cm across. [CS/GC]

DISTRIBUTION: Mexico, Puebla, S of Petlalzingo.

OTHER NAMES: *M. pectinifera fa. solisioides.*

Mammillaria sonorensis Craig

Heads globose, to 8 cm across, clumping. Rsp 8–15, 1–20 mm; csp 1–4, 5–45 mm. [K243/IP/K]

DISTRIBUTION: Mexico, in the region where Sonora, Chihuahua and Sinaloa meet.

OTHER NAMES: *M. bellisiana.*

Mammillaria sphacelata Mart.

Stems cylindric to 20 cm long by 3 cm, clumping. [K226-1/IP/K]

DISTRIBUTION: Mexico, around Tehuacan, Puebla and S into adjacent Oaxaca.

Mammillaria sphaerica Dietr.

Heads flattened-globose to 5 cm across, clumping. Fl 6 cm across. [CS/PM]

DISTRIBUTION: SE Texas into Tamaulipas, Mexico.

OTHER NAMES: *Dolichothele sphaerica.*

Mammillaria spinosissima Lem.

Clustering, stems to 30 cm or more high by 10 cm, spines very variable in colour from whitish through yellowish-brown, pink or reddish-brown to ruby-red. [Repp772/CS/PM]

DISTRIBUTION: Mexico: Mexico DF; Morelos and S into Guerrero in scattered localities on cliffs.

OTHER NAMES: *M. auricoma, M. flava, M. kladiwae.*

Mammillaria standleyi (B. & R.) Orcutt

Solitary, to 10 cm across, depressed-spherical. [W]

DISTRIBUTION: Mexico, Sonora, near Alamos.

Mammillaria subducta (Hunt) Repp.

Solitary or sparingly clumping, heads to 7 cm across. Spines hard. [CS/PM]

DISTRIBUTION: Mexico, Tamaulipas, between Ciudad Victoria and Jaumave.

OTHER NAMES: *M. lauii fa. subducta.*

**Mammillaria subducta
v. dasyacantha** (Hunt) Repp.

Heads to 5 cm across, strongly clumping in cultivation. Spines relatively soft. [E]

DISTRIBUTION: Mexico, Tamaulipas, between Ciudad Victoria and Jaumave.

OTHER NAMES: *M. lauii fa. dasyacantha.*

Mammillaria supertexta Mart. ex Pfeiff.

Solitary, to 12.5 cm high by 9.5 cm. [K5/IP/K]

DISTRIBUTION: Mexico, N Oaxaca and adjacent Puebla.

OTHER NAMES: *M. lanata, M. martinezii.*

Mammillaria surculosa Boed.

Heads to 2 cm across, strongly offsetting to form mats. [CS/P]

DISTRIBUTION: Mexico: Tamaulipas, Miquihuana and San Luis Potosi, between Huizache and Tula.

OTHER NAMES: *Dolichothele surculosa.*

Mammillaria swinglei (B. & R.) Boed.
Stems to 30 cm high by 5 cm, sparingly clustering from the base. [L606/CS/PM]
DISTRIBUTION: Mexico, Sonora, Guaymas.
OTHER NAMES: *M. inaiae.*

Mammillaria tayloriorum Glass & Foster
Stems globose to cylindric to 25 cm high by 11 cm, eventually clustering. [K242/IP/K]
DISTRIBUTION: Mexico, Sonora, Isla San Pedro Nolasco.

Mammillaria tegelbergiana
Gates ex Lindsay
Solitary (clumping in cultivation) stems to 9 cm tall by 6 cm. [IP/K]
DISTRIBUTION: Mexico, Chiapas, W of Ocozocautla and other sites; S Oaxaca.

Mammillaria tesopacensis Craig
Solitary, spherical to oblong, to 18 cm high by 13 cm. Fl cream or pink (*v. rubriflora*, illus.). Possibly only a form of **M. sonorensis**. [K179/IP/K]
DISTRIBUTION: Mexico, Sonora, near Tesopaco.

Mammillaria tetrancistra Englm.
Stems to 25 cm high by 7.5 cm, clustering. [CS/E]
DISTRIBUTION: California near San Felipe, otherwise widely distributed in SW USA and NW Mexico.
OTHER NAMES: *Phellosperma tetrancistra.*

Mammillaria theresae Cutak
Stem to 4 cm high by 2 cm, sparingly clustering. [IP/GC]
DISTRIBUTION: Mexico, Durango, E slope of Coneto Mts.
OTHER NAMES: *M. saboae v. theresae.*

Mammillaria thornberi Orcutt

Stems cylindric, to 10 cm high by 2.5 cm, densely clustering. [CS/PM]

DISTRIBUTION: S Arizona and Mexico, N Sonora.

OTHER NAMES: *M. fasciculata.*

Mammillari tlalocii Repp.

Solitary, to 20 cm high by 7 cm. Fl not opening widely, 8–10 mm across, carmine. [L1109/IP/K]

DISTRIBUTION: Mexico, Oaxaca, Barranca Ixcatlan.

Mammillaria tonalensis D.R. Hunt

Slender cylindric, to 12 cm or more long by 3 cm. Fl 12 mm across, petals carmine with whitish margins. [IP/W]

DISTRIBUTION: Mexico, Oaxaca, Puente de Tonala.

Mammillaria tropica Repp.

Stem to 10 cm high by 8 cm, forming large clumps; spines 4(–5), glassy yellow tipped brown. Fl yellowish, 1.5 cm broad. Closely related to **M. knippeliana.** [Repp677/H]

DISTRIBUTION: Mexico, Jalisco, Tomatlan.

Mammillaria uncinata Zuc. ex Pfeiff.

Stems depressed-globose, to 10 cm across, occasionally offsetting sparingly from the base. [PM26/HS/PM]

DISTRIBUTION: Mexico, Hidalgo, near Pachuca and widely distributed in CS Mexico.

Mammillaria vallensis Repp.

Clumping, body to 6 cm high by 8 cm; rsp 2–3, 1–3 mm long; rsp 1, 1–4.5 cm long. **v. brevispina** Repp. (lower illus. [Repp1119/CS/PM]) is solitary; rsp 4–6, csp 1, 5–20 mm long (Tamaulipas, Abra Celeya). [Repp1117/IP/Repp]

DISTRIBUTION: Mexico, San Luis Potosi, Abra/Valles.

Mammillaria variabilis Repp.

Stem to 8 cm high by 4 cm, clumping; rsp 14−19, 6−10 mm long, white; csp 4−9, 7−10 mm long, the lowest longest and hooked, all glassy white to reddish- or dark-brown. Fl 12−16 mm broad, whitish, yellowish or pinkish. [Repp1393/IP/Repp]

DISTRIBUTION: Mexico, Guanajuato, Absylon.

Mammillaria varieaculeata Buchenau

Stems to 13 cm high by 9 cm forming large clumps. Fl 17−18 m long, reddish-purple. [K145-1/IP/K]

DISTRIBUTION: Mexico, Puebla, S of Chilac.

Mammillaria vetula Mart.

Stems to 4 cm across, clustering. Fl 12 mm across, dirty yellowish-cream. [W]

DISTRIBUTION: Mexico, Hidalgo, San Jose del Oro.

OTHER NAMES: *M. kuentziana, M. magneticola.*

Mammillaria viereckii Boed.

Stems to 5 cm high by 4 cm, sparingly clumping. Related to **M. picta**. [CS/PM]

DISTRIBUTION: Mexico, Tamaulipas, near Nogales.

Mammillaria viperina Purpus

Stems slender-cylindric, to 2 cm across. Fl 11 mm long, light carmine, not opening widely. Probably only an extreme southern form of **M. sphacelata**. [HS/PM]

DISTRIBUTION: Mexico, Puebla, Rio de Zapotitlan.

Mammillaria virginis Fittkau & Kladiwa

Usually solitary, to 25 cm high by 8 cm. A member of the complex of plants centred on **M. spinosissima**. [CS/W]

DISTRIBUTION: Mexico, Guerrero, near Ancon.

Mammillaria viridiflora (B. & R.) Boed.

Stem usually solitary but sometimes clustering, heads to 10 cm high by 7.5 cm. [CS/W]

DISTRIBUTION: Arizona, near Boundary Monument.

OTHER NAMES: *M. chavezii, M. orestera, M. wilcoxii v. viridiflora, M. wrightii v. viridiflora.*

Mammillaria voburnensis Scheer

Heads to 20 cm long by 8 cm, freely offsetting. Fl 2 cm long, yellow with brownish dorsal stripe. **v. eichlamii** (Quehl) Repp., **v. collinsii** (B. & R.) Repp. and **v. quetzalcoatl** Repp. differ in a number of minor details. [CS/W]

DISTRIBUTION: Guatemala. Mexico, Oaxaca, Tehuantepec (**v. collinsii**); Oaxaca, Mixtequilla (**v. quetz.**); Chiapas, Rio Grijalva, Tuxtla Gutierrez. (**v. eichl.**).

OTHER NAMES: *M. collinsii, M. eichlamii.*

Mammillaria wagneriana Boed.

Solitary, depressed-globose to 10 cm across. Fl 1.5 cm broad, dirty white with pale pink midstripes. [Repp1508/CS/W]

DISTRIBUTION: Mexico, Zacatecas.

Mammillaria weingartiana Boed.

Stems globose, 4–5 cm across, usually solitary, perhaps offsetting with age. Fl pale greenish-yellow with pinkish-brown midstripe. [CS/E]

DISTRIBUTION: Mexico, Nuevo Leon, Ascension.

OTHER NAMES: *M. unihamata.*

Mammillaria wiesingeri Boed.

Solitary, depressed-globose, to 4 cm tall by 8 cm. [K247-1/IP/K]

DISTRIBUTION: Mexico, Hidalgo, near Metzquititlan.

Mammillaria wilcoxii Toumey ex Sch.

Stem spherical to elongated to 10 cm high by 5 cm, solitary or clumping. Fl 4 cm across. [L778/CS/PM]

DISTRIBUTION: SW New Mexico, S Arizona. N Sonora and adjacent Chihuahua, Mexico.

OTHER NAMES: *M. wrightii v. wilcoxii, M. meridiorosei.*

Mammillaria wildii A. Dietrich

In habitat small, in cultivation to 15 cm long by 6 cm, clumping. [SB144/CS/PM]

DISTRIBUTION: Mexico, Hidalgo, Barranca of the Rio Grande, E of Metztitlan.

OTHER NAMES: *M. calleana.*

Mammillaria winterae Boed.

Solitary, depressed-globose, up to 30 cm across. [K289/IP/K]

DISTRIBUTION: Mexico, Coahuila around Saltillo and in Nuevo Leon near Monterrey.

OTHER NAMES: *M. zahniana.*

Mammillaria wohlschlageri Repp.

Solitary, body flattened-globular to 3 cm high by 6 cm. Spines 26–36, 2–6 long. Fl not widely opening, 18–20 mm long, dirty white. [K291/IP/K]

DISTRIBUTION: Mexico, Zacatecas, La Cardona.

Mammillaria wrightii Englm. & Bigelow

Usually solitary, globular to short-columnar, to 8 cm across. Flower 2.5 cm broad, deep pink. **v. wolfii** (Hunt) Repp. (illus.) from Santa Clara Canyon, Chihuahua, Mexico, has white flowers. [CS/E]

DISTRIBUTION: Arizona and New Mexico.

OTHER NAMES: **v. wolfii**: *M. wrightii fa. wolfii,* 'M. wolfii'.

Mammillaria xaltianguensis Sanchez-Mejorada

Stem to 20 cm high by 8 cm, solitary or occasionally clustering. Fl small, yellowish with purple stripes on the outer petals. [CS/W]

DISTRIBUTION: Mexico: Guerrero, near Xaltianguis and other localities; Michoacan, near Aguililla and between Playa Azul and Arteaga.

Mammillaria xochipilli Repp.

Solitary, to 20 cm high by 9 cm; spines 4–6, 3–20 mm long, brown to black. Fl 12–15 mm across, carmine. Closely related to **M. magnimamma.** [Repp1709/H]

DISTRIBUTION: Mexico, Hidalgo, San Jose del Oro.

Mammillaria yaquensis Craig

Joints to 7 cm by 1.5 cm, clustering freely. Probably a southern variety of **M. thornberi.** [CS/PM]

DISTRIBUTION: Mexico, Sonora, Rio Yaqui and S of Guaymas.

Mammillaria yucatanensis (B. & R.) Orcutt

Stems to 15 cm high by 6 cm. [IP/K]

DISTRIBUTION: Mexico, Yucatan, Progreso, possibly extinct.

Mammillaria zacatecasensis Shurly

Solitary, to 12 cm high by 7 cm. [CS/PM]

DISTRIBUTION: Mexico, mountains near the city of Zacatecas.

Mammillaria zeilmanniana Boed.

In cultivation heads to 12 cm high by 8 cm, solitary or clustering. [CS/P]

DISTRIBUTION: Mexico, Guanajuato, near San Miguel Allende.

Mammillaria zephyranthoides Scheidw.

Solitary, to 8 cm high by 10 cm. Fl 4 cm across. [CS/P]

DISTRIBUTION: Mexico: Oaxaca; Puebla; Hidalgo and Queretaro.

OTHER NAMES: *Dolichothele zephyranthoides.*

Mammillaria zeyeriana Haage ex Sch.

Solitary, up to 10 cm or more across, flattened-globose. [CS/PM]

DISTRIBUTION: Mexico, Coahuila, Viesca.

Mammillaria zubleri Repp.

Body to 5 cm high by 4.5 cm, clumping; rsp 20–24, 4–7 mm long, white tipped yellow; csp 5–6, 5–9 mm long, glassy yellow. Fl 14–16 mm across, bright yellow. Closely related to **M. picta**. [IP/Repp]

DISTRIBUTION: Mexico, Tamaulipas, Ocampo.

Mammillaria zuccariniana Mart.

Solitary, to 20 cm high by 10 cm or more; rsp 3–4, 2–6 mm long; csp 2, the upper 25 mm, the lower slightly longer. Fl 25 mm long, rose-purple. The plant illustrated is the one which currently best fits this original description. [CS/W]

DISTRIBUTION: Mexico, Hidalgo, reported originally from Ixmiquilpan; recent collections from between Zimapan and Encarnacion.

Matucana aurantiaca (Vpl.) Ritt.

Usually solitary, to 15 cm high and broad. Fl to 9 cm long. [CS/PM]

DISTRIBUTION: Peru: Cajamarca between Chota and Hualgayoc; Huancabamba near Sondor.

OTHER NAMES: *Borzicactus aurantiacus, B. calvescens, M. calvescens, Submatucana aurantiaca, 'S. bagalaensis', 'S. calmada', S. calvescens, 'S. grandiflora', 'S. nivosa'.*

Matucana aureiflora Ritt.

Flattened-globular, to 13 cm across. Fl to 4.5 cm long. [L104/IP/GC]

DISTRIBUTION: Peru, Cajamarca, Banos del Inca.

OTHER NAMES: *Submatucana aureiflora, Borzicactus aureiflorus.*

Matucana comacephala Ritt.

Solitary, becoming columnar, usually to 75 cm high by 8 cm. Fl pink to carmine (L103, L185) or pinkish-orange (L173). [L185/IP/DHS]

DISTRIBUTION: Peru; mountains above the Rio Maranon, from Balsas to Llamellin and Huari (*M. huarinensis n.n.*).

OTHER NAMES: *M. calocephala, M. winteri.*

Matucana crinifera Ritt.

Globular to elongated, 30 cm high by 10 cm. Fl 6–7 cm long. Probably only an extension of the range of the previous species. [IP/F]

DISTRIBUTION: Peru, Dept. of Ancash, Machac.

Matucana formosa Ritt.

Globular, up to 15 cm across. Fl 9−10 cm long, carmine.

DISTRIBUTION: Peru, Dept. of Cajamarca, Balsas.

OTHER NAMES: *Submatucana formosa, Borzicactus formosus.*

Matucana haynei (Otto) B. & R.

Usually solitary to 60 cm high by 15 cm. Fl 5−7 cm long, red. 'v. breviflora' (*M. breviflora* Rauh & Bkbg.) is globular, 15 cm tall and broad; fl only 4 cm long (W of Incuio). [IP/GC]

DISTRIBUTION: Peru, various valleys running inland from the sea e.g. Pisco Valley, Fortaleza Valley.

OTHER NAMES: *M. blancii, M. cereoides, M. elongata, M. herzogiana, M. hystrix* & *vars., M. multicolor, M. supertexta, M. variabilis, M. yanganucensis, Borzicactus haynei, B. variabilis.*

Matucana huagalensis (Don. & Lau) Bregman *et al*

Solitary, short-cylindric. Fl originally described as pale pink but all subsequent collections seem to be as illustrated. [CS/PM]

DISTRIBUTION: Peru, Hacienda Huagal, near junction of the Rio Crisnejas and Rio Maranon.

OTHER NAMES: *Borzicactus huagalensis.*

Matucana intertexta Ritt.

Solitary, to 36 cm high by 7−18 cm. Fl 7.5−10.5 cm long, petals golden yellow, blood-red above. [KK/IP/GC]

DISTRIBUTION: Peru, Puente Crisnejas, N of Cajamarca.

OTHER NAMES: *Borzicactus inter., Submatucana inter.*

Matucana intertexta v. celendinensis (Ritt.) Bregman *et al*.

Solitary, to 12 cm across. Fl 7.5 cm long. [IP/GC]

DISTRIBUTION: Peru, between Celendin and Balsas.

OTHER NAMES: *Borzicactus intertextus v. celendinensis, M. celen.*

Matucana krahnii (Don.) Bregman

Heads 5−6 cm across, depressed-globose, solitary. Fl to 8.5 cm long. [KK758/IP/GC]

DISTRIBUTION: Peru, Dept. of Amazonas, East of Balsas.

OTHER NAMES: *M. calliantha, Borzicactus krahnii.*

Matucana madisoniorum
(Hutch.) Rowley
Spherical, later becoming elongated, to 7 cm across. Fl 8−10 cm long. [HS/GC]

DISTRIBUTION: Peru, Dept. of Amazonas, near the Rio Maranon.

OTHER NAMES: *Submatucana mad., Borzicactus mad.*

Matucana myriacantha (Vpl.) Bux.
Usually solitary, body globose to short cylindric, 8 cm across; rsp white, pale yellow or light brown; csp ginger with darker tips. [CS/GC]

DISTRIBUTION: Peru, 20 km NE of Balsas.

OTHER NAMES: *M. purpureoalba, M. roseoalba.*

Matucana oreodoxa (Ritt.) Slaba
Flattened globular, to 8 cm across, solitary. Fl 4−6 cm long. [CS/PM]

DISTRIBUTION: Peru, Dept. of Ancash, Rahuapampa Gorge.

OTHER NAMES: *Borzicactus oreodoxus.*

Matucana pallarensis Ritt.
Globular, to 10 cm across, solitary. Probably only a form of **M. aurantiaca**. [CS/PM]

DISTRIBUTION: Peru, Dept. of La Libertad, El Pallar.

OTHER NAMES: *Borzicactus weberbaueri v. pall.*

Matucana paucicostata Ritt.
Body to 14 cm high by 7 cm, freely clustering. Fl 6 cm long. [L187a/IP/GC]

DISTRIBUTION: Peru, Dept. of Ancash, Rahuapampa.

OTHER NAMES: *Borzicactus pauc., Submatucana pauc., 'M. caespitosa', 'M. eriodisca', 'M. huaricensis', 'M. paucispina', 'M. senile', 'M. senilis', 'M. turbiniformis'.*

Matucana polzii Diers, Don. & Zecher
Strongly offsetting, heads to 5 cm high by 8 cm. Fl to 7 cm long, red. [IP/DHS]

DISTRIBUTION: Peru, above the Rio Maranon in SW part of Dept. of Huanuco.

Matucana pujupatii
(Don. & Lau) Bregman

Similar to **M. madisoniorum** but ribs more tuberculate, body greener, spines always present. LAU IP/GC.

DISTRIBUTION: Peru, Dept. of Amazonas, near Puente Julio 24 on the Chamaya to Bagua road.

OTHER NAMES: *Borzicactus mad. v. pujupatii.*

Matucana ritteri   Buin.

Depressed globose, to 14 cm broad, eventually clumping. Fl to 9 cm long. [IP/GC]

DISTRIBUTION: Peru, Dept. of La Libertad, Otuzco.

OTHER NAMES: *Submatucana ritteri, Borzicactus ritteri.*

Matucana tuberculosa   Ritt.

Stems 4–6 cm across, globular to elongated, clumping Fl 5.5 cm long. [IP/F]

DISTRIBUTION: Peru, Dept. of La Libertad, El Chagual.

Matucana weberbaueri   (Vpl.) Bkbg.

Body to 7 cm high by 15 cm, sometimes offsetting. Fl 5.5 cm long, lemon-yellow. 'v. **flammeus**' has orange-yellow flowers. [IP ex Lau/GC]

DISTRIBUTION: Peru, Dept. of Amazonas, Balsas.

OTHER NAMES: *Borzicactus weberbaueri.* 'v. **flammeus**': *M. weber. fa. flam.*

Melocactus azureus   Buin. & Bred.

Solitary, to 17 cm high by 14 cm. [IP/Hovens]

DISTRIBUTION: Brazil, Bahia, Serro do Espinhaco above the Rio Jacare.

Melocactus caesius   Wendl.

Solitary. [PM137/H]

DISTRIBUTION: Widespread along the coast of Venezuela and inland into the drier areas.

Melocactus glaucescens Buin. & Bred.

Solitary, to 14 cm high and broad. [H]

DISTRIBUTION: Brazil, C Bahia, in W Serro do Espinhaco.

Melocactus matanzanus Leon

To 8 cm high and 9 cm across. [IP/Hovens]

DISTRIBUTION: Cuba, Matanzas.

Melocactus oreas Miqu.

To 12 cm or more high, spines noticeably long. [PM123/H]

DISTRIBUTION: Brazil, Bahia, particularly common around Jequie on the Rio do Contas.

OTHER NAMES: *M. cremnophilus, M. erythracanthus, M. longispinus, M. rubrisaetosus.*

Melocactus oreas subsp. ernestii (Vpl.) Braun

Spines longer and more twisting than in the species, brownish to yellowish. [PMI30/H]

DISTRIBUTION: Brazil, Bahia, Rio das Contas valley.

OTHER NAMES: *M. azulensis, M. ernestii, M. nitidus.*

Melocactus peruvianus Vpl.

DISTRIBUTION: Widespread in Peru.

OTHER NAMES: *'M. alpestris', M. amstutziae, M. chalensis, M. huallancaensis, M. jansenianus, M. trujilloensis, M. unguispinus.*

Melocactus salvadorensis Werd.

Solitary, hemispherical, to 12 cm across.

DISTRIBUTION: Brazil, Bahia.

Mila caespitosa   B. & R.

Stems to 30 cm long by 3 cm, spination very variable in colour and length. Fl 2 cm across. [PM61/H]

DISTRIBUTION: Peru, in several river valleys, e.g. Rimac, Lurin, Santa and Pisco.

OTHER NAMES: Any other **Mila** name is now regarded as this species.

Neolloydia conoidea   (DC.) B. & R.

Stems usually clustering, to 15 cm high by 5 cm. Flower to 6 cm across. [PM54/HS/PM]

DISTRIBUTION: From Texas and throughout a large area of Tamaulipas and San Luis Potosi in Mexico, with many local forms.

OTHER NAMES: *N. ceratites, N. grandiflora, N. matehualensis, N. texensis.*

Neoporteria aspillagai   (Sohr.) Bkbg.

Stem to 15 cm across, flattened, sparingly offsetting. Probably a variety of **N. horrida.** Fl 4 cm long. [L880/IP/F]

DISTRIBUTION: Chile, Hacienda Tanume.

OTHER NAMES: *Neochilenia aspill., Pyrrhocactus aspill.*

Neoporteria atroviridis
(Ritt.) R.M. Ferryman comb. nov. *Pyrrhocactus atroviridis* Ritt. 1960, Succulenta, 8: 89.

Solitary, to 10 cm across, becoming elongated. Fl 4–5 cm across, petals pink edged yellow. [PM234/H].

DISTRIBUTION: Chile, around Vallenar.

OTHER NAMES: *Horridocactus atrov., Neop. tuberisulcata v. atrov., Pyrrhocactus atrov.*

Neoporteria calderana
(Ritt.) Don. & Rowley

Solitary, 5–8 cm across, globose to elongate; rsp 8–10, 1–3.5 cm long, csp 3–5, 2–4 cm long. Fl 3.5 cm broad, white to pink. [RMF171/IP/F].

DISTRIBUTION: N Chile, Caldera to Chanaral.

OTHER NAMES: *Neochilenia cald., Pyrrhocactus cald., Neoc. intermedia, Neop. int., Pyrrh. int., Neoc. pilispinas, Pyrrho. pil, Pyrrho. pygmaeus., Neop. pilispina & fa. pygm., Horridocactus scoparius, Neoc. scoparia, Neop. scop., Pyrrh. scop., Neoc. gracilis, Neop. cald. fa. grac., Pyrrho. grac.*

Neoporteria chilensis
(Hildm.) Don. & Rowley

Solitary or clumping to 30 cm high and 10 cm across. Fl pink or white, 5 cm across. [PM258/H]

DISTRIBUTION: Coast of Chile to N and S of Pichidangui.

OTHER NAMES: *Neochilenia chilensis, Pyrrhocactus chilensis, P. chilensis v. albidiflorus.*

Neoporteria chorosensis
(Ritt.) Don. & Rowley

Solitary, flattened-globular, to 6 cm across. Fl 4 cm across, light yellow. [RMF7/IP/F]

DISTRIBUTION: Chile, Choros to Trapiche.

OTHER NAMES: *Neochilenia choro., Neoc. deherdtiana, Neoc. subikii n.n., Neoc. minima n.n., Pyrrhocactus choro., P. trapichensis.*

Neoporteria clavata (Sohr.) Werd.

At first globular then to 1.5 m high by 15 cm. Fl 5 cm long. **v. procera** Ritt. has smaller flowers and is less spiny. [RMF117/IP/F]

DISTRIBUTION: Chile, Elqui Valley.

Neoporteria coimasensis Ritt.

Solitary, to 30 cm and more high by 12 cm. Fl 5−7.5 cm long, 4 cm broad, widely opening. **v. robusta** (Ritt.) Ritt., (upper, [RM182/IP/F]) tends to have thicker and darker spination; fl to 8 cm long (E of Montenegro). [RMF105/IP/F]

DISTRIBUTION: Chile, Las Coimas and from Las Chilcas in the S to N of Illapel.

OTHER NAMES: **v. robusta**: *Neoporteria robusta.*

Neoporteria confinis
(Ritt.) Don. & Rowley

Solitary, body green or black, globular later elongated, 6−8 cm broad. Fl 3 cm across. [RMF173/IP/F]

DISTRIBUTION: Chile, Monte Amargo.

OTHER NAMES: *Neochilenia confinis, Pyrrhocactus confinis.*

Neoporteria crispa (Ritt.) Don. & Rowley

Solitary, flattened-globular to 7 cm across, spination hair-like. Fl 3.5 cm across, pale yellow with a narrow purple midstripe. [IP/F]

DISTRIBUTION: Chile, Freirina.

OTHER NAMES: *Pyrrhocactus crispus, Horridocactus crispus, Neochilenia nigriscoparia.*

Neoporteria curvispina
(Bert.) Don. & Rowley

Solitary, globular to over 15 cm across, spination very variable fl 3.5 cm across, straw coloured (often with a red midstripe). [RMF221/IP/F]

DISTRIBUTION: Chile. A very variable taxon widespread in the mts. around Santiago, and a long way N and S.

OTHER NAMES: *Horridocactus curvisp., H. andicolus & vars., H. lissocarpus & v. gracilis, (= H. engleri v. krausii & Neop. eng. v. kr.) Neop. curv. v. acon., N. curv. v. and., N. curv. v. liss., Pyrrhocactus curvisp., P. coliguayensis.*

Neoporteria curvispina v. grandiflora
(Ritt.) Don. & Rowley

Solitary, globose to 15 cm broad. Fl to 7 cm across.
[PM192/H]

DISTRIBUTION: Chile, Cerro Ramon, over 2000 m.

OTHER NAMES: *Horridocactus grandif., Pyrrhocactus grandif.*

Neoporteria echinus
(Ritt.) R.M. Ferryman comb. nov. *Pyrrhocactus echinus* Ritt. 1963, Taxon 12(1), 33.

Solitary, globular to elongated, 6–9 cm across, rsp 8–14, csp 1–8. Fl to 3 cm long, 2 cm wide, white with pink midstripe, sometimes flushed yellow. [RMF42/IP/F]

DISTRIBUTION: Chile, Cerro Coloso and El Cobre, near Antofagasta.

OTHER NAMES: *Horridocactus echinus, N. curvispina v. echinus, N. eriocephala v. glaucescens, Neoc. glaucescens, Pyrrhocactus echinus, P. glaucescens.*

Neoporteria echinus v. floccosa
(Ritt.) R.M. Ferryman comb. nov. *Pyrrhocactus floccosus* Ritt. 1963, Taxon 12(1), 32.

Mainly distinguished from the species by the generally larger amount of hair, which can be quite dense in the crown, but may often be absent or nearly so. [CS/PM]

DISTRIBUTION: Chile, coastal mountains Prov. of Antofagasta.

OTHER NAMES: *Neochilenia flocc., Pyrrhocactus flocc., Neop. eriocephala* (Bkbg.) Don. & Rowley wrongly applied here (= **Neop. odieri v. malleolata**).

Neoporteria engleri   (Ritt.) Don. & Rowley

Solitary, to 30 cm high by 18 cm, spines, white, yellow, or brown with black tips. Fl 4.5 cm across, yellow usually with pink midstripe. [IP/F]

DISTRIBUTION: Chile, mountains between Santiago and Valparaiso.

OTHER NAMES: *Horridocactus engleri, Pyrrhocactus engleri.*

Neoporteria eriosyzoides
(Ritt.) Don. & Rowley

Solitary, green, globular to elongated, 9–12 cm wide. Fl 3 cm broad, brownish-yellow with a reddish-brown midstripe. **v. domeykoensis** (Ritt.) R.M. Ferryman comb. nov. (*Pyrrhocactus eriosyzoides v. domeykoensis* Ritt. 1980, Kak. in Sudam. 3: 938.); body with blackish tints, spines paler, more rsp. Fl larger (Domeyko). [RMF123/IP/F]

DISTRIBUTION: Chile, Elqui Valley, Huanta.

OTHER NAMES: *Pyrrhocactus erios., Horridocactus erios., Neochilenia erios.*

Neoporteria esmeraldana
(Ritt.) Don. & Rowley

Solitary or offsetting, flattened, heads to 4 cm across. Fl to 5 cm long, pale greenish-yellow. [RMF159/IP/F]

DISTRIBUTION: N Chile, Esmeralda.

OTHER NAMES: *'Neochilenia esmer.', 'Chileorebutia esmer.', 'Thelocephala esmer.'*

Neoporteria garaventai
(Ritt.) R.M. Ferryman comb. nov. *Pyrrhocactus garaventai* Ritt. 1959, Succulenta, 10: 131.
Solitary or sparingly clumping, heads to 25 cm high by 12 cm. Fl 4 cm across, pale yellow often with a reddish midstripe. [RMF232/IP/F]

DISTRIBUTION: Chile, Cerro La Campana.

OTHER NAMES: *Horridocactus garav., Pyrrhocactus subaianus, N. curvispina v. garav., N. subaiana.*

Neoporteria heinrichiana
(Bkbg.) R.M. Ferryman comb. nov. *Horridocactus heinrichianus* Bkbg. 1942, Kakt.-kde., 8.
Solitary, globular, to 6 cm or more across. Fl 4 cm broad yellow with red tips. [RMF266/IP/F]

DISTRIBUTION: Chile, Chaniaral de Aceitunas.

OTHER NAMES: *Horridocactus hein., Pyrrhocactus heinr., Neop. curvispina v. hein., Pyrrho. chaniarensis.*

Neoporteria horrida
(Remy ex Gay) D. Hunt
Usually solitary, to 20 cm high and broad, but dwarf clustering forms occur. Spination very variable in number, length and spine diameter. Some populations are similar to forms of **N. curvispina** with probable hybrids between the two. [FK208/IP/F]

DISTRIBUTION: Over a wide area of C Chile.

OTHER NAMES: See Appendix 4.

Neoporteria huascensis
(Ritt.) Don. & Rowley
Solitary, hemispherical to oblong, to 8 cm across. Fl to 4.5 cm long. [CS/PM]

DISTRIBUTION: N Chile, near Huasco.

OTHER NAMES: *Neochilenia huascensis, Pyrrhocactus huasc.*

Neoporteria iquiquensis
(Ritt.) Don. & Rowley
Solitary, globular to elongated, 5–6 cm across; rsp 8–10, csp 2–4(–6). Fl 2 cm across. [RMF36/IP/F]

DISTRIBUTION: N Chile, Arica to Pisagua.

OTHER NAMES: *Neochilenia aricensis, Neoc. iquiquensis, Neop. aricensis, Neop. reichei fa. floribunda, Pyrrhocactus florib., P. aricensis, P. saxifragus, 'Reicheocactus florib.'*

Neoporteria islayensis
(Foerst.) Don. & Rowley
Solitary, 5–7 cm broad, oblong. Fl 2 cm long. [IP/F]

DISTRIBUTION: S Peru, Islay.

OTHER NAMES: *Islaya copiapoides, I. flavida, I. islayensis, I. longicarpa, I. maritima, I. minuscula, I. mollendensis, I. minor, I. grandiflorens, Neop. islayensis v. islayensis fa. brevicylindrica, fa. grandiflorens, fa. minor, fa. mollendensis, fa spinosior.*

Neoporteria islayensis v. divaricatiflora (Ritt.) Don. & Rowley

Solitary, globose, to 7 cm broad; fl 2–3 cm broad, greenish-yellow or reddish. [IP/GC]

DISTRIBUTION: Peru, Camana.

OTHER NAMES: *Islaya divaricatiflora.*

Neoporteria jussieui (Monv.) B. & R.

Solitary, short-cylindric to 7 cm high by 4 cm. Fl 4 cm broad. [RMF115/IP/F]

DISTRIBUTION: Chile, Elqui Valley, above Vicuna, Las Rojas etc.

OTHER NAMES: *Neochilenia juss., N. neofusca, N. vanbaelii, Pyrrhocactus juss.*

Neoporteria jussieui v. wagenknechtii (Ritt.) Hoffmann.

Usually solitary, globular to elongated to 9 cm across. Fl 3.5 cm wide, shades of yellow, to reddish. **v. dimorpha** (Ritt.) Hoffmann has an almost spineless 'juvenile' form and a spiny 'adult' form. [RMF308/IP/F]

DISTRIBUTION: Chile, from Coquimbo to La Serena.

OTHER NAMES: *Neochilenia wagenknechtii, Pyrrhocactus wagen., Neop. ritteri.* **v. dim.:** *Neoc. dimorpha, Pyrrho. dimorphus.*

Neoporteria krainziana (Ritt.) Don. & Rowley

Solitary, becoming short-cylindric in cultivation. Fl 3 cm broad, scented. [IP/F]

DISTRIBUTION: N Chile, near Poconchile close to the Peruvian border.

OTHER NAMES: *Islaya krainziana, I. unguispina.*

Neoporteria kunzei (Foerst.) Bkbg.

Solitary to 12 cm across becoming short-cylindric. Fl to 3–3.5 cm across. Plants purporting to be this species often turn out to be **N. eriosyzoides**. [IP ex Ritt./F]

DISTRIBUTION: Chile, around Copiapo.

OTHER NAMES: *Neochilenia kunzei, Pyrrhocactus kunzei.*

Neoporteria limariensis (Ritt.) R.M. Ferryman comb. nov. *Pyrrhocactus limariensis* Ritt. 1980, Kak. in Sudam. 3: 956–7.

Solitary, globular becoming slightly elongated, 5–15 cm across. Fl 4.5–5.5. cm long. [RMF260/IP/F]

DISTRIBUTION: Chile midway between Frai Jorge and the Pan American Highway; also from Ovalle (smaller flowers) and Incienso.

OTHER NAMES: *Pyrrhocactus limariensis, P. pamaensis.*

Neoporteria marksiana
(Ritt.) Don. & Rowley

Globular, to 24 cm across. Fl 4 cm broad, lemon or reddish-yellow. Closely related to **N. curvispina**. [PM251/H]

DISTRIBUTION: Chile, Vila Prat to San Fernando.

OTHER NAMES: *Horridocactus marksianus & v. tunensis, Neop. marksiana v. tunensis, Pyrrhocactus marks. v. tunensis, P. truncatipetalus.*

Neoporteria microsperma   Ritt.

Solitary, to 50 cm high by 10 cm, sometimes clumping. Fl 2.5 cm long. [RMF366/IP/F]

DISTRIBUTION: Chile, Elqui Valley.

OTHER NAMES: *Neop. subgibbosa v. microsperma, N. micros. v. serenana & v. graciana.*

Neoporteria napina   (Phil.) Bkbg.

Solitary, club-shaped, to 3.5 cm across, elongating in cultivation. Fl 4 cm across, white to pink, yellow or brownish. [RMF184/IP/F]

DISTRIBUTION: Chile, Dept. of Copiapo, near the coast in many localities, and N to Carrizal Bajo, Dept. of Freirina.

OTHER NAMES: *Neochilenia napina & v. spinosior, Neoc. glabrescens, Neoc. mitis; Neop. napina v. mitis & fa. glabrescens, Neop. napina v. spinosior; Chileorebutia napina; Thelocephala napina, T. nuda, T. tenebrica.*

Neoporteria napina v. fankhauseri
(Ritt.) Hoffmann.

Usually solitary, flattened, to 7 cm across. Fl 4 cm long. [RMF79/HS/GC]

DISTRIBUTION: Chile, near Domeyko.

OTHER NAMES: *Thelocephala fankhauseri, N. napina v. laniger n. n.*

Neoporteria neohankeana (Ritt.)
R.M. Ferryman comb. nov. *Pyrrhocactus neohankeanus* Ritt. 1980, Kak. in Sudam. 3: 959.

Solitary, spherical to oblong, 4–7 cm across, either green or black. Fl 3.5 cm long, pale yellowish or reddish. [RMF149/IP/F]

DISTRIBUTION: Chile, various canyons N of Taltal.

OTHER NAMES: *Neochilenia hankeana & vars., Pyrrhocactus neohankeanus, Neoc. taltalensis v. flaviflora, 'Delaetia woutersiana'.*

Neoporteria nidus   (Sohr.) B. & R.

Solitary, spherical, becoming cylindric in cultivation, to 12 cm high by 7 cm, spination extremely variable, soft and wavy or harder and curved. Colour white, gold, brown or black. Fl 4–5 cm long. [RMF251/IP/F]

DISTRIBUTION: Chile, around Ovalle.

OTHER NAMES: *Neop. senilis, Neop. nidus v. matancillana, Neop. nidus v. senilis.*

Neoporteria nidus v. gerocephala (Ito) Ritt.

Distinguished from the species by its much smaller size and softer spination. Spines white, grey or black. [RMF302/IP/F]

DISTRIBUTION: Chile, Elqui Valley.

OTHER NAMES: *Neop. gerocephala.*

Neoporteria nidus v. multicolor (Ritt.) Hoffmann

Solitary, to 20 cm high by 8 cm. Range of spination as for the species. Fl 6–8 cm long. [RMF248, left; RMF249, right/IP/F]

DISTRIBUTION: Chile, E of Salamanca and in the mountains E of Illapel.

OTHER NAMES: *N. multicolor.*

Neoporteria nigrihorrida (Bkbg.) Bkbg.

Solitary, to 20 cm high by 10 cm. Fl 4–7 cm long. [RMF192/IP/F]

DISTRIBUTION: Chile along the coast on both sides of Coquimbo.

OTHER NAMES: *Neop. subgibbosa v. nigri.* All the named varieties fall within the species.

Neoporteria occulta (Sch.) B. & R.

Body flattened, to 4.5 cm across, sometimes clumping. Fl 2.5 cm long, pale yellow. [CS/PM]

DISTRIBUTION: N Chile, Taltal to Paposo.

OTHER NAMES: *Neochilenia occulta, Pyrrhocactus occultus.*

Neoporteria odieri (Lem.) Berg.

Solitary, flattened to 6 cm across, rsp 6–10. Fl 3 cm broad, white to pink. **v. malleolata** (Ritt.) R.M. Ferryman comb. nov. (*Chieleorebutia malleolata* Ritt. 1963, Taxon 12(3): 123.) often clumps, rsp 4–8, fl pale brownish-yellow to pale orange-red (Chanaral). [RMF338/IP/F]

DISTRIBUTION: Chile, coasts N and S of Copiapo.

OTHER NAMES: See Appendix 5.

Neoporteria odieri v. monte-amargensis (Bkbg.) R.M. Ferryman comb. nov. *Basionym Neochilenia monte-amargensis* Bkbg. 1963, Cact. Nov. III: Holotype Das Kakteen Lexicon 1965 p632 Ill 259.

Stems depressed-spherical to 5 cm across, spines often longer than in the plant pictured, offsetting to form small clumps. [RMF339/IP/F]

DISTRIBUTION: Chile, Monte Amargo.

OTHER NAMES: *'Neop. monte-amargensis'.*

Neoporteria omasensis
(Ostolaza & Mischler) R.M. Ferryman comb.
nov. *Islaya omasensis* Ostolaza & Mischler
1983, KuaS 34, 3: 54–57.

Solitary, to 30 cm high by 14 cm. Fl 1.7 cm across. [IP/GC]

DISTRIBUTION: Peru: Omas Valley, 90 km S of Lima;
Pacoto and Topara Gorges; Huatiana Gorge at Chincha
Alta. Extends the distribution of Neoporteria 400 km
northwards.

OTHER NAMES: *Islaya omasensis.*

Neoporteria paucicostata
(Ritt.) Don. & Rowley

Solitary, to 30 cm high by 8 cm, body bluish-grey or green.
Fl 5 cm across. [RMF57/IP/F]

DISTRIBUTION: Chile, along the coast to the N & S of
Paposo.

OTHER NAMES: *Horridocactus pauc., Neochilenia pauc.,
Pyrrhocactus pauc.* & *var. viridis* for all of these.

Neoporteria pulchella
(Ritt.) R.M. Ferryman comb. nov. *Pyrrhocactus
pulchellus* Ritt. 1980, Kak. in Sudam. 3:
965–6.

Solitary, globular later somewhat elongated to 7 cm across.
Fl 2.5 cm across, white with a reddish midstripe. [H]

DISTRIBUTION: Rare, in scattered localities from Cifuncho
to Barquito, Chile.

OTHER NAMES: *Neochilenia pulchella, Pyrrhocactus pulchellus.*

Neoporteria recondita
(Ritt.) Don. & Rowley

Solitary, dwarf, 2.5–4.5 cm across, csp 1–2, 1–1.5 cm
long. Fl 3.5 cm across, white to yellowish. **v. residua** (Ritt.)
Hoffmann is up to 8 cm across, csp 2–5(–8), 1–3 cm long
(Antofagasta to Tocopilla). [IP ex Ritt./F]

DISTRIBUTION: Chile, mountains N of Antofagasta.

OTHER NAMES: *Neochilenia recond., Pyrrhocactus recond.*
v. residua: *Neoc. residua, Pyrrho. residuus.*

Neoporteria recondita v. vexata
(Ritt.) Hoffmann

Solitary, flattened-globular, to 3 cm (rarely to 5 cm) across.
Fl 3 cm long. [RMF40/IP/F]

DISTRIBUTION: Chile, Morro Moreno, NW of
Antofagasta.

OTHER NAMES: *Pyrrhocactus vexatus.*

Neoporteria reichei (Sch.) Bkbg.

Usually solitary, often becoming unnaturally elongated in
cultivation, to 10 cm or more long by 3–4.5 cm. Fl 2.5 cm
across. **v. aerocarpa** (Ritt.) R.M. Ferryman comb. nov.
(*Chileorebutia aerocarpa* Ritt. 'Cactus' 64,1 Suppl. Aug.
1959.) is usually clumping and has a larger carmine flower
(Carrizal Alto to Totoral). [RMF176/IP/F]

DISTRIBUTION: Chile, Vallenar to Huasco.

OTHER NAMES: See Appendix 6.

Neoporteria setosiflora
(Ritt.) Don. & Rowley

Body flattened to globular, to 6 cm across, sometimes offsetting. Fl to 4–6 cm across, yellowish to brick-red. Close to N. jussieui and possibly only a variety of it. [RMF98/IP/F]

DISTRIBUTION: C Chilean coastal region.

OTHER NAMES: *Neochilenia setosif. & v. intermedia, Pyrrhocactus setosif. & v. intermedius.*

Neoporteria simulans
(Ritt.) Don. & Rowley

Solitary, to 20 cm long and 8 cm across. Fl 4 cm across. [RMFl87/IP/F]

DISTRIBUTION: Chile, near Choros.

OTHER NAMES: *Neochilenia simulans, Pyrrhocactus simulans.*

Neoporteria sociabilis   Ritt.

Solitary or sparingly clumping, heads to 40 cm high and 8 cm across. Fl 2.2–3.3 cm long, pink. [RMF267/IP/F]

DISTRIBUTION: Chile, Totoral Bajo to Huasco.

OTHER NAMES: *N. sociabilis v. napina.*

Neoporteria subgibbosa   (Haw.) B. & R.

Usually solitary, at first globular, later to 1 m and more long by 10 cm. Fl 4 cm long. [RMFl99/IP/F]

DISTRIBUTION: Chile, from Coquimbo S along the coast.

OTHER NAMES: *Neop. subgib. v. orientalis, N. litoralis & v. intermedia, N. subgib. fa. litoralis.*

Neoporteria subgibbosa v. castanea
(Ritt.) R.M. Ferryman comb. nov.
Neoporteria castanea Ritt. 1963, Taxon 12(1): 34.

Solitary, globular becoming elongated to 15 cm across; spines dark gingerish-brown or glassy whitish-grey. Fl 6–7 cm long. [PM260/IP/F]

DISTRIBUTION: Chile, near Vila Prat.

OTHER NAMES: *Neop. castanea, N. subgib. v. subgib. fa. castanea.*

Neoporteria taltalensis   Hutch.

Solitary, to 12 cm high by 8 cm, body black or green. Fl 2.5–3 cm across. pinkish-purple. [RMFl63/IP/F]

DISTRIBUTION: Chile, from near Paposo to N of Chanaral.

OTHER NAMES: *Neochilenia taltal., Pyrrhocactus taltal., Neoc. rupicola, Pyrrho. rupic., Neop. rupic., Neoc. violaciflora n.n. Pyrrho tenuis.*

Neoporteria totoralensis
(Ritt.) Don. & Rowley

Solitary or sparingly offsetting, flattened to globular to 5 cm across; rsp 6–8, 15–10 mm long; csp 0–1 (rarely 2–3), 2–3 cm long. Fl 4 cm across. [RMF292/IP/F]

DISTRIBUTION: Chile, Totoral Bajo.

OTHER NAMES: *Neochilenia totoral., Pyrrhocactus totoral.*

Neoporteria totoralensis v. carrizalensis
(Ritt.) R.M. Ferryman comb. nov.
Pyrrhocactus carrizalensis Ritt. 1963, Taxon 12(1): 33.

Solitary, 13 cm high by 7 cm; rsp 12–18, 10–25 mm long; csp 4–8, 2–4 cm long. Fl 4.5–7 cm across. [RMF281/IP/F]

DISTRIBUTION: Chile, around Carrizal Bajo.

OTHER NAMES: *Horridocactus carrizal., Pyrr. carriz.*

Neoporteria transiens
(Ritt.) R.M. Ferryman comb. nov.
Pyrrhocactus transiens Ritt. 1980, Kak. in Sudam. 3: 977–8.

Solitary, globular 5–7 cm across. Fl 2.5–3 cm long. [RMF134/IP/F]

DISTRIBUTION: Chile, N of Caldera.

OTHER NAMES: *Pyrrhocactus transiens.*

Neoporteria transitensis
(Ritt.) R.M. Ferryman comb. nov.
Pyrrhocactus transitensis Ritt. 1963, Taxon, 12(1): 33.

Solitary, to 16 cm high by 11 cm. Fl 3 cm across. [RMF354/IP/F]

DISTRIBUTION: Chile, around Transito.

OTHER NAMES: *Neochilenia transitensis, Neop. curvispina v. transitensis, Pyrrhocactus transitensis.*

Neoporteria vallenarensis
(Ritt.) Hoffmann

Solitary, globular to elongated to 10 cm across. Fl 3.5–5.5 cm broad, yellow, greenish-yellow or orange-yellow, often with a reddish midstripe. [RMF122/IP/F]

DISTRIBUTION: Chile, Elqui Valley above and below Vicuna.

OTHER NAMES: *Horridocactus vallen., Neop. curvispina v. vallen., Pyrrhocactus vallen.*

Neoporteria villosa (Monv.) Berg.

Solitary, at first globular then cylindric to 15 cm high by 8 cm. Fl 2 cm long. [RMF185/IP/F]

DISTRIBUTION: Chile, around Huasco and to Carrizal Bajo.

OTHER NAMES: *Neop. atrispinosa, N. cephalophora, N. laniceps, ?N. polyrhaphis.*

Neoporteria wagenknechtii Ritt.

Solitary, to 30 cm high by 11 cm. Fl 2.2 cm long. [RMFl91/IP/F]

DISTRIBUTION: Chile, N of La Serena, Juan Soldado Gorge.

OTHER NAMES: *N. wagen. v. napina, N. rapifera.*

Neoporteria wagenknechtii v. vallenarensis (Ritt.) Hoffmann

Solitary, at first globular, later elongated up to 6 cm across. Ribs 11–12. Fl 3.5 cm long. [RMFl77/IP/F]

DISTRIBUTION: Chile, between Vallenar and Freirina. Rare due to grazing and trampling by goats.

OTHER NAMES: *Neoporteria vallenarensis.*

Neowerdermannia chilensis Bkbg.

Solitary, 3–4 cm across. [IP/F]

DISTRIBUTION: N Chile, Ticnamar.

OTHER NAMES: *Weingartia chilensis.*

'Neowerdermannia chilensis v. putrensis' n.n.

Much larger and with thinner spines than the species. Fl flushed pink. [RMF/IP/F]

DISTRIBUTION: Chile, Putre.

Neowerdermannia vorwerkii Fric

Solitary, flattened (becoming globular-elongate in cultivation). [IP ex Lau/F]

DISTRIBUTION: Over a large area of the Andean Altiplano from N Argentina to N Bolivia.

OTHER NAMES: *Weingartia vorwerkii.*

Notocactus buenekeri (Buin.) Bux.

Solitary, to 5 cm high by 6 cm. Fl 4 cm across, yellow. [RM]

DISTRIBUTION: All from S Brazil, Rio Grande do Sul.

OTHER NAMES: *Brasiliparodia buenek., Parodia buenek.*

Larger, to 8 cm broad is **N. alacriportanus** (Bkbg. & Voll) Bux.

OTHER NAMES: *Brasilip. alac., Par. alac.*

Spines to only 4 mm is **N. brevihamatus** (W. Hge.) Bux.

OTHER NAMES: *Brasilip. brev., Par. brev.*

Notocactus buiningii Bux.

Solitary, to 8 cm high and 12 cm across. Fl 5–8 cm across. [CS/PM]

DISTRIBUTION: Uruguay, near Livramento, rare.

Notocactus caespitosus Speg.

Clumping, to 8 cm high and 3 cm across. Fl 4 cm long. [IP/GC]

DISTRIBUTION: Brazil, Rio Grande do Sul, near Alegrete and in N Uruguay.

OTHER NAMES: *N. minimus, N. tenuicylindricus.*

Notocactus concinnus (Monv.) Berg.

Solitary, 10 cm across and 6 cm high. Spination fairly variable from quite short and neat to untidy and interlacing. Fl 7 cm long, canary yellow. [DV9c/IP/G]

DISTRIBUTION: S Brazil and Uruguay.

OTHER NAMES: *N. agnetae, N. apricus, N. blauuwianus, N. bommelje, N. eremeticus, N. multicostatus, N. tabularis.*

Notocactus crassigibbus Ritt.

Solitary, flattened, to 10 cm across. Fl to 10 cm long. [CS/PM]

DISTRIBUTION: Brazil, Rio Grande do Sul, Lavras.

OTHER NAMES: *N. arachnites.*

Notocactus erinaceus (Haw.) Krainz

Globular, to 15 cm high and broad. Fl to 7 cm broad, canary yellow. [CS/PM].

DISTRIBUTION: S Brazil, Uruguay and Argentina.

OTHER NAMES: *Malacocarpus corynodes, Wigginsia cory., Noto. cory., M. courantii, W. cour., M. erinaceus, W. erinacea, N. erinaceus v. spinosior, M. fricii, N. fricii, W. fricii, M. hennisii, M. kovaricii, N. kov., W. kov., W. longispina, M. sellowi, N. sell., W. sell., M. sessiflorus, N. sess., M. stegmannii, N. steg., W. steg., W. sess., M. tephracanthus, Wig. teph., M. turbinatus, W. turb., M. vorwerckiana, W. vorw.*

Notocactus fuscus Ritt.

Solitary, 4–7 cm across. Fl 3 cm or more long. [HU29/CS/PM]

DISTRIBUTION: Brazil, Rio Grande do Sul, 15 km W of Sao Francisco de Assis.

Notocactus graessneri   (Sch.) Berg.

Usually solitary, to 10 cm high by 15 cm; spines usually hard and yellow but paler and softer in '*v. albisetus*'. Fl greenish or yellow. **fa. microdasys** P.J. Braun has extremely short spines. [IP/G]

DISTRIBUTION: Brazil, Rio Grande do Sul, Jaquerana.

OTHER NAMES: *Brasilicactus graessneri.*

Notocactus haselbergii   (F. Hge.) Berg.

Solitary, to 10 cm high by 15 cm, spines white or yellowish ('*v. stellatus*'). [GC]

DISTRIBUTION: Brazil, Rio Grande do Sul.

OTHER NAMES: *Brasilicactus haselbergii.*

Notocactus herteri   Werd.

Spherical to elongated, 15 cm or more across, solitary. **fa. pseudoherteri** (Buin.) Herm. has yellow fl. [Schl162/CS/PM]

DISTRIBUTION: Uruguay, Cerro Galgo.

OTHER NAMES: **fa. pseudoherteri:** *N. pseudoherteri.*

Notocactus horstii   Ritt.

Usually solitary, to 30 cm high by 14 cm. Fl orange to purple. [CS/PM]

DISTRIBUTION: Brazil, Rio Grande do Sul, Serra Geral.

OTHER NAMES: *Noto. purpureus*, '*N. muegelianus*'.

Notocactus leninghausii   (Hge. jr.) Berg.

Clumping, heads to 1 m high by 10 cm. Fl 5 cm across. Related is **N. nigrispinus** (Sch.) Buin.; clumping, to 40 cm high by 16 cm across, ribs 24, spines thicker and fewer (between Carepegua and Acaay). [CS/PM]

DISTRIBUTION: Brazil, Rio Grande do Sul, to Paraguay, Cerro Santo Thomas and Cerro Acaay.

OTHER NAMES: *Eriocactus leninghausii.*

Notocactus magnificus   (Ritt.) Krainz

Clumping, body to 20 cm across, globular later becoming elongated. Fl 5–6 cm across. [E]

DISTRIBUTION: Brazil, Rio Grande do Sul, Serra Geral, Julio de Castilho.

OTHER NAMES: *Eriocactus magnificus.*

Notocactus mammulosus (Lem.) Berg.

Solitary, to 10 cm high by 6 cm. Fl 4 cm long. Similar but less free-flowering is **N. allosiphon** Marchesi (Uruguay, Rivera, Valle Ar. Platon). [R346/1G]

DISTRIBUTION: Argentina and Uruguay.

OTHER NAMES: *N. erythracanthus*, *N. floricomus*, '*N. orthacanthus*', *N. pampeanus*, *N. submammulosus* & *v. pampeanus*.
N. megalanthus Schl. & Bred. from the Cerro Mosquitos, Uruguay appears to be an intermediate between **N. mammulosus** and **N. concinnus**.

Notocactus mueller-melchersii Fric ex Bkbg.

Solitary, to 8 cm high by 6 cm. Fl 5 cm across, pale golden yellow. [SCHL151/IP/G]

DISTRIBUTION: Uruguay, Sierra de los Animos.

Notocactus muricatus (Otto) Berg.

Clumping, heads to 20 cm and more high. Fl 3 cm long. [HU19/CS/PM]

DISTRIBUTION: S Brazil, Rio Grande do Sul, near Taquarichim.

Notocactus neoarechavaletai (Sch. ex Speg.) Elsner

Solitary, spherical to elongated, csp dark brown or black. Fl 5 cm across. [CS/PM]

DISTRIBUTION: Uruguay, near Maldonado.

OTHER NAMES: *Malacocarpus arechavaletai*, *Wigginsia arech.*

Notocactus neohorstii (Ritt.) Theun.

Solitary, globular to elongated. Fl 3.5 cm wide.
v. juveniliformis Ritt. resembles, when adult, a juvenile form of the species (Cacapava).

DISTRIBUTION: Brazil, Rio Grande do Sul, Mine Camaqua.

OTHER NAMES: *Wigginsia horstii.*

Notocactus ottonis (Lehm.) Berg.

Exceedingly variable yet instantly recognizable because of the general characteristics so obvious in the plate. Fl to 6 cm or more across. The most distinctive forms are those with more sharply-angled ribs, (e.g. *N. securituberculatus*). [CS/PM]

DISTRIBUTION: S Brazil, Uruguay, Paraguay, and NE Argentina.

OTHER NAMES: See Appendix 7.

Notocactus ottonis v. tortuosus
(Link & Otto) Berg.
Flower smaller, 3–4 cm across, deeper lemon-yellow than the species. [HU22/G]

DISTRIBUTION: Brazil, Rio Grande do Sul.

OTHER NAMES: *N. carambeiensis, N. linkii, N. megapotamicus.*

Notocactus rauschii van Vliet
Solitary, globular to 7 cm across, elongating somewhat to 10 cm. Fl 5–6 cm across. [CS/PM]

DISTRIBUTION: Uruguay, Cuchilla Negra.

Notocactus rechensis Buin.
Forming small clumps, heads to 7 cm long by 5 cm. Fl 3–3.5 cm across. [CS/PM]

DISTRIBUTION: Brazil, Rio Grande do Sul, near Ana Reche.

OTHER NAMES: *Brasiliparodia rechensis.*

Notocactus roseiflorus Schl. & Bred.
Solitary, to 12 cm high by 6.5 cm. Fl 3.5 cm across. [CS/CG]

DISTRIBUTION: Uruguay, Prov. of Artigas, Cuchilla Yacare.

Notocactus roseoluteus van Vliet
Solitary, body globose, to 18 cm high and broad. Fl to 8 cm across. [CS/PM]

DISTRIBUTION: Uruguay, near Tranqueras.

Notocactus rutilans Daen. & Krainz
Solitary, slightly elongated, to 5 cm high by 4 cm. Fl to 6 cm across. [CS/PM]

DISTRIBUTION: Uruguay, Cerro Largo.

Notocactus schlosseri van Vliet

Solitary, short-cylindric to 18 cm high by 11 cm. Fl 5 cm
across. [Schl157/G]

DISTRIBUTION: Uruguay, near Garzon.

Notocactus schumannianus
(Sch.) Berg. emend. Buin.

Body columnar, to 30 cm broad. Fl 4 cm across, pale
golden-yellow. [R]

DISTRIBUTION: Paraguay, Cerro Santo Thomas and Cerro
Acaay.

OTHER NAMES: *Eriocactus ampliocostatus, E. claviceps,
E. grossei, Noto. claviceps.*

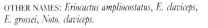

Notocactus scopa (Spreng.) Berg.

Solitary, to 25 cm and more high by 10 cm. Csp brown to
white. Fl 4 cm across. Many vars. − more properly just
forms − most distinct being **v. marchesii** Abraham:
strongly clumping, heads to 10 cm long, 4 cm across. Csp
white to orange. Fl 5 cm across (Dept. of Treinta y Tres,
Uruguay). [CS/P]

DISTRIBUTION: S Brazil and Uruguay.

OTHER NAMES: *?N. rudibuenekeri.*

Notocactus sucineus Ritt.

Solitary, spherical to oblong, 3−7 cm across. Fl 3.5 cm
long. [FR1399/CS/PM]

DISTRIBUTION: Brazil, Rio Grande do Sul, Sao Gabriel.

OTHER NAMES: *N. neobuenekeri.*

Notocactus uebelmannianus Buin.

Solitary, to 12 cm high by 17 cm. Fl to 5 cm across, purple
or yellow. [CS/PM].

DISTRIBUTION: Brazil, Rio Grande do Sul, near Cacapava.

OTHER NAMES: *N. uebelman. v. flaviflorus.*

Notocactus vanvlietii Rausch

Solitary, to 10 cm high by 6 cm. Fl to 5.5 cm across.
v. gracilior Rausch is smaller, with curly spines and flowers
yellow to orange yellow (between Minas de Corales and
Ansina). [DV18/G]

DISTRIBUTION: Uruguay, Cuchilla de los Once Cerros.

Notocactus veenianus Van Vliet

Solitary, to 20 cm high by 8 cm. Fl 5 cm across. [CS/PM]

DISTRIBUTION: Uruguay, Tacuarembo.

OTHER NAMES: '*N. erizo*', *N. eugeniae, N. paulus, N. winkleri.*

Notocactus warasii Ritt.

Solitary, to 50 cm high by 20 cm or more. Fl 6 cm across. [CS/PM]

DISTRIBUTION: Brazil, Rio Grande do Sul.

OTHER NAMES: *Eriocactus warasii.*

Notocactus werdermannianus Herter

Solitary, to 13 cm high by 10 cm. Fl over 7 cm across. [G]

DISTRIBUTION: Uruguay, Tacuarembo.

Obregonia denegrii Fric

Solitary, to 12 cm across. Fl 2.5 cm across. [CS/P]

DISTRIBUTION: Mexico, Tamaulipas, San Vicente near Ciudad Victoria.

OTHER NAMES: *Ariocarpus denegrii, Strombocactus denegrii.*

Oroya borchersii (Boed.) Bkbg.

Solitary, to over 20 cm high and broad, spines brown or yellow. Fl 1 cm across. [L114a/IP]

DISTRIBUTION: N Peru, Cordillera Blanca and Cordillera Negra.

Oroya peruviana (Sch.) B. & R.

Solitary, depressed-spherical, to 14 cm across. Fl to 2.2 cm broad, pink and yellow, lemon-yellow (e.g. '*O. citriflora*') or carmine. [IP/F]

DISTRIBUTION: C Peru, around Oroya.

OTHER NAMES: '*O. acollana*', '*O. baumannii*', *O. gibbosa* & *vars., O. laxiareolata* & *var., O. neoperuviana* & *vars., O. subocculata* & *vars., vars.* of **O. peruviana.**

Ortegocactus macdougallii Alex.

Heads globular, to 4 cm across, clustering, Fl 2.5 cm broad. [GC]

DISTRIBUTION: Mexico, Oaxaca, near San Jose Lacheguiri.

Parodia argerichiana Wesk.

Solitary, 6 cm across. Fl 5 cm wide, red. [DH108/CS/DHS]

DISTRIBUTION: N Argentina, Salta, Sierra del Muerto, between Santa Barbara and Santa Rosa.

Parodia aureicentra Bkbg.

Becoming elongated to 15 cm across, usually clumping, spination very variable. Fl 4 cm broad, light blood-red. [P252/CS/DHS]

DISTRIBUTION: N Argentina, Salta, Cachipampa.

OTHER NAMES: *P. aureic, v. omniaurea* & *rubrispina, P. muhrii, P. rauschii, P. uhligiana, P. variicolor.*

Parodia aureispina Bkbg.

Solitary, globose, to 6.5 cm across. Fl also red. Plants circulated as *P. mutabilis* are invariably this species. [WR707b/CS/DH]

DISTRIBUTION: N Argentina, Salta.

OTHER NAMES: *'P. aurihamata', P. mutabilis, P. scopaoides.*

Parodia ayopayana Card.

Stems to 8 cm high by 9 cm, prolifically clumping. [CS/PM]

DISTRIBUTION: Bolivia, Puente Pilatos.

OTHER NAMES: *P. cotacajensis, P. elata, P. pseudoayopayana.*

Parodia campestrae Brandt

Solitary, to 11 cm high by 7 cm, spines straight. [CS/PM]

DISTRIBUTION: Argentina, meeting point of Salta, Tucuman and Santiago del Estero Provinces on the road E of Antilla.

Parodia chrysacanthion (Sch.) Bkbg.

Solitary, spherical Fl small, yellow. [CS/PM]

DISTRIBUTION: N Argentina, Jujuy.

Parodia columnaris Card.

Solitary, to 30 cm high by 7 cm. Fl 3 cm across, light yellow. [Donald IP/DHS]

DISTRIBUTION: Bolivia, Dept. Cochabamba, Angosto de Perez.

OTHER NAMES: *P. legitima.*

Parodia comarapana Card.

Solitary, to 5 cm high by 8 cm. Fl 5 mm across, orange-yellow. [KK1462/IP/DHS]

DISTRIBUTION: Bolivia, Comarapa.

OTHER NAMES: *P. neglecta, P. neglectoides.*

Parodia commutans Ritt.

Solitary, to 30 cm by 16 cm. Fl to 3.5 cm long, yellow.

DISTRIBUTION: Bolivia, near Impora.

OTHER NAMES: *P. maassii v. commutans, P. obtusa.*
Illustrated but probably only a variety is **Parodia maxima** Ritt. which is solitary, cylindric, to 25 cm high. Csp in seedlings hooked, straight in mature plants. Fl 4 cm across. [L928/IP/DHS]

DISTRIBUTION: Bolivia, Cieneguillas.

OTHER NAMES: *P. maassii v. commutans fa. maxima.*

'Parodia dextrohamata' Bkbg.

Solitary, to 5 cm high by 3.5 cm. Fl 2 cm across, yellow. [P44a/CS/DHS]

DISTRIBUTION: N Argentina.

Parodia dichroacantha Brandt & Wesk.

Hemispherical or later elongated. Fl 6 cm across, brilliant yellow or red. [B53/IP/DHS]

DISTRIBUTION: N Argentina, N of Salta and Tucuman.

OTHER NAMES: *P. rigida.*

Parodia echinopsoides Brandt

Solitary, to 40 cm high by 10 cm, ribs always 13. Fl 3.5–4 cm long, yellow. [CS/DHS]

DISTRIBUTION: Bolivia, Prov. Mendez, Colpana on the Rio Pilaya.

OTHER NAMES: *P. separata, P. tredecimcostata.*

Parodia faustiana Bkbg.

Solitary, to 6 cm across. Fl scarlet outside, golden-yellow inside. [B160/IP/DHS]

DISTRIBUTION: N Argentina, Salta, Quebrada del Toro.

OTHER NAMES: *P. cruci-nigricentra n.n..*

'Parodia fechseri' Bkbg.

Solitary, to 8 cm high by 4 cm. Fl 4 cm across, yellow. [IP ex Fechser/DHS]

DISTRIBUTION: N Argentina.

OTHER NAMES: *P. mesembrina.*

Parodia formosa Ritt.

Solitary, globular to elongated, to 8 cm across. Spination rather variable. Fl to 4 cm long, sulphur-yellow. [CS/DHS]

DISTRIBUTION: Widespread in C and S Bolivia.

OTHER NAMES: *P. carapariana, P. cardenasii, P. chaetocarpa, P. chirimoyarana, P. pachysa, P. parvula, P. purpureo-aurea, P. pusilla, P. setispina, P. tillii.*

'Parodia fuscato-viridis' Bkbg.

Solitary, spherical to 4.5 cm broad. Fl 3.5–6 cm broad, yellow. [P239/CS/DHS]

DISTRIBUTION: N Argentina, Quebrada de Belen.

Parodia gibbulosoides Brandt

Broadly spherical, to 10 cm across. Fl 1 cm across. [CS/DHS]

DISTRIBUTION: Bolivia, Dept. Cochabamba in the mountains N of the Rio Grande.

OTHER NAMES: *P. gibbulosa.*

Parodia hausteiniana Rausch

Solitary, short-cylindric, to 5 cm across. Fl 10 mm across, yellow. [CS/PM]

DISTRIBUTION: Bolivia, near Mizque.

Parodia herzogii Rausch

Solitary, to 6 cm high by 9 cm. Fl 4 cm across, golden-yellow to orange. [WR707a/CS/DHS]

DISTRIBUTION: Argentina, Salta, E of Cafayate.

Parodia heteracantha Ritt. & Wesk.

Solitary, 9.5 cm high by 5.5 cm. Fl yellowish-orange. [P62/CS/DHS]

DISTRIBUTION: N Argentina, Salta, near Cachi.

Parodia horrida Brandt

Solitary, slim-cylindric to 9 cm or more high. Fl yellow. [Muhr IP/DHS]

DISTRIBUTION: N Argentina, Salta, Rio Calchaqui.

OTHER NAMES: *P. piltziorum.*

Parodia hummeliana Lau & Wesk.

Solitary, 6 cm high by 7 cm. Related to **P. microsperma**. [L567/CS/DHS]

DISTRIBUTION: Argentina, Salta, Amblayo.

Parodia krahnii Wesk.

Solitary or clumping, to 30 cm high by 8 cm. Fl yellow. [CS/DHS]

DISTRIBUTION: Bolivia, Prov. Tarata, La Vina on the Rio Caine.

Parodia lauii Brandt

Solitary, to 7 cm high by 9 cm. Fl to 4 cm across, salmon to red. [CS/PM]

DISTRIBUTION: Bolivia, between Mizque and Mine Asientos, above the Rio Caine.

Parodia maassii (Heese) Berg.

Very variable, solitary or clumping, body large or small, spines long or relatively short, white to brown to black. Fl various shades of red. [H]

DISTRIBUTION: Over a wide area of C and S Bolivia and N Argentina.

OTHER NAMES: *P. belliata, P. bermejoensis, P. camargensis, P. castanea, P. cintiensis, P. escayachensis, P. fulvispina, P. haageana, P. knizei, P. lamprospina, P. mendezana, P. otaviana, P. perplexa, P. ritteri & v. cintiensis, P. rostrumsperma, P. rubida, P. suprema, P. thieleana, P. tojoensis.*

Parodia macrancistra (Sch.) Wesk.

Solitary, to 8 cm high by 6.5 cm, csp to 3.7 cm long. Undoubtedly a long-spined form of **P. microsperma**. [B24/IP/DHS]

DISTRIBUTION: N Argentina, Tucuman at the foot of the Sierra Medina.

OTHER NAMES: *P. talaensis.*

Parodia mairanana Card.

Broadly spherical to over 5 cm across, greyish-green to glossy dark green. Fl to 3.5 cm across, orange to golden-yellow. Plants distributed under the name *'P. mairanana v. atra'* are often nothing to do with this species. [FR744/HS/DHS]

DISTRIBUTION: Bolivia, Mairana.

OTHER NAMES: *'P. mairanana v. atra'.*

Parodia malyana Rausch

Solitary, to 6 cm high by 5 cm, csp straight, Fl to 4 cm across, yellow or red. [CS/DHS]

DISTRIBUTION: Argentina, Catamarca, near Ancasti.

Parodia mercedesiana Wesk.

Solitary, to 5.5 cm high by 6.5 cm. Fl 6 cm across, red or yellow. [DH116/CS/DHS]

DISTRIBUTION: N Argentina, Salta, NW of Las Curtiembres.

Parodia microsperma (Web.) Speg.

Solitary, to 20 cm high by 10 cm. Fl yellow to red to 4 cm across. [B155/IP/DHS]

DISTRIBUTION: N Argentina, Tucuman.

OTHER NAMES: *P. amblayensis, P. betaniana, P. catamarcensis, P. chlorocarpa, P. glischrocarpa, P. rubellihamata, P. sanagasta, P. setifera, P. spanisa, P. thionantha, P. tuberculosi-costata, P. weskampiana.*

Parodia miguillensis Card.

Solitary, to 6 cm high by 4 cm. Fl only 7 mm broad, pale yellow. [L1001/IP/DHS]

DISTRIBUTION: Widespread in river gorges in C N Bolivia.

OTHER NAMES: *P. borealis, P. comosa, P. echinus, P. macednosa.*

Parodia minuscula Rausch

Solitary, globosc, to 4 cm broad, csp hooked. Closely related to **P. malyana**. [WR757/CS/DHS]

DISTRIBUTION: Argentina, Catamarca, along the Rio Guayamba.

OTHER NAMES: *P. minima* Rausch *non* Brandt.

Parodia nivosa Fric ex Bkbg.

Solitary, to 15 cm high by 8 cm. Fl 5 cm broad, red. [B41/IP/DHS]

DISTRIBUTION: N Argentina, Salta.

Parodia ocampoi Card.

Stem to 7 cm high by 6 cm, forming cushions to 40 cm across. Fl 3 cm long, golden yellow. *P. compressa* Ritt. (illus.) appears to be merely a red-flowered slightly spinier form from only a few miles distant. [H]

DISTRIBUTION: Bolivia, Puente Arce.

OTHER NAMES: ?*P. caineana, P. compressa, P. ignorata.*

Parodia occulta Ritt.

Solitary, flattened, to 2.5(−5) cm across. Fl to 2−4 cm across, red, reddish-orange or yellow. The smallest of the parodias. [H]

DISTRIBUTION: Bolivia, between Camargo and Culpina.

Parodia otuyensis Ritt.

Solitary, flattened-globular, to 11 cm broad. [H]

DISTRIBUTION: Bolivia, Dept. Potosi, near Otuyo.

OTHER NAMES: *P. backebergiana, P. firmissima, P. idiosa, P. quechua, ?P. sotomayorensis, P. stereospina, P. yamparaezi.*

Parodia penicillata Fechs. & v.d. Steeg

Solitary, to 70 cm long by 12 cm, spines usually (on cultivated plants) glassy straw-coloured but can be fulvous. Fl red. **v. nivosa** Fechser; spines thicker, white. Fl more orange. [CS/PM]

DISTRIBUTION: N Argentina, Salta.

Parodia pluricentralis Bkbg. & Brandt

Solitary, to 12 cm high by 5 cm. Fl 5 cm across, yellow. [P169/CS/DHS]

DISTRIBUTION: Argentina, Salta, near Amblayo.

Parodia prestoensis Brandt

Solitary, 8 cm high by 10 cm. Fl 3 cm broad, golden yellow. [L384/IP/DHS]

DISTRIBUTION: Bolivia, Presto.

Parodia procera Ritt.

Solitary, to 30 cm high by 5 cm. Fl to 3 cm long. [IP/DHS]

DISTRIBUTION: Bolivia, Dept. Chuquisaca, mouth of Rio Challamarca.

OTHER NAMES: *P. challamarcana, P. pseudoprocera.*

Parodia punae Card.

Solitary, 8 cm high by 7 cm. Fl 2 cm broad, dark orange to red. [Lau IP/DHS]

DISTRIBUTION: Bolivia, Dept. Cochabamba, near Mine Asientos.

OTHER NAMES: *P. eleachista, P. zecheri.*

Parodia riojensis Ritt. & Wesk.

Clumping. Fl 4 cm wide, yellow. [P27/DHS]

DISTRIBUTION: Argentina, border between Catamarca and La Rioja.

OTHER NAMES: *P. mazanensis n.n.*

Parodia roseoalba Ritt.

Solitary or forming large clumps, heads to 15 cm across. Fl 3.5 cm long. Probably only a white-spined phase of **P. maassii**. [H]

DISTRIBUTION: Bolivia, from near Tupiza to near Camargo.

OTHER NAMES: *P. agasta, P. roseo. v. australis.*

Parodia rubristaminea Ritt.

Solitary, to 5 cm across. Fl 3–4 cm across, scented. [MLV59/HS/PM]

DISTRIBUTION: Argentina, Salta, SW of Alemania.

Parodia saint-pieana Bkbg.

Clumping, stems to 6 cm across. Fl 2.5 cm long, yellow. Not positively rediscovered in the wild. [Offset from original collection IP/DHS]

DISTRIBUTION: N Argentina, Jujuy.

Parodia sanguiniflora Fric ex Bkbg.

Solitary, globular to elongated, to over 5 cm across. Fl 4 cm across. Probably only a form of **P. microsperma**. [CS/PM]

DISTRIBUTION: N Argentina, Salta.

OTHER NAMES: *P. rubriflora.*

Parodia sanguiniflora v. comata Ritt.

Solitary, globose. Fl 4 cm broad. [B168/IP/DHS]

DISTRIBUTION: N Argentina, Tucuman, Tafi del Valle.

OTHER NAMES: *P. tafiensis.*

Parodia schwebsiana (Werd.) Bkbg.

Solitary, to 11 cm high by 7 cm. Fl 2 cm broad, wine to rust red. [KK1663/IP/DHS]

DISTRIBUTION: Bolivia, Cochabamba, occurs even within the city limits.

OTHER NAMES: *P. applanata*, '*P. eriodesa*', *P. minima*, *P. schweb. v. applanata*.

'Parodia setosa' Bkbg.

Solitary, to 25 cm high by 12 cm. Fl red. [P171/CS/DHS]

DISTRIBUTION: Argentina, Tumbaya.

Parodia spegazziniana Brandt

Solitary, to 9 cm high by 7 cm. Fl 5 cm across, red. [P51/CS/DHS]

DISTRIBUTION: Argentina, Jujuy.

OTHER NAMES: *P. capillitaensis*, '*P. gigantea v. jujuyana*'.

Parodia stuemeri (Werd.) Bkbg.

Usually solitary, to 20 cm high by 15 cm; rsp to 25, thin. Fl 4 cm long, yellow to orange. **v. robustior** Bkbg.; spines stouter; rsp 12–13. Fl red, 2–5 cm across (Maimara). [B91/IP/DHS]

DISTRIBUTION: N Argentina.

OTHER NAMES: *P. friciana*, *P. gigantea*, *P. gokrauseana*, *P. pseudostuemeri*, *P. rigidispina*, *P. rubricentra*, *P. scoparia*, *P. tilcarensis*.

Parodia subterranea Ritt.

In habitat small and flattened, in cultivation becoming larger and elongated, 6 cm across; csp hooked or straight. Fl to 3 cm long. [CS/PM]

DISTRIBUTION: Bolivia, near Culpina.

OTHER NAMES: *P. culpinensis*, *P. maassii v. subterranea*, *P. nigresca*, *P. salitrensis*, *P. zaletaewana*.

Parodia taratensis Card.

In cultivation becoming cylindric and clumping. Fl 1.5 cm across, yellow. [L979/IP/DHS]

DISTRIBUTION: Bolivia, road from Tarata to the Rio Caine.

OTHER NAMES: *P. bilbaoensis*.

Parodia tuberculata Card.

Solitary, to 5 cm high by 7 cm. Fl to 1.8 cm long, yellowish-red. [KK874/IP/DHS]

DISTRIBUTION: Bolivia, Oropeza, Hacienda Ressini and around Sucre.

OTHER NAMES: *P. krasuckana, P. sucrensis.*

Parodia uebelmanniana Ritt.

Solitary, globose to elongated, to 8 cm across. Fl 3.5 cm wide, golden yellow. [P153/CS/DHS]

DISTRIBUTION: Argentina, Salta, Lumbreras.

OTHER NAMES: *P. rubellihamata Ritt. n.n., P. rufidihamata n.n.*

Parodia weberiana Brandt

Solitary, to 7 cm high by 10 cm. Fl yellow [P247/CS/DHS]

DISTRIBUTION: N Argentina, valley of the Rio Grande de Sauce.

Pediocactus knowltonii Benson

Stems 0.7–5.5 cm tall, 1–3 cm across, clumping. Fl 1–2.5 cm broad. [Withers coll.]

DISTRIBUTION: Near the Los Pinos River in Colorado and New Mexico, USA.

OTHER NAMES: *P. bradyi v. knowltonii.*

Pediocactus papyracanthus (Englm.) Benson

Solitary, to 10 cm high by 2.5 cm. Fl 1.25 cm across, white. [H]

DISTRIBUTION: New Mexico and N Arizona, rare.

OTHER NAMES: *Toumeya papyracantha.*

Pediocactus peeblesianus (Croiz.) Benson

Solitary, to 6 cm high by 4 cm; csp 0. Fl to 17 mm long, cream to yellow. [GC]

DISTRIBUTION: N Arizona, between Holbrook and Joseph City. **v. fickeisenii** (Bkbg.) Benson is more densely spined; csp. 1.

DISTRIBUTION: N Arizona, Grand Canyon area.

OTHER NAMES: *Navajoa peeblesianus.* **v. fickeisenii**: *N. fickeisenii.*

Pediocactus simpsonii (Englm.) B. & R.

Globular, solitary to clumping. Fl yellowish, greenish-pink, pink or white. [H]

DISTRIBUTION: Washington and Oregon, S Idaho, Montana, Wyoming to C Nevada, Colorado, N Arizona, Utah, W Kansas, New Mexico.

Pelecyphora aselliformis Ehrenbg.

Up to 10 cm high by 5.5 cm, clumping. Fl 3 cm across. [IP/GC]

DISTRIBUTION: Mexico, San Luis Potosi.

Pelecyphora strobiliformis (Werd.) Kreuz.

Spherical. Fl 3 cm long. [IP/F]

DISTRIBUTION: Mexico, Nuevo Leon, near Dr. Arroyo.

OTHER NAMES: *Encephalocarpus strobil.*

'Pyrrhocactus andreaeanus' (Bkbg.) Ritt.

Solitary, to 15 cm high by 5 cm. Fl 3–4 cm broad, light scarlet to coppery-red. [GC]

DISTRIBUTION: Argentina, La Rioja, Famatina Massif.

OTHER NAMES: *Neochilenia andreaeana.*

Pyrrhocactus bulbocalyx (Werd.) Bkbg.

Solitary, spherical to elongated. Fl to 4 cm long. [L504/IP/F]

DISTRIBUTION: N Argentina.

OTHER NAMES: *P. sanjuanensis.*

Pyrrhocactus megliolii Rausch

Solitary, 45 cm high by 12 cm. Fl 2.5 cm across. [WR559/IP/GC]

DISTRIBUTION: Argentina, San Juan, near Marayes.

Pyrrhocactus strausianus (Sch.) Berg.

Solitary, to 16 cm high by 9 cm. [IP/F]

DISTRIBUTION: Argentina.

OTHER NAMES: *P. atrospinosus* (= *Neoporteria backebergii*
Don. & Rowley), *N. catamarcensis*, *P. catamarc., P. dubius,
P. pachacoensis, P. platyacanthus, N. setiflora, P. setif.*

Pyrrhocactus umadaeve (Fric) Bkbg.

Solitary, to 10 cm high by 11 cm. Fl to 3.5 cm long, pale
yellowish. [IP/F]

DISTRIBUTION: N Argentina.

Rebutia albiflora Ritt. & Buin.

Heads very small, forming mats. [PM]

DISTRIBUTION: Bolivia, NE Tarija, Rio Pilaya.

OTHER NAMES: *Aylostera albiflora.*

Rebutia albipilosa Ritt.

Sparingly offsetting. Fl 3 cm across, orange, to red. [IP/P]

DISTRIBUTION: Bolivia, Narvaez.

OTHER NAMES: *Aylostera albipilosa.*

Rebutia albopectinata Rausch

Density of spination somewhat variable. [CS/PM]

DISTRIBUTION: Bolivia, Culpina.

Rebutia archibuiningiana Ritt.

Prolifically offsetting, fl 2.5 cm across. [L404/CS/PM]

DISTRIBUTION: Bolivia, Padcaya.

Rebutia brunescens Rausch

Fl 3 cm across. [L383/IP/DHS]

DISTRIBUTION: Bolivia, Tarabuco.

Rebutia buiningiana Rausch

Fl 3 cm across. [KK860/IP/DHS]

DISTRIBUTION: Argentina, Jujuy, near Iruya.

Rebutia deminuta (Web.) B. & R.

A very variable species. (see Appendix 8). [DHS]

DISTRIBUTION: N Argentina and S Bolivia, widespread.

OTHER NAMES: *Aylostera deminuta, R. albiareolata,*
'R. boliviensis', R. cajasensis, R. maxima, R. nitida,
R. nogalesensis, R. patericalyx, R. pseudominuscula,
R. rubiginosa, R. tamboensis, R. tuberosa.

Rebutia donaldiana Lau & Rowley

Fl 2.5 cm across. [CS/PM]

DISTRIBUTION: Bolivia, Pucara.

Rebutia einsteinii Fric

Stem cylindric, stems to 2 cm or more across, spine length
extremely variable. Fl 3.5 cm across. [WR159/IP/DHS]

DISTRIBUTION: N Argentina, Salta, Volcan Chani.

OTHER NAMES: *Cylindrorebutia einst., Mediolobivia*
schmiedcheniana & vars., Lobivia einst.

'Rebutia einsteinii v. aureiflora'
published as *R. aureiflora* Bkbg.

Heads globular, to 3 cm across. Fl 4 cm across, yellow,
violet-pink or orange-red. [CS/PM]

DISTRIBUTION: Argentina, Salta, Quebrada del Toro.

OTHER NAMES: *R. sarothroides, Mediolobivia aureif. & vars.,*
M. duursmaiana, M. rubelliflora, M. rubriflora,
'Reb. albilongiseta', 'R. longiseta', Lobivia einst. v. aureiflora.

Rebutia einsteinii v. gonjianii
(Kies.) Don.

Stems only 1 cm across, spines short. [WR578/IP/DHS]

DISTRIBUTION: Argentina, Salta, from Purmamarca to Tilcara.

OTHER NAMES: *R. gonjianii*, *Lobivia einst. v. gonj.*

Rebutia euanthema   (Bkbg.) Buin. & Don.
[CS/PM]

DISTRIBUTION: Argentina, Volcan and Tumbaya.

OTHER NAMES: *Digitorebutia euanth.*, *Mediolobivia euanth.*, *R. oculata.*

Rebutia fabrisii
Rausch. & **v. aureiflora** Rausch

Heads small, only 2 cm across, flower red. The variety has a smaller, yellow flower. [WR688 upper; WR687 lower/F]

DISTRIBUTION: Argentina, Jujuy, between Santa Ana and Valle Colorado.

Rebutia fiebrigii   (Guerke) B. & R.

Some plants have much longer, straighter golden spines than the one pictured. [CS/PM]

DISTRIBUTION: Bolivia, widespread and very variable.

OTHER NAMES: *Aylostera fiebr.* & *v. densiseta*, *A. spinosissima*, 'R. aureispina', *R. cintiensis*, *R. fiebr. v. densiseta*, *R. spinosissima.*

Rebutia flavistyla   Ritt.
Fl 3 cm long. [CS/PM]

DISTRIBUTION: Bolivia, near Cajas.

Rebutia fulviseta   Rausch

Body dark blackish-green. Fl 2.5 cm across. [CS/PM]

DISTRIBUTION: Bolivia, Arce, near Padcaya.

OTHER NAMES: *Aylostera fulviseta.*

Rebutia heliosa Rausch

Fl orange. [CS/PM]

DISTRIBUTION: Bolivia, road to Narvaez.

OTHER NAMES: *Aylostera heliosa.*

Rebutia heliosa v. condorensis Don.

Spination longer and less neat than in the species, heads larger forming bigger clumps in cultivation. Fl orange or red. [L405/CS/PM]

DISTRIBUTION: Bolivia, Condor Pass and Cajas Pass.

OTHER NAMES: *R. heliosa v. cajasensis.*

Rebutia hoffmannii Diers & Rausch

Probably only a form of **R. fiebrigii**. Fl to 4.5 cm across. [Hoff2018/IP/DHS]

DISTRIBUTION: Argentina, Salta, near Santa Viktoria.

Rebutia huasiensis Rausch

Fl to 3.5 cm across. [WR313a/IP/DHS]

DISTRIBUTION: Bolivia, near Inca Huasi.

Rebutia ithyacantha (Card.) Diers

Spine-length rather variable. Fl 2.5 cm across. [L350/IP/DHS]

DISTRIBUTION: Bolivia, near Comarapa.

OTHER NAMES: *Mediolobivia ithyacantha.*

Rebutia jujuyana Rausch

[WR220/CS/PM]

DISTRIBUTION: Argentina, widespread in Jujuy Province.

OTHER NAMES: *Aylostera jujuyana.*

Rebutia kieslingii Rausch

Fl orange or red. [CS/PM]

DISTRIBUTION: Argentina, Salta, Caspala.

Rebutia krainziana Kessel.

A cultivar, not known from the wild. [CS/PM]

Rebutia kupperiana Boed.

Fl 3.5 cm across. [CS/PM]

DISTRIBUTION: Bolivia, near Tarija.

OTHER NAMES: *Aylostera kupperiana.*

Rebutia leucanthema Rausch

Fl 2.5 cm broad, white or pink. **v. cocciniflora** Ritt. has longer, denser spination and a scarlet flower (N of Camargo). [WR305/IP/DHS]

DISTRIBUTION: Bolivia, Cana Cruz.

Rebutia mamillosa Rausch

Fl 4 cm across. The plant illustrated is possibly a cultivar since wild plants normally have pure orange-red flowers. [CS/PM]

DISTRIBUTION: Bolivia, near Camargo.

OTHER NAMES: *R. graciliflora* & *vars.*

Rebutia margarethae Rausch

Spination rather variable, from short and soft to long and needle-like. Fl orange to red. [L530/IP/DHS]

DISTRIBUTION: Argentina, Salta, near Santa Victoria.

Rebutia marsoneri Werd.

Solitary or only sparingly offsetting, heads to 5 cm or more across. Fl usually yellow, also red. [DHS]

DISTRIBUTION: N Argentina, Jujuy.

Rebutia minuscula Sch.

Fl to 4 cm long. [DHS]

DISTRIBUTION: Argentina, Tucuman.

Rebutia minuscula v. grandiflora (Bkbg.) Buin. & Don. Fl to 6.5 cm long.

DISTRIBUTION: Argentina, Salta, Quebrada Escoipe.

OTHER NAMES: *R. grandiflora.*

Rebutia muscula Ritt. & Thiele.

Spination very soft. [CS/PM]

DISTRIBUTION: Bolivia, Narvaez.

OTHER NAMES: *Aylostera muscula.*

Rebutia narvaecensis (Card.) Don.

Fl pale to deep pink. [KK1518/IP/DHS]

DISTRIBUTION: Bolivia, near Narvaez.

OTHER NAMES: *Aylostera narvaecensis*, 'R. espinosae'

Rebutia padcayensis Rausch

Fl 3.5 cm across. [CS/PM]

DISTRIBUTION: Bolivia, W of Padcaya.

OTHER NAMES: *Aylostera padcay., R. singularis.*

Rebutia perplexa Don.

Heads small, to 1.5 cm across. Initially distributed as R. narvaecensis. [L329a/IP/F]

DISTRIBUTION: Bolivia, Mine Asientos.

Rebutia pseudodeminuta Bkbg.

Clumping, stems to 10 cm long. Fl red. [R642/DHS]

DISTRIBUTION: N Argentina, Salta. (See also Appendix 8).

Rebutia pulchella Rausch

A distinctive short-spined member of the **fiebrigii** complex. [DHS]

DISTRIBUTION: Bolivia, N of Padilla.

OTHER NAMES: *Aylostera pulchella.*

Rebutia pulvinosa Ritt. & Buin.

Forming mats of small heads. Fl 1.5 cm across. [DHS]

DISTRIBUTION: Bolivia, Narvaez.

OTHER NAMES: *Aylostera pulvinosa.*

Rebutia pygmaea (Fries) B. & R.

Fl 2.5 cm across, bright red to dark purple-red (*fide* Rausch). [IP/DHS]

DISTRIBUTION: N Argentina, Jujuy, Yavi.

OTHER NAMES: *Lobivia digitiformis, L. pygmaea, R. gracilispina, 'R. oligitiformis' R. pauciareolata, R. pectinata, R. torquata.*

'Rebutia pygmaea v. colorea'
Published as *Rebutia colorea* Ritt.

Distinguished from the species by its dark body colour and brown spines. [CS/PM]

DISTRIBUTION: Bolivia, Iscayache, Abra de Sama.

OTHER NAMES: *Lobivia pygmaea v. colorea.*

'Rebutia pygmaea v. diersiana'
Published as *Rebutia diersiana* Rausch.

Body bright grey-green, spines white. Fl yellow. A small-bodied form also from Yuquina is traded as *R. diersiana v. minor* (=*Lobivia pygmaea v. minor* (Rausch) Rausch.) [CS/PM]

DISTRIBUTION: Bolivia, Yuquina near Culpina.

OTHER NAMES: *Digitorebutia diersiana, Lobivia pygmaea v. diersiana, R. rutiliflora.*

'Rebutia pygmaea v. eos'
published as *Rebutia eos* Rausch.

'v. canacruzensis' pub. as *Rebutia canacruzensis* Rausch is virtually identical (Cana Cruz). [CS/PM]

DISTRIBUTION: S Bolivia, Talina and Tafna.

OTHER NAMES: *Lobivia haagei v. eos, R. rosalbiflora, R. mixta.* **'v. canacruzensis'**: *L. haagei v. can.*

'Rebutia pygmaea v. friedrichiana'
Published as *Rebutia friedrichiana* Rausch.

Body larger than any other variety, to 5 cm high by 3 cm. Fl 3 cm across. [CS/PM]

DISTRIBUTION: Bolivia, La Cueva.

OTHER NAMES: *Lobivia pygmaea v. friedrichiana, R. odontopetala.*

'Rebutia pygmaea v. haagei'
published as *Rebutia haagei* Fric & Schelle.

Fl 4 cm broad. [RK84–4/IP]

DISTRIBUTION: Argentina, Jujuy.

OTHER NAMES: *Mediolobivia pygmaea* Bkbg. *Lobivia haagei.*

'Rebutia pygmaea v. iscayachensis'
Published as *Rebutia iscayachensis* Rausch

Body broader, squatter and paler green than its near neighbour **v. colorea**. Fl larger and less glossy than in the latter. [CS/PM]

DISTRIBUTION: Bolivia, Iscayache, Abra de Sama.

OTHER NAMES: *Lobivia pygmaea v. iscayachensis.* See Appendix 9 for other varieties.

Rebutia ritteri (Wessn.) Don.

Fl 4.5 cm across, flame to crimson. **Rebutia raulii** Rausch, similar, but larger stems, to 4 cm across and a smaller, redder flower (Rio Honda). Similar; **R. yuquinensis** Rausch with greener epidermis and smoky-red flower (Culpina). [WR650/IP/DHS]

DISTRIBUTION: Bolivia, near Iscayache.

OTHER NAMES: *Lobivia atrovirens v. ritteri, Mediolobivia ritteri, R. nigricans, 'R. sphaerica', ?R. tarijensis, R. zecheri. Lobivia atrovirens v. raulii. L. atrov. v. yuquin.*

Rebutia schatzliana Rausch

Closely related to **Rebutia albopectinata** but spines more bristly. [DHS]

DISTRIBUTION: Bolivia, Nord Cinti, Pucara.

Rebutia senilis Bkbg.

Body to 8 cm high by 7 cm, spines relatively long and dense, glassy-white. Fl 3.5 cm across. **'v. breviseta'** Bkbg. is pictured below the species. For other varieties see Appendix 10. [Upper P181/CS/PM] [Lower CS/PM]

DISTRIBUTION: N Argentina, Salta, upper Quebrada Escoipe.

Rebutia spegazziniana Bkbg.

Fl 4 cm across. [L547/CS/PM]

DISTRIBUTION: N Argentina, Salta.

OTHER NAMES: *Aylostera speg.*, *R. fusca*, *R. poecilantha*, *R. sanguinea*, *R. speg. v. atroviridis*, *R. robustispina*, *R. theresae*, *R. vulpina*, *R. wahliana*.

Rebutia steinmannii
(Solms-Laubach) B. & R.

Body 2 cm high by 1.5−2.5 cm. Spines 8−11. Fl 2 cm long, red. For varieties other than those illustrated see Appendix 11. [L421/IP/P]

DISTRIBUTION: Bolivia, between Oruro and Cochabamba, Eucaliptos.

OTHER NAMES: *Aylostera steinmannii*, *Mediolobivia eucaliptana*, *R. eucaliptana*, *?R. iridescens*, *?R. lanosiflora*, *?R. potosina*, *R. salpingantha*.

'Rebutia steinmannii v. christinae'
Published as *Rebutia christinae* Rausch.

With a neat, hard, interlacing spination. [CS/PM]

DISTRIBUTION: N Argentina, Salta, Nazareno and Rodeo.

OTHER NAMES: *Rebutia christinae*.

Rebutia sumayana Rausch

Fl 2.5 cm across. [WR738/IP/DHS]

DISTRIBUTION: Bolivia, Sud Cinti, Sumaya.

Rebutia supthutiana Rausch

Fl 4 cm broad. [WR629/IP/DHS]

DISTRIBUTION: Bolivia, N of Culpina and Inca Huasi.

Rebutia tarvitaensis Ritt.

Flower is one of the largest in the genus, to 5 cm or more across. [CS/PM]

DISTRIBUTION: Bolivia, Tarvita.

Rebutia tropaeolipicta Ritt.

Fl 3.5 cm long. [CS/DHS]

DISTRIBUTION: Bolivia, Mal Paso.

Rebutia violaciflora Bkbg.

Solitary in the wild, later clumping in cultivation. [CS/PM]

DISTRIBUTION: N Argentina.

OTHER NAMES: *?R. kariusiana, R. minuscula fa. violaciflora.*

Rebutia violascens Ritt.

Fl 3–4 cm across. [CS/PM]

DISTRIBUTION: Bolivia, near Camargo N to Llallagua.

OTHER NAMES: *Lobivia haagei v. viol.*

Rebutia walteri Diers

Closely related to **R. hoffmannii**. [WR784/DHS]

DISTRIBUTION: Argentina, Salta, Santa Viktoria.

Rebutia wessneriana Bew.

Characterized by its rather dense spination. Fl 5.5 cm across. **v. calliantha** (Bew.) Don. has a flame-coloured fl. [Holotype/DHS]

DISTRIBUTION: N Argentina.

OTHER NAMES: *R. hyalacantha.* **v. calliantha:** *R. calliantha.*

Rebutia wessneriana v. beryllioides
(Buin. & Don.) Don.

Body flattened, glossy-green. Fl scarlet.

DISTRIBUTION: N Argentina.

OTHER NAMES: *R. call. v. beryllioides*, '*R. beryllioides*'.

Rebutia xanthocarpa   Bkbg.

Fl only 2 cm across. **fa. dasyphrissa** (Card.) Buin. & Don.; spines longer, fl bluish-red. **fa. salmonea** (Bkbg.) Buin. & Don.; fl salmon-red. **fa. violaciflora** (Bkbg.) Buin. & Don.; fl brilliant violet. **fa. graciliflora** (Bkbg.) Don.; fl only 1.7 cm across, light red tinged yellowish. [WR1/IP/DHS]

DISTRIBUTION: N Argentina, Salta, Quebrada del Toro.

OTHER NAMES: **fa. dasy**: *R. dasy*. **fa. gracil.**: *R. graciliflora* Bkbg.

Sclerocactus parviflorus   Clover & Jotter

Stem solitary or 2–3; upper csp pink. Fl averages 4–4.5 cm across. **v. intermedius** (Peeb.) Woodruff & Benson (illus.); upper csp white; fl averages 3 cm across (higher altitude juniper-pinon woodland in Colorado, Utah and N Arizona and New Mexico. [H]

DISTRIBUTION: Lower parts of Navajoan Desert Arizona.

Sclerocactus whipplei
(Englm. & Big.) B. & R.

Solitary, to 7.5 cm high by 9 cm. Fl 2.5–3.5 cm across. [H]

DISTRIBUTION: Lower parts of Navajoan Desert, Arizona.

Sclerocactus wrightiae   Benson

Solitary. Fl 2 cm broad. [H]

DISTRIBUTION: Utah.

Stenocactus albatus   (Dietr.) A.W. Hill

The plant pictured is commonly circulated as this species; it does not fit the original description and is of unknown wild provenance. [CS/P]

Stenocactus coptonogonus
(Lem.) A.W. Hill

The only member of the genus which is easily and quickly referable to a specific identity. Characterized by the non-wavy ribs. [CS/PM]

DISTRIBUTION: Mexico, San Luis Potosi State.

Stenocactus crispatus (DC) A.W. Hill

So variable that we are including several plates of the more distinctive forms, which are best acquired under collection numbers rather than names. Fl with purple pigments (L1377; fl large, purple!). The plant pictured, Lau738, is an 'average' form. [L738/CS/PM]

DISTRIBUTION: Mexico, from Puebla and Oaxaca northwards to N San Luis Potosi and Zacatecas.

OTHER NAMES: Too uncertain to state.

Stenocactus crispatus 'lloydii'

One of the more distinctive members of the complex in cultivation, with its long, curved csps. The plant illustrated, Lau1008, is virtually indistinguishable from the 'lloydii' in trade. [L1008/CS/PM]

OTHER NAMES: *Echinofossulocactus lloydii*.

Stenocactus crispatus 'Huizache form'.

One of a number of forms from widely scattered localities noted for their long csps. This plant is in trade as PM49 and SB437. [PM49/HS/PM]

Stenocactus multicostatus
(Hildman ex Sch.) A.W. Hill

Ribs numerous, to 100 or more, no more than 1 mm wide. Fl 2.5 cm long, white with purple midstripes. [P288/CS/PM]

DISTRIBUTION: Scattered in Zacatecas, Coahuila, Nuevo Leon and Durango, Mexico.

Stenocactus multicostatus 'zacatecasensis'

Solitary, globular, to 10 cm across. Fl 3–4 cm broad. [SB7/HS/PM]

DISTRIBUTION: Mexico, N Zacatecas.

OTHER NAMES: *Echinofossulocactus zacatecasensis*.

Stenocactus ochoterenaus   Tiegel

Globose, 7 cm high and 10 cm across; upper csp to 6 cm long and 2 mm broad. Fl whitish-pink. [H]

DISTRIBUTION: Mexico, Sierra Madre Occidental.

Stenocactus phyllacanthus
(Dietr. & Otto) A.W. Hill

Usually solitary, 4–10 cm across. Fl to 2 cm long, white to pale yellow, sometimes with a thin, brown midstripe. [PM28/HS/PM]

DISTRIBUTION: Mexico: Hidalgo; Guanajuato; San Luis Potosi and Zacatecas.

OTHER NAMES: *E. tricuspidatus.*

Stenocactus vaupelianus
(Werd.) A.W. Hill

Solitary, flattened-globose, to 10 cm across. Fl to 22 mm across very pale yellow. [H]

DISTRIBUTION: Mexico, the plant pictured was growing a few miles N of Zimapan, Hidalgo.

Strombocactus disciformis   (DC.) B. & R.

Slow-growing. Fl 4 cm across. [IP/DHS]

DISTRIBUTION: Mexico, Hidalgo.

Sulcorebutia alba   Rausch

Fls only red. [WR472/IP/DHS]

DISTRIBUTION: Bolivia, road from Sucre to Los Alamos.

OTHER NAMES: *S. verticillacantha v. chatajillensis.*

Sublcorebutia albissima   (Brandt) Pilbeam

Spine colour and arrangement very variable. [Upper HS24/IP/DHS: Lower KK1567/IP/DHS]

DISTRIBUTION: Bolivia, Province Mizque.

OTHER NAMES: *Weingartia albissima, S. albida n.n.*

Sulcorebutia arenacea (Card.) Ritt

Only sparingly offsetting, spine-length variable.
[Card.4400/IP/DHS]

DISTRIBUTION: Bolivia, Province Ayopaya, near Tiquipaya.

OTHER NAMES: *Rebutia arenacea.*

Sulcorebutia augustinii G. Hentzschel

[HS152/IP/DHS]

DISTRIBUTION: Bolivia, Province Campero, at Vana
Kunichico.

Sulcorebutia breviflora Bkbg.

Fl size and spine length variable. Fl usually yellow but also
white, rose, pink and pink with white. [Upper Card.
IP/DHS: Lower L315/IP/DHS]

DISTRIBUTION: Bolivia, Province Tarata, by the Rio Caine,
La Vina.

OTHER NAMES: *S. caineana, S. haseltonii.*

Sulcorebutia candiae
(Card.) Buin. & Don.

Spine-length very variable. [WR245/IP/DHS]

DISTRIBUTION: Bolivia, Province Ayopaya, near Tiquipaya.

OTHER NAMES: *Rebutia candiae, S. xanthoantha.*

Sulcorebutia canigueralii
(Card.) Buin. & Don.

[KR217-2/IP/DHS]

DISTRIBUTION: Bolivia, Sucre.

OTHER NAMES: *Rebutia canig.*

Sulcorebutia canigueralii v. applanata
Don. & Krahn

Noted for its flattened stems and deep magenta-red fl.
[KR217a/IP/DHS]

DISTRIBUTION: Bolivia, Sucre, on the road from the Rio
Chico valley.

OTHER NAMES: *S. verticillacantha v. applanata.*

Sulcorebutia caracarensis sensu Rausch

No recent collections which are definitely this plant have been made. The plant illustrated is Rausch's concept of the species, WR598. [WR598/IP/DHS]

DISTRIBUTION: Bolivia, originally given as Province Zudanez, Caracara Hills.

OTHER NAMES: *Rebutia caracarensis.*

Sulcorebutia cardenasiana Vasq.

[WR609/IP/DHS]

DISTRIBUTION: Bolivia, Province Campero, near Pasorapa.

Sulcorebutia cochabambina Rausch

Rather variable, spines long or short, epidermis green or bronze. Fl always magenta. [WR611-7/IP/DHS]

DISTRIBUTION: Bolivia, Dept. Cochabamba, around Cliza and Arani and near Arque.

OTHER NAMES: *S. clizensis* nom. prov.

Sulcorebutia crispata Rausch

Spine and fl colour variable (see illus.). [L390/IP/DHS]

DISTRIBUTION: Bolivia, Dept. Chuquisaca, Tomina.

Sulcorebutia cylindrica Don. & Lau

The original Lau collection illustrated has a slim, cylindrical body and a yellow fl, though white fl forms also occur. Later collections from other localities have turned up broader plants with magenta fls, e.g., *'v. crucensis'* n.n. [L335/IP/DHS]

DISTRIBUTION: Bolivia, between Vila Vila and Cruce.

Sulcorebutia fischeriana Augustin

[HS79/IP/DHS]

DISTRIBUTION: Bolivia, Dept. Chuquisaca, Cerro Kaspichancha.

Sulcorebutia flavissima Rausch

Flower pink or white. This species almost certainly is a yellow-spined form of **S. mentosa**. [L338/IP/DHS]

DISTRIBUTION: Bolivia, between Aiquile and Mizque, near Orkho Abuelo.

OTHER NAMES: *S. cupreata n.n.*, *S. flavida.*

Sulcorebutia frankiana Rausch

[HS75/IP/DHS]

DISTRIBUTION: Bolivia, Sucre, road to Los Alamos.

Sulcorebutia glomeriseta (Card.) Ritt.

Though distinctive in cultivation it seems to be merely a form of **S. menesesii**. [Card. IP/DHS]

DISTRIBUTION: Bolivia, Province Ayopaya, near Naranjito.

OTHER NAMES: *Rebutia glomeriseta.*

Sulcorebutia glomerispina (Card.) Buin. & Don.

Doubtfully distinct from **S. steinbachii**, which is often the plant passed off as **glomerispina** in trade. [WR249/IP/DHS]

DISTRIBUTION: Bolivia, Huakani.

OTHER NAMES: *Rebutia glomerispina.*

Sulcorebutia inflexiseta (Card.) Don.

[Card.6308/IP/DHS]

DISTRIBUTION: Bolivia, Dept. Chuquisaca.

OTHER NAMES: *Rebutia inflexiseta.*

Sulcorebutia jolantana *nom. nud.*

Merely a yellow-spined population of the very variable **S. purpurea**. [HS68a/IP/DHS]

DISTRIBUTION: Bolivia, near Laguna.

Sulcorebutia krahnii Rausch

[HS33/IP/DHS]

DISTRIBUTION: Bolivia, Dept. Santa Cruz, N of Comarapa, Cerro Tukiphalla.

Sulcorebutia kruegeri (Card.) Ritt.

Flower yellow or reddish. [Card.5495/IP/DHS]

DISTRIBUTION: Bolivia, near Cochabamba.

Sulcorebutia kruegeri v. hoffmanniana (Bkbg.) Don.

Spines very variable in density, and colour which ranges from yellowish-white to various shades of brown. [DHS]

DISTRIBUTION: Bolivia, Cuchu Punata, La Villa and Tacachi.

OTHER NAMES: *Lobivia hoffmanniana, S. seinoiana, S. vanbaelii, S. hoffmanniana.*

Sulcorebutia langeri
Neumann & Falkenburg *nom. prov.*

[Langer IP/DHS]

DISTRIBUTION: Bolivia, Dept. Santa Cruz, near Pampa Grande, on the Rio Chico.

OTHER NAMES: '*S. koehresii*'.

Sulcorebutia losenickyana Rausch

Stem solitary, to 7 cm tall, sparingly clustering only with age. Fl bright red. The pinkish-magenta fl plants often sold under this name are not this species. [WR477/IP/DHS]

DISTRIBUTION: Bolivia, near the road from Sucre to Ravelo.

OTHER NAMES: *S. sucrensis* Ritt. *n.n.*

Sulcorebutia mariana Swoboda

Probably only a form of **S. totorensis**. [HS15/IP/DHS]

DISTRIBUTION: Bolivia, Dept. Cochabamba, W of Mizque.

Sulcorebutia markusii Rausch

Spination very variable in colour and density (see plate). Fl 3.5 cm across deep magenta or scarlet. [Upper WR195/IP/DHS: Lower HS64/IP/DHS]

DISTRIBUTION: Bolivia, Prov. Mizque, near Vila Vila.

'Sulcorebutia markusii v. cuprea'
Published as *S. verticillacantha v. cuprea* Rausch.

Spines longer than in the species. Fl 4.5 cm across, red with an orange throat. [WR476/IP/DHS]

DISTRIBUTION: Bolivia.

Sulcorebutia menesesii
(Card.) Buin. & Don.

Many plants labelled incorrectly as **S. haseltonii** in collections should be referred here. [IP/DHS]

DISTRIBUTION: Bolivia, Prov. Ayopaya, near Naranjito.

OTHER NAMES: *S. menesesii v. kamiensis.*

Sulcorebutia menesesii v. muschii
(Vasqu.) Don.

[WR607/IP/DHS]

DISTRIBUTION: Bolivia, Prov. Ayopaya, Chicote Grande.

Sulcorebutia mentosa Ritt.
[HS104/IP/DHS]
DISTRIBUTION: Bolivia, Aiquile.

Sulcorebutia mizquensis Rausch
[WR194/IP/DHS]
DISTRIBUTION: Bolivia, Dept. Cochabamba, near Mizque.

Sulcorebutia ocnantha Rausch

Solitary, to 10 cm across. [KK/IP/DHS]

DISTRIBUTION: Bolivia, Dept. Cochabamba, S of Totora.

Sulcorebutia pampagrandensis Rausch

Solitary, 7–8 cm across. Occurs but a few miles from the preceding species into which it grades. [WR466/IP/DHS]

DISTRIBUTION: Bolivia, Dept. Cochabamba, S of Totora, Hacienda Pampagrande.

OTHER NAMES: 'S. weingartioides'.

Sulcorebutia perplexiflora Brandt

Collectors may be more familiar with this plant as one of the contenders for the confused **S. pulchra** (see next entry). [L387/IP/DHS]

DISTRIBUTION: Bolivia, Presto-Pasopaya.

Sulcorebutia pulchra (Card.) Don.

Plants exactly matching the original description have yet to be relocated. Plants commonly bearing this name in cultivation are most often Rausch's 593 & 599. However, the plant illustrated, HS78a, seems a better contender. [HS78a/IP/DHS]

DISTRIBUTION: Bolivia, Dept. Chuquisaca, between Rio Grande and Presto.

OTHER NAMES: Originally published in error as S. pulchera.

Sulcorebutia purpurea Don.

Usually solitary, to 9 cm or more across, very variable. [Upper HS67/IP/DHS: Lower L336/IP/DHS]

DISTRIBUTION: Bolivia, Dept. Cochabamba, Lagunillas to within 12 km of Aiquile, near Novillero and almost as far W as Cauta.

OTHER NAMES: S. unguispina, Weingartia rubriflora.

Sulcorebutia rauschii Frank

Body green to purple, spines black or gold. [CS/PM]

DISTRIBUTION: Bolivia, Dept. Chuquisaca, near Zudanez.

Sulcorebutia santiaginiensis Rausch

A small-bodied member of the **S. purpurea** complex. [JD178a/IP/DHS]

DISTRIBUTION: Bolivia, Aiquile.

Sulcorebutia steinbachii (Werd.) Bkbg.

So variable that it seems pointless to uphold any of the named varieties except see right. Within a single population fl may vary from gold, to gold-orange, flame orange, magenta or scarlet; spines from almost pectinate to long and dagger-like. [Card. IP/DHS]

DISTRIBUTION: Bolivia, widespread around Cochabamba.

OTHER NAMES: *S. stein. v. australis, v. gracilior, v. horrida, v. violaciflora, 'S. bicolor', S. tuberculato-chrysantha, Weingartia clavata.*

Sulcorebutia steinbachii v. polymorpha (Card.) Pilbeam

A population with the two flower colours depicted in the plate and rather fresh-green bodies. [Upper KK875/IP/DHS: Lower KK869/IP/DHS]

DISTRIBUTION: Bolivia, Kayrani.

OTHER NAMES: *S. polymorpha.*

Sulcorebutia swobodae Augustin

Spines light or dark. Closely related to **S. mentosa** and probably better treated as a variety thereof. [HS27a/IP/DHS]

DISTRIBUTION: Bolivia, Dept. Cochabamba, between Aiquile and Mizque.

Sulcorebutia tarabucoensis Rausch

Spination usually rather untidy and curly. Fl red. Closely related to **S. canigueralii**. [L382/IP/DHS]

DISTRIBUTION: Bolivia, Dept. Chiquisaca, near Tarabuco.

'Sulcorebutia tarabucoensis v. aureiflora' Published as *S. verticillacantha v. aureiflora* Rausch.

Heads smaller and slimmer than in the species. Fl yellow. [L389/IP/DHS]

DISTRIBUTION: Bolivia, Dept. of Chuquisaca, near Tarabuco.

OTHER NAMES: See heading. Also *Weingartia callecallensis, W. rubro-aurea.*

Sulcorebutia taratensis (Card.) Bkbg.

Typically a dark bodied plant. [Vasqez IP ex Krahn/DHS]

DISTRIBUTION: Bolivia, around Tarata.

Sulcorebutia tarijensis Ritt.

Body can be much blacker than in the plant illustrated. [KK864/IP/DHS]

DISTRIBUTION: Bolivia, Cuesta de Sama

OTHER NAMES: *Weingartia tarijensis, W. oligacantha, W. sanguineo-tarijensis.*

Sulcorebutia tiraquensis (Card.) Ritt.

Spines dark-yellow to dark-brown; fl purple to red. **'v. bicolorispina'** Knize *nom. prov.*; (illus.), fl magenta sometimes red. [KK1770/IP/DHS]

DISTRIBUTION: Bolivia, near Monte Puncu.

OTHER NAMES: *S. tiraqu. v. spinosior. Weingartia nigrofuscata* **v. bicolorispina**: *Weingartia aglaia, S. 'camachoi', S. 'senilis*

'Sulcorebutia tiraquensis v. electracantha' Bkbg.

Spines white to yellow, fl orange to red. Not really a good variety as it grows mixed in with the species. [KK1801/IP/DHS]

DISTRIBUTION: As for the species.

Sulcorebutia tiraquensis v. longiseta (Card.) Don.

Described as being long-spined but short-spined forms also occur [Krahn IP/DHS]

DISTRIBUTION: Bolivia, Cochabamba, isolated on islands near Lopez Mendoza.

Sulcorebutia torotorensis (Card.) Bred. & Don.

The largest of the sulcorebutias, to 15 cm across. [KK1771/IP/GC]

DISTRIBUTION: Bolivia, Dept. Potosi, near Toro-Toro.

OTHER NAMES: *Weingartia torotorensis.*

Sulcorebutia totorensis (Card.) Ritt.

Body dark-green, csp 3–6, to 2 cm long. Fl dark reddish-purple, 3.5 cm long. **v. lepida** (Ritt.) Pilbeam ex Don. (illus.); body very dark-green or purplish-brown, csp usually 0(–6), 5–8 mm long. Fl dark red, 3 cm long. (50 km E of Copachuncho.) [WR190a/IP/DHS]

DISTRIBUTION: Bolivia, Dept. Cochabamba, from Copachuncho S towards Lagunillas.

OTHER NAMES: *Rebutia totorensis*. **v. lepida**: *S. lepida*.

Sulcorebutia tunariensis (Card.) Buin. & Don.

[L.971/IP/DHS]

DISTRIBUTION: Bolivia, Dept. Cochabamba, around Tunari.

OTHER NAMES: *Rebutia tunariensis*.

Sulcorebutia vasqueziana Rausch

Spine colour variable, see plate. **v. albispina** Rausch has white spines. [Upper HS72/IP/DHS: Lower WR474/IP/DHS]

DISTRIBUTION: Bolivia, Dept. Chuquisaca, Sucre, near the road to Los Alamos.

OTHER NAMES: **v. albispina**: *S. ritteri*, 'S. sucrensis', *S. verticillacantha v. albispina*.

Sulcorebutia verticillacantha Ritt.

Fl pale violet-purple or vermilion with an orange throat. **v. minima** Pilbeam ex Rausch has tiny stems and magenta-pink fl (Prov. Arque, at Anzaldo). [IP/DHS]

DISTRIBUTION: Bolivia, Dept. Cochabamba, near Arque and near Izata.

Thelocactus bicolor (Gal. ex Pfeiff.) B. & R.

Spination so variable that most varieties can be sunk within the species. **v. flavidispinus** Bkbg.; a dwarf plant restricted to a unique soil type near Marathon, Texas. [CS/PM]

DISTRIBUTION: Widely distributed in SW Texas and N Mexico.

OTHER NAMES: *T. bicolor v. schottii, v. texensis, v. tricolor & v. wagnerianus, T. wagnerianus; Ferocactus bicolor*. **v. flavidispinus**: *Fero. bicolor v. flavid. T. flavid*.

Thelocactus bicolor v. bolaensis (Runge) Knuth

Noted for its beautiful dense covering of pale, yellowish-white spines. Fl lacks the red centre usually found in the species. [CS/W]

DISTRIBUTION: Mexico, Coahuila, Sierra Bola.

OTHER NAMES: *Ferocactus bicolor v. bolaensis*.

Thelocactus bicolor v. schwarzii
(Bkbg.) Anderson

Csp usually absent. [CS/PM]

DISTRIBUTION: Mexico, Tamaulipas, S of Llera.

OTHER NAMES: *T. schwarzii, Ferocactus bicolor v. schwarzii.*

Thelocactus conothelos
(Regel & Klein) Bkbg. & Knuth

Solitary, fl magenta, purple or white. **v. aurantiacus** Glass & Foster (illus.), is very similar but fl yellow. In some populations pink and yellow flowered forms grow together so it may not be a good variety (Nuevo Leon, near Aramberri.) [CS/PM]

DISTRIBUTION: Mexico: Nuevo Leon; Tamaulipas and San Luis Potosi.

OTHER NAMES: *T. saussieri.*

Thelocactus conothelos v. argenteus
Glass & Foster

Solitary, spines glassy, silvery greyish-white. [CS/PM]

DISTRIBUTION: Under pines near La Ascension, Nuevo Leon, Mexico.

Thelocactus hastifer
(Werd. & Boed.) Knuth

Stem solitary, long-cylindrical. Fl 3.5–5 cm across. [IP/K]

DISTRIBUTION: Mexico, Queretaro.

OTHER NAMES: *Ferocactus hastifer.*

Thelocactus heterochromus
(Web.) van Oosten

Seemingly intermediate between **T. bicolor** and **T. hexaedrophorus**. Fl to 10 cm across, light violet with a darker centre. [NPT499/H]

DISTRIBUTION: Mexico, Chihuahua to Coahuila.

OTHER NAMES: *Ferocactus heterochromus.*

Thelocactus hexaedrophorus
(Lem.) B. & R.

Spination and body form rather variable. Fl white. **v. lloydii** (B. & R.) Kladiwa & Fittkau has very conspicuous broad tubercles and a pink flower (Zacatecas, e.g., near Fresnillo). [CS/PM]

DISTRIBUTION: Mexico, widespread in San Luis Potosi, Tamaulipas and Nuevo Leon.

OTHER NAMES: *T. fossulatus, T. hex. v. foss.* **v. lloydii**: *T. lloydii.*

Thelocactus leucacanthus
(Zucc. ex Pfeiff.) B. & R.

Eventually clumping. Fl 4.5 cm across, yellow, or pinkish-violet to carmine in 'v. schmollii & v. sanchezmejoradai'.
[CS/PM]

DISTRIBUTION: Mexico: Hidalgo and Queretaro.

OTHER NAMES: Ferocactus leucacanthus, T. ehrenbergii.

Thelocactus macdowellii
(Rebut ex Quehl) Glass

Solitary or clumping, fl 5 cm across, pink. [CS/PM]

DISTRIBUTION: Mexico: Coahuila and Nuevo Leon, especially between Monterrey and Saltillo.

OTHER NAMES: T. conothelos v. macdow.

Thelocactus rinconensis   (Poselg.) B. & R.

Solitary, to 20 cm across, spines variable in length from short in 'v. phymatothelos' to as much as 6 cm in 'v. nidulans'.
[CS/PM]

DISTRIBUTION: Mexico: Coahuila and Nuevo Leon.

OTHER NAMES: T. lophothele, & v. nidulans, T. nidulans, T. phymatothelos.

Thelocactus setispinus
(Englm.) Anderson

Solitary, to 12 cm high by 9 cm. Fl 3–4.2 cm across.
[SB858/CS/PM]

DISTRIBUTION: S Texas and Mexico in Coahuila, Nuevo Leon and Tamaulipas.

OTHER NAMES: Ferocactus set., Hamatocactus set.

Thelocactus tulensis   (Poselger) B. & R.

Solitary or clumping, elongate. Fl 3.5–4.2 cm across, white with pale pink midstripe. Yellow-flowered plants labelled v. nova are in cultivation. **v. bueckii** (Klein) Anderson; body squat, tubercles pointed, less spiny (Nuevo Leon, e.g. Aramberri). [IP/W]

DISTRIBUTION: Mexico: Tamaulipas and San Luis Potosi.

OTHER NAMES: **v. bueckii**: T. bueckii.

Thelocactus tulensis v. matudae
(Sanchez-Mej. & Lau) Anderson

Solitary, to 15 cm across. Fl 7.5–8 cm across.
[L744/CS/PM]

DISTRIBUTION: Mexico, Nuevo Leon, Valley of Rayones.

OTHER NAMES: T. matudae.

Turbinicarpus laui   Glass & Foster

Solitary, globose, to 3.5 cm across. Fl 3–3.5 cm wide.
[CS/PM]

DISTRIBUTION: Mexico, San Luis Potosi, near Villa Juarez.

OTHER NAMES: *Neolloydia laui.*

Turbinicarpus lophophoroides
(Werd.) Bux. & Bkbg.

Solitary, to 3.5 cm high and 4.7 cm broad. Fl 3.5 cm across.
[CS/PM]

DISTRIBUTION: Mexico, San Luis Potosi, Las Tablas.

OTHER NAMES: *Neolloydia loph.*

Turbinicarpus pseudomacrochele
(Bkbg.) Bux. & Bkbg.

Usually solitary, to 4 cm high by 3.5 cm. Fl 3–3.5 cm wide.
[CS/PM]

DISTRIBUTION: Mexico: Hidalgo and Queretaro.

OTHER NAMES: *Neolloydia pseudomac.*

**Turbinicarpus pseudomacrochele
v. krainzianus**   (Frank) Glass & Foster

Almost invariably clumping in cultivation, to 4 cm high by
3 cm. Fl yellow. This form not refound in the wild but a
miniature pink-flowered form has recently been found in
Hidalgo. [CS/PM]

DISTRIBUTION: Mexico, Queretaro.

OTHER NAMES: *Turbinicarpus krainz., Toumeya pseudomac.
v. krainz., Strombocactus pseudomac. v. krainz.*

Turbinicarpus pseudopectinatus
(Bkbg.) Glass & Foster

Solitary, to 5 cm high by 2–3.5 cm. '*v. rubriflora*' has
reddish-pink fl. [CS/PM]

DISTRIBUTION: Mexico: Tamaulipas and Nuevo Leon.

OTHER NAMES: *Neolloydia pseudo., Normanbokea pseudo.,
Pelecyphora pseudo.*

Turbinicarpus schmiedickeanus
(Berg.) Bux. & Bkbg.

Solitary, to 2.5 cm high and broad. Fl 1.8–2.8 cm across,
white to pinkish with light magenta mid-veins. [IP/P]

DISTRIBUTION: Mexico, Tamaulipas, near Miquihuana.

OTHER NAMES: *Neolloydia schmied.*

**Turbinicarpus schmiedickeanus
v. dickisoniae** Glass & Foster

Solitary, 2.5 cm high by 3.5 cm. Fl 1.7 cm across. [CS/P]

DISTRIBUTION: Mexico, Nuevo Leon, near Aramberri.

OTHER NAMES: *Neolloydia schmied. v. dick.*, *'Turbinicarpus dick.'*, *'T. gracilis. v. dick.'*

**Turbinicarpus schmiedickeanus
v. flaviflorus** (Frank & Lau) Glass & Foster

Solitary, to 3 cm high by 2 cm. Fl 1−1.5 cm across. [IP/GC]

DISTRIBUTION: Mexico, San Luis Potosi, near Santa Rita.

OTHER NAMES: *Neolloydia schmied. v. flav.*, *Turbinicarpus flav.*

**Turbinicarpus schmiedickeanus
v. gracilis** Glass & Foster

Solitary, to 2.5 cm high by 3 cm. Fl 1.5 cm across. [CS/P]

DISTRIBUTION: Mexico, Nuevo Leon, near Aramberri.

OTHER NAMES: *Neolloydia schmied. v. gracilis, T. gracilis.*

**Turbinicarpus schmiedickeanus
v. klinkerianus** (Bkbg. & Jacobs.) Glass & Foster

Solitary, to 3 cm high by 5 cm. [IP/DHS]

DISTRIBUTION: Mexico, San Luis Potosi.

OTHER NAMES: *Neolloydia schmied. v. klink. T. klinkerianus.*

**Turbinicarpus schmiedickeanus
v. macrochcle** (Werd.) Glass & Foster

Solitary, to 3 cm high by 4 cm. Fl to 3.2 cm across. [IP/GC]

DISTRIBUTION: Mexico, San Luis Potosi, Matehuala.

OTHER NAMES: *Neolloydia schmied. v. macro., T. macro.*

**Turbinicarpus schmiedickeanus
v. schwarzii** (Shurly) Glass & Foster

Solitary, to 3 cm high by 4 cm. Fl 2.5−3.2 cm across. [IP/DHS]

DISTRIBUTION: Mexico, E San Luis Potosi.

OTHER NAMES: *Neolloydia schmied, v. schwarzii, Thelocactus macrochele v. schwarzii, Toumeya mac. v. schw., T. schw., 'T. polaskii'.*

Turbinicarpus valdezianus
(Moell.) Glass & Foster
Solitary, to 2.5 cm high. [CS/PM]

DISTRIBUTION: Mexico, Coahuila, Saltillo.

OTHER NAMES: *Gymnocactus vald. & v. albiflorus, Neolloydia vald. Normanbokea vald., Pelecyphora vald., Thelocactus vald.*

Uebelmannia buiningii Don.
Solitary, short-cylindric to 8 cm broad. Fl to 2 cm across, yellow. [CS/GC]

DISTRIBUTION: Brazil, Minas Geraes, Serra Negra.

Uebelmannia flavispina Buin. & Bred.
Solitary, to 35 cm high by 11 cm. Fl 7 mm broad, light yellow. [CS/GC]

DISTRIBUTION: Brazil, Minas Geraes, W of Diamantina.

Uebelmannia gummifera
(Bkbg. & Vol.) Buin.
Solitary, to 10 cm high by 6 cm. Fl 1.5 cm wide, yellow. [H]

DISTRIBUTION: Brazil, Minas Geraes, Serra de Ambrosia.

OTHER NAMES: *P. gummifera.*

Uebelmannia meninensis Buin.
Solitary, to 50 cm long and 10 cm broad. Fl 3 cm across, pale yellow. [CS/GC]

DISTRIBUTION: Brazil, Minas Geraes, near Pedra Menina.

Uebelmannia pectinifera Buin.
Solitary, to 50 cm high by 15 cm. Fl greenish-yellow.
v. pseudopectinifera Buin. is smaller, body greener, spines spreading sideways. [GC]

DISTRIBUTION: Brazil, Minas Geraes, near Diamantina.

OTHER NAMES: *U. ammatrophus, U. multicostatus.*

Weingartia buiningiana Ritt.

Solitary, 5–10 cm across, becoming elongated.
[FR816/GC]

DISTRIBUTION: Bolivia, Capadala on the Rio Pilcomayo.

Weingartia cintiensis Card.

[KK722/IP/DHS]

DISTRIBUTION: Bolivia, N. Cinti.

OTHER NAMES: *W. fidaiana subsp. cintiensis.*

Weingartia fidaiana (Bkbg.) Werd.

Usually solitary, to 12 cm or more across. Fl to 3 cm long,
yellow. [IP ex Lau/GC]

DISTRIBUTION: S Bolivia, Tupiza.

Weingartia kargliana Rausch

Solitary, globular, to 5 cm across. Fl 3.5 cm across, yellow.
[WR677/IP/GC]

DISTRIBUTION: Bolivia, N of Tupiza on the Pampa
Mochara.

OTHER NAMES: *W. pygmaea.*

Weingartia lanata Ritt.

Usually solitary, globular, to 17 cm across. Fl to 3 cm
across, yellow. *W. riograndensis* is merely a small-headed
clumping form of this species. [IP/GC]

DISTRIBUTION: Bolivia, near Chuquichuqui.

OTHER NAMES: *'W. chuquichuquinensis', W. corroana
(Cardenas 1971), W. longigibba.*

Weingartia neocumingii Bkbg.

Solitary, to 20 cm high by 10 cm. Fl orange to golden
yellow. **subsp. pulquinensis** (Card.) Don.; globose,
woollier, spines thinner, fl yellow. [KK1201/IP/GC]

DISTRIBUTION: Bolivia, widespread in NC Bolivia.

OTHER NAMES: *W. brachygraphisa.* **subsp. pulquinensis:**
*W. multispina, W. pulquinensis, W. knizei, W. corroanus,
W. erinacea* & *v. catarirensis.*

Weingartia neocumingii subsp. pulquinensis v. mairanensis Don.

A particularly attractive form with its orange to brown spines. [L.958/GC]

DISTRIBUTION: Bolivia, near Mairana.

OTHER NAMES: '*W. hajekiana*'.

Weingartia neocumingii subsp. sucrensis (Ritt.) Don.

Solitary, depressed-spherical, to 15 cm across. Fl 3 cm broad, yellow. **v. trollii** (Oeser) Don. (illus.); fl yellow to red. [GC]

DISTRIBUTION: Bolivia, E of Sucre, Questa del Desmeador.

OTHER NAMES: *W. gracilispina*, *W. hediniana*, *W. neocumingii subsp. sucrensis v. hediniana*, *W. sucrensis*. **v. trolli:** *W. trollii*.

Weingartia neumanniana (Bkbg.) Werd.

Solitary, to 7 cm high by 5 cm. Fl 2.5 cm broad, yellow to reddish-orange. [IP/GC]

DISTRIBUTION: N Argentina, N of Humahuaca.

Weingartia pilcomayoensis Card.

Solitary, to 13 cm high by 12 cm. Fl 4 cm long, yellow. The plant illustrated is the small-flowered form of this species from Millares known as *W. platygona*. [KK829/IP/GC]

DISTRIBUTION: Bolivia, Dept. Potosi, between Puente Pilcomayo and Otuyo.

Weingartia westii Hutch.

Solitary, to 20 cm high by 8 cm. Fl 3.5 cm broad, yellow. [West 6367, type plant/DHS]

DISTRIBUTION: Bolivia, Cuchu Ingenio.

OTHER NAMES: *W. lecoriensis*, *W. vilcayensis*.

APPENDICES

APPENDIX 1.

Echinopsis obrepanda (S-D) Sch.
Its wide distribution through the highlands of C and S Bolivia has caused this species to show a perplexingly broad range of variation. As a result, many individual populations showing their own distinctive characteristics of body morphology, spination and flower colour have been named as discrete species or varieties. A number of these names was based mainly on flower colour, but as populations are now known where a full range of colours — from white through pink and magenta to red and scarlet — can be found on adjacent plants, this form of splitting now seems untenable. Only where body and spine details differ in a consistent way within a population, which may also exhibit a single flower colour, is a name now retained, albeit at a varietal rather than specific level.

A general description of the species is as follows. Body depressed-spherical, glossy dark-green. Around Cochabamba and at Zudanez the heads may reach a diameter of 30 cm, at which point they begin to form clumps. In some of these populations only a single flower colour is found, e.g. white or magenta, while in others the full range described above occurs. Rsp generally 9−11 up to 1 cm long, csp 1−3 up to 5 cm long, whitish to dark brown often with 1 csp hooked; fl 20 cm long. At Culpina a giant form occurs with more globular bodies up to 50 cm or more across and 30 cm high; spines longer than normal, straw-coloured, fl white.
OTHER NAMES: *E. calliantholilacina, E. callichroma, E. carmineoflora, E. coronata, E. cristata, E. fiebrigii, Pseudolobivia frankii, E. mataranensis, E. pseudomamillosa, E. riviere de caraltii, E. rojasii, E. roseo-lilacina & E. toralapana; E. obrepanda v. purpurea.*

APPENDIX 2.

Escobaria albicolumnaria Hester
Solitary or very sparingly branching; rsp 25−30; csp 11−15, to 18 mm long. Fl to 1.8 cm across, pinkish.
DISTRIBUTION: W Texas.

Escobaria orcuttii Boed.
Stem to 15 cm high by 6 cm, solitary or clumping; rsp 30−41; csp 15−18; fl 12 mm wide, pinkish, **v. macraxina** Castetter *et al* and **v. koenigii** Castetter *et al*; spine count higher, seeds larger otherwise similar (SW New Mexico).
DISTRIBUTION: SE Arizona and SW New Mexico.
OTHER NAMES: *Coryphantha orcutti, C. strobiliformis v. orcuttii.*

Escobaria sandbergii Castetter *et al*
Stem to 7 cm across. Fl to 2.5 cm across, light pink to purple.
DISTRIBUTION: New Mexico, San Andres Mts.

APPENDIX 3.

Lobivia aurea.
Lobivia aurea is one of those plants which shows such a bewildering degree of variation from population to population over its wide range that it is virtually impossible to draw any firm and distinct lines of differentiation between them. When a plant from any particular population varies from that of a neighbouring population in details of body morphology, spination and flower, and there are dozens of such populations, it can surely only be an arbitrary decision as to which of these merit specific or varietal status. Nevertheless, at present around twelve varieties are accepted, but it should be realized that a plant of this species acquired merely as **Lobivia aurea** may differ as much from the plant in the original description as do many of the named varieties. In view of this it is well worth obtaining plants from different localities distinguished only by the different collector's number.

A brief description of the named varieties other than those illustrated is as follows:

v. albiflora Rausch
Fl 7 cm long, white.
DISTRIBUTION: Argentina, Sierra de Cordoba.

v. callochrysea (Ritt.) Rausch.
Solitary, cylindrical, up to over 20 cm high, with an 11 cm long yellow fl.
DISTRIBUTION: Argentina, Salta, Quebrada de las Conchas, the most northerly locality for this group.
OTHER NAMES: *Hymenorebutia aurea v. callochrysea.*

v. catamarcensis (Ritt.) Rausch
Single or sparingly clumping, body to 20 cm high by 8 cm. Fl 6−9 cm long, yellow.
DISTRIBUTION: Argentina, Catamarca.
OTHER NAMES: *Hymenorebutia aurea v. catamarcensis.*

v. dobeana (Doelz) Rausch
Clumping and characterized by the bright red flower.
DISTRIBUTION: Argentina, Sierra Ancasti.
OTHER NAMES: *Lobivia dobeana.*

v. sierragrandensis Rausch
Solitary, globular, up to 8 cm across, dense, needle-like spination, csp to 2.5 cm. Fl yellow.
DISTRIBUTION: Argentina, Sierra Grande de Cordoba.

v. tortuosa Rausch
Simple, up to 8 cm high by 7 cm; spines black, up to 3 cm long, twisted. Fl yellow.
DISTRIBUTION: Argentina, Santiago del Estero, near Ojo de Agua.

APPENDIX 4.

Neoporteria horrida (Remy ex Gay) D. Hunt.
OTHER NAMES: *Horridocactus aconcaguensis, H. horridus, H. tuberisulcatus, H. choapensis, Neochilenia odoriflora, Neoporteria choapensis, Neop. odorif., Neop. tuberis., Pyrrhocactus aconcaguensis, P. choapensis, P. horridus, P. odorif. P. tuberis., Neop. tuberisulcata v. cupreata, v. robusta & v. vegasana; Pyrrho. horridus v. aconcaguensis & v. robustus, Horrido. robustus & v. vegasanus, Neoc. robusta & v. vegasana, Pyrrho. robustus & v. vegasanus, Neop. curvispina v. aconcaguensis* (wrongly applied), *Neop. horrida v. armata, H. armatus, Neop. armata, N. tuberisulcata v. armata, P. armatus.*

APPENDIX 5.

Neoporteria odieri (Lem.) Berg.
OTHER NAMES: *Neochilenia imitans, Noec. odieri, Neoc. mall. & v. solitaria, 'Neoc. krausii', Neop. reichei v. mall. & fa. krausii & fa. solit., Chileorebutia odieri, C. krausii, C. malleolata & v. solitaria, Thelocephala odieri, T. krausii, T. longirapa, T. malleolata & v. solitaria, Chiloerebutia fulva, Neoc. fulva, Thelo. fulva.* Wrongly applied to **N. reichei v. aerocarpa** was *Neoc. aerocarpa v. fulva* which belongs here.

APPENDIX 6.

Neoporteria reichei (Sch.) Bkbg.
OTHER NAMES: *Neochilenia reichei, 'Neoc. atra', Thelocephala reichei, Chileorebutia reichei, 'Neoc. lembckei', Thelo. lemb., 'Neoc. neoreichei', 'N. pseudoreichei', Neop. reichei v. reichei fa. lembckei, fa. neoreichei, fa. duripulpa & fa. pseudoreichei; Chileorebutia duripulpa, Neoc. duri., Thelo. duri.* **v. aerocarpa:** *Chileorebutia aeroc., Neoc. aeroc., Neop. reichei v. reichei fa. aeroc.*

APPENDIX 7.

Notocactus ottonis (Lehm.) Berg.
OTHER NAMES: *N. acutus, N. arechavelatai & vars., N. campestrensis, N. glaucinus, N. globularis, N. harmonianus, N. ibicuiensis, 'N. incomptus', N. laetivirens* Ritt. *N. oxycostatus, N. securituberculatus.*

APPENDIX 8.

Rebutia deminuta (Web.) Br. & R.
KGP-M's observations of a population of flowering rebutias near Iscayache in Bolivia, along with those on plants in cultivation, seem to indicate an incredible degree of variation within this species. Spination, body-form and flower vary to such an extent that no two plants are completely alike and a dozen so-called species can be found in a single locality, with bees flying at random from the flower of one to another. Previous collectors do not seem to have accepted that cacti can show this degree of variation and seem to have elected instead to select a number of the most similar looking plants from the population to name as species.

It seems almost certain that **R. fulviseta, R. kupperiana, R. pseudodeminuta & R. spegazziniana** also fall within this variation, since plants corresponding quite closely to all these 'species' were also part of the same single population. However, as these three are distinctive enough to be valued by collectors, we are keeping them separate here, though they probably only deserve cultivar status.

APPENDIX 9.

Rebutia pygmaea vars.
'v. crassa' published as *Lobivia haagei v. crassa* Rausch.
A slightly larger form with more tuberculate ribs and a larger, red-orange fl.
DISTRIBUTION: Bolivia, Iscayache.

'v. elegantula' published as *Lobivia haagei v. elegantula* Rausch.
Smaller in all of its parts and noted for its prolific clumping habit.
DISTRIBUTION: Argentina, Rio San Juan de Oro.

'v. mudanensis' published as *Rebutia mudanensis* Rausch.
The largest variety, stems to 3 cm across and more globular, spination whitish-silver, quite dense. Fl large, very pale salmon-pink.
DISTRIBUTION: Argentina, Jujuy, Cerro Mudana.
OTHER NAMES: *Lobivia haagei v. mudanensis.*

'v. nazarenoensis' published as *Rebutia nazarenoensis* Rausch.
Similar to the last but with more upstanding spination, with 1 csp and darker orange fl.
DISTRIBUTION: N Argentina, near Nazareno.
OTHER NAMES: *Lobivia haagei v. nazarenoensis.*

'v. orurensis' published as *Lobivia orurensis* Bkbg.
Body with violet tints. Fl rich orange with paler throat.
DISTRIBUTION: N Bolivia, Oruro and Pazna.
OTHER NAMES: *Mediolobivia orurensis, Med. pectinata v. orurensis, Lobivia haagei v. orurensis.*

'v. pallida' published as *Rebutia pallida* Rausch.
Body tinted pinkish-violet, spination pinkish-brown. Fl smaller, bright orange-pink.
DISTRIBUTION: Bolivia, Culpina, La Cueva.
OTHER NAMES: *Lobivia haagei v. pallida.*

'v. pelzliana' published as *Lobivia haagei v. pelzliana* Rausch.
A thinner spined **v. eos** with a bright orange-red flower.
DISTRIBUTION: Argentina, Jujuy, Tafna.

APPENDIX 10.

Rebutia senilis vars.
Numerous varieties of **Rebutia senilis** have been described and are in cultivation. These all breed true and are often worth collecting, so we are listing the more distinctive examples below. This does not

however imply any certainty that these are more than just forms from a very variable population.

v. iseliniana Krainz.
Body more rounded, fl orange-red.

v. kesselringiana Bewg.
Fl yellow. 'Rose of York' has white flowers.

v. lilacino-rosea Bkbg.
Fl light lilac-pink.

v. schieliana Bewg.
Fl 4 cm broad, outer petals crimson, inner orange-red.

v. stuemeri Bkbg.
Fl with a brick-red throat, petals often bordered yellowish.

APPENDIX 11.

Rebutia steinmannii (Solms-Laub.) Bkbg.
None of the following varieties has yet been placed in the genus **Rebutia**, so we are not quoting the authority after the combination. Instead this is quoted for the original publication in the 'OTHER NAMES' section for each variety.

'v. applanata'
Body thickened and rather flattened. Fl large, red.
DISTRIBUTION: Bolivia, Rio Honda.
OTHER NAMES: *Lobivia steinmannii v. applanata* Rausch.

'v. cincinnata'
A small form with curly white spines and reddish-orange flowers.
DISTRIBUTION: Bolivia, Cuchu Ingenio.
OTHER NAMES: *R. cincinnata* Rausch., *Lobivia stein. v. cinc.*

'v. costata'
Fresh-green, fl 3.5 cm across, orange with carmine edges.
DISTRIBUTION: Bolivia, Potosi.
OTHER NAMES: *R. costata* Werd., *Lobivia stein. v. cost.*

'v. major'
The largest form, 5 cm high and 3 cm across with scented orange-red fls.
DISTRIBUTION: Argentina, La Quiaca, Tafna.
OTHER NAMES: *Lobivia stein. v. major* Rausch.

'v. rauschii'
The smallest form, fl only 2 cm long, orange.
DISTRIBUTION: Bolivia, Huari.
OTHER NAMES: *Reb. rauschii* Zecher, *Lobivia stein. v. rauschii.*

INDEX OF
ALTERNATIVE NAMES

Acanthocalycium andreaeanum (Bkbg.) Don. = **Pyrrhocactus andreaeanus** (Bkbg.) Ritt.

A. aurantiacum Rausch = **Acanthocalycium thionanthum v. aurantiacum** (Rausch) Don.

A. brevispinum Ritt. = **Acanthocalycium thionanthum v. brevispinum** (Ritt.) Don.

A. catamarcense Ritt. = **Acanthocalycium thionanthum** (Speg.) Bkbg.

A. chionanthum (Speg.) Bkbg. = **Acanthocalycium thionanthum v. chionanthum** (Speg.) Hoss.

A. ferrarii Rausch = **'Acanthocalycium thionanthum v. ferrarii'**

A. glaucum Ritt. = **Acanthocalycium thionanthum v. glaucum** (Ritt.) Don. ex Rausch.

A. griseum Bkbg. = **Acanthocalycium thionanthum** (Speg.) Bkbg.

A. klimpelianum (Weidl. & Werd.) Bkbg. = **Acanthocalycium spiniflorum** (K. Sch.) Bkbg.

A. peitscherianum Bkbg. = **Acanthocalycium spiniflorum** (K. Sch.) Bkbg.

A. variiflorum Bkbg. = **Acanthocalycium thionanthum v. variiflorum** (Bkbg.) Don.

A. violaceum (Werd.) Bkbg. = **Acanthocalycium spiniflorum fa. violaceum** (Werd.) Don.

Acantholobivia incuiensis (R. & B.) Rauh & Bkbg. = **Lobivia tegeleriana** Bkbg.

A. tegeleriana (Bkbg.) Bkbg. = **Lobivia tegeleriana** Bkbg.

Ancistrocactus brevihamatus (Engelm.) B. & R. = **Ancistrocactus scheerii** (S–D) B. & R.

A. megarhizus (Rose) B. & R. = **Ancistrocactus scheerii** (S–D) B. & R.

Arequipa erectocylindrica Rauh & Bkbg. = **Arequipa hempeliana** (Guerke) Oehme.

A. leucotricha (Phil.) B. & R. is an **Oreocereus**.

A. rettigii (Quehl) Oehme = **Arequipa hempeliana** (Guerke) Oehme.

A. spinosissima Ritt. – **Arequipa hempeliana** (Guerke) Oehme.

A. weingartiana Bkbg. = **Arequipa hempeliana** (Guerke) Oehme.

Ariocarpus elongatus (S–D) M.H. Lee = **Ariocarpus trigonus** (Weber) Sch.

A. intermedius Bkbg. = **Ariocarpus fissuratus v. lloydii** (Rose) And.

A. lloydii (Rose) Berg. = **Ariocarpus fissuratus v. lloydii** (Rose) And.

Astrophytum niveum Kays. = **Astrophytum capricorne v. niveum** (Kays.) Ok.

Aylostera albiflora (Ritt. & Buin.) Bkbg. = **Rebutia albiflora** Ritt. & Buin.

A. albipilosa (Ritt.) Bkbg. = **Rebutia albipilosa** Ritt.

A. deminuta (Web.) Bkbg. = **Rebutia deminuta** (Web.) Br. & R.

A. fiebrigii (Guerke) Bkbg. = **Rebutia fiebrigii** (Guerke) B. & R.

A. fiebrigii v. densiseta Cullm. = **Rebutia fiebrigii** (Guerke) B. & R.

A. fulviseta Rausch = **Rebutia fulviseta** Rausch.

A. heliosa Rausch = **Rebutia heliosa** Rausch.

A. jujuyana Rausch = **Rebutia jujuyana** Rausch.

A. kupperiana (Boed.) Bkbg. = **Rebutia kupperiana** Boed.

A. muscula (Ritt. & Thiele) Bkbg. = **Rebutia muscula** Ritt. & Thiele.

A. narvaecensis Card. = **Rebutia narvaecensis** (Card.) Don.

A. padcayensis Rausch = **Rebutia padcayensis** Rausch.

A. pseudodeminuta (Bkbg.) Bkbg. = **Rebutia pseudodeminuta** Bkbg.

A. pseudominuscula (Speg.) Speg. = **Rebutia deminuta** (Web.) Br. & R.

A. pulchella Rausch = **Rebutia pulchella** Rausch.

A. pulvinosa (Ritt. & Buin.) Bkbg. = **Rebutia pulvinosa** Ritt. & Buin.

A. rubiginosa (Ritt.) Bkbg. = **Rebutia deminuta** (Web.) Br. & R.

A. spegazziniana (Bkbg.) Bkbg. = **Rebutia spegazziniana** Bkbg.

A. spinosissima (Bkbg.) Bkbg. = **Rebutia fiebrigii** (Guerke) B. & R.

A. steinmannii (Solms-Laub.) Bkbg. = **Rebutia steinmannii** Solms-Laub.

A. tuberosa (Ritt.) Bkbg. = **Rebutia tuberosa** Ritt.

Bartschella schumannii (Hildm.) B. & R. = **Mammillaria schumannii** Hildm.

Blossfeldia atroviridis Ritt.
B. campaniflora Bkbg.
'B. fechseri' Bkbg.
B. minima Ritt.
B. pedicellata Ritt.
} = **Blossfeldia liliputana** Werd.

Borzicactus aurantiacus (Vpl.) Kim. & Hutch. = **Matucana aurantiaca** (Vpl.) Bux.

B. aureiflorus (Ritt.) Don. = **Matucana aureiflora** Ritt.

B. calvescens Kim. & Hutch. = **Matucana aurantiaca** (Vpl.) Bux.

B. formosus (Ritt.) Don. = **Matucana formosa** Ritt.

B. haynei (Otto) Kim. & Hutch. = **Matucana haynei** (Otto) B. & R.

B. huagalensis Don. & Lu = **Matucana huagalensis** (Don. & Lau) Bregman *et al.*

B. intertextus (Ritt.) Don. = **Matucana intertexta** Ritt.

B. intertextus v. celendinensis (Ritt.) Don. = **Matucana intertexta v. celendinensis** (Ritt.) Bregman *et al.*

B. krahnii Don. = **Matucana krahnii** (Don.) Bregman.

B. madisoniorum Hutch. = **Matucana madisoniorum** (Hutch.) Rowley.

B. madisoniorum v. pujupatii Don. & Lau = **Matucana pujupatii** (Don. & Lau) Bregman.

B. oreodoxus (Ritt.) Don. = **Matucana oreodoxa** (Ritt.) Slaba.

B. paucicostatus (Ritt.) Don. = **Matucana paucicostata** Ritt.

B. ritteri (Buin.) Don. = **Matucana ritteri** Buin.

B. variabilis (Rauh & Bkbg.) Don. = **Matucana haynei** (Otto) B. & R.

B. weberbaueri (Vpl.) Don. = **Matucana weberbaueri** (Vpl.) Bkbg.

Brachycalycium tilcarense (Bkbg.) Bkbg. = **Gymnocalycium saglione** (Cels) B. & R.

Brasilicactus graessneri (Sch.) Bkbg. = **Notocactus graessneri** Sch.
B. haselbergii (Haage) Bkbg. = **Notocactus haselbergii** Haage.

Brasiliparodia alacriportana (Bkbg. & Voll) Ritt. = **Notocactus alacripotanus** (Bkbg. & Voll) Bux.
B. brevihamata (W. Haage) Ritt. = **Notocactus brevihamatus** (W. Haage) Bux.
B. buenekeri (Buin.) Ritt. = **Notocactus buenekeri** (Buin.) Bux.
B. rechensis (Buin.) Ritt. = **Notocactus rechensis** Buin.

Chamaecereus silvestrii (Speg.) B. & R. = **Lobivia silvestrii** (Speg.) Rowley.

Chileorebutia aerocarpa Ritt. = **Neoporteria reichei v. aerocarpa** (Ritt.) R. M. Ferryman
'*C. carneoflora*' = hort. hybrid.
C. duripulpa Ritt. = **Neoporteria reichei** (Sch.) Bkbg.
C. esmeraldana Ritt. = **Neoporteria esmeraldana** (Ritt.) Don. & Rowley.
C. fulva Ritt. n.n. = **Neoporteria odieri** (Lem.) Berg.
C. glabrescens Ritt. = **Neoporteria napina** (Phil.) Bkbg.
C. krausii Ritt. = **Neoporteria odieri v. malleolata** (Ritt.) R.M. Ferryman.
'*C. lembckei*' = catalogue name = **Neoporteria reichei** (Sch.) Bkbg.
C. malleolata & v. solitaria Ritt. = **Neoporteria odieri v.malleolata** (Ritt.) R.M. Ferryman.
C. napina (Phil.) Ritt. = **Neoporteria napina** (Phil.) Bkbg.
C. odieri (S–D) Ritt. = **Neoporteria odieri** (Lem.) Berg.
C. reichei Ritt. = **Neoporteria reichei** (Sch.) Bkbg.

Cochemiea halei (K. Brand.) Walt. = **Mammillaria halei** K. Brandegee.
C. maritima Lindsay = **Mammillaria maritima** (Lindsay) D. Hunt.
C. pondii (Greene) Walt. = **Mammillaria pondii** Greene.
C. poselgeri (Hildm.) B. & R. = **Mammillaria poselgeri** Hildm.
C. setispina (Coult.) Walt. = **Mammillaria setispina** (Coult.) K. Brandegee.

Copiapoa alticostata Ritt. = **Copiapoa dura** Ritt.
C. applanata Bkbg. = **Copiapoa cinerascens** (S–D) B. & R.
C. atacamensis Middleditch = **Copiapoa boliviana** (Pfeiff.) Ritt.
'*C. barquitensis*' Ritt. n.n. = **Copiapoa hypogaea v. barquitensis** Ritt.
C. carrizalensis Ritt. = **Copiapoa dealbata** Ritt.
C. chaniaralensis Ritt. = **?Copiapoa cinerascens** (S–D) B. & R.
C. cinerea v. dealbata (Ritt.) Bkbg. = **Copiapoa dealbata** Ritt.
C. columna-alba Ritt. = **Copiapoa cinerea v. columna-alba** (Ritt.) Bkbg.
C. conglomerata (Phil.) Lembcke = status doubtful.
C. coquimbana (Karw. ex Ruemp.) B. & R. = *nom. dub.*, plants obtained as this are usually forms of **Copiapoa pendulina**.
C. cuprea Ritt. = **Copiapoa dura** Ritt.
C. cupreata (Poselg. ex Hildm.) Bkbg. = status doubtful.
'*C. domeykoensis*' = **Copiapoa pendulina** Ritt.
C. echinoides (Lem. ex S–D) B. & R. = status doubtful.
C. eremophila Ritt. = **Copiapoa cinerea v. haseltoniana** (Bkbg.) N.P. Taylor.
C. ferox Lembcke & Bkbg. = **Copiapoa solaris** (Ritt.) Ritt.
C. haseltoniana Bkbg. = **Copiapoa cinerea v. haseltoniana** (Bkbg.) N.P. Taylor.
C. gigantea Bkbg. = **Copiapoa cinerea v. haseltoniana** (Bkbg.) N.P. Taylor.
'*C. imbricata*' = catalogue name = **?Copiapoa dura** Ritt.
C. intermedia Ritt. n.n. = **Copiapoa cinerascens** (S–D) B. & R.
C. lembckei Bkbg. = **Copiapoa calderana** Ritt.
C. longispina Ritt. = **Copiapoa humilis** (Phil.) Hutch.
C. malletiana (Lem. ex S–D) Bkbg. = status doubtful.
C. melanohystrix Ritt. = **Copiapoa cinerea v. columna-alba** (Ritt.) Bkbg.
'*C. militaris*' = catalogue name = **?Copiapoa pendulina** Ritt.
C. mollicula Ritt. = **Copiapoa hypogaea** Ritt.
C. montana Ritt. = **Copiapoa hypogaea** Ritt.
'*C. multicolor*' hort. = a name of no value.
'*C. paposoensis*' Ritt. = **Copiapoa humilis** (Phil.) Hutch.
C. pepiniana (Lem. [ex S–D]) Bkbg. = status doubtful.
C. pepiniana v. fiedleriana (Sch.) Bkbg. = **Copiapoa fiedlerana** (Sch.) Bkbg.
C. pseudocoquimbana Ritt. = **Copiapoa pendulina** Ritt.
C. rarissima Ritt. = **Copiapoa hypogaea** Ritt.
C. rubriflora Ritt. = **Copiapoa rupestris** Ritt.
C. scopulina Ritt. = **Copiapoa krainziana** Ritt.
C. serena Voldan = **Copiapoa pendulina** Ritt.
C. streptocaulon (Hook.) van Oosten = **Copiapoa marginata** (S–D) B. & R.
C. taltalensis (Werd.) Looser = **Copiapoa humilis** (Phil.) Hutch.
C. tenebrosa Ritt. = **Copiapoa cinerea** (Phil.) B. & R.
C. totoralensis Ritt. = **Copiapoa echinata v. borealis** Ritt.
'*C. vulgata*' = **Copiapoa pendulina** Ritt.
C. wagenknechtii Ritt. n.n. = distinctive form of **Copiapoa pendulina** Ritt.

Coryphantha clava (Pfeiff.) Lem. see under **Coryphantha clavata**.
C. columnaris Lahman = **Escobaria vivipara v. radiosa** (Engelm.) D.R. Hunt.
C. duncanii (Hester) Benson = **Escobaria dasyacantha** (Engelm.) B. & R.

C. hesteri Wright = **Escobaria hesteri** (Wright) Bux.

C. minima Baird = **Escobaria minima** (Baird) D. Hunt.

C. muehlenpfordtii B. & R. = **Coryphantha scheerii** (Muehlof.) Lem.

C. nelliae Croiz. = **Escobaria minima** (Baird) D.R. Hunt.

C. organensis Zimmerman = **Escobaria organensis** (Zimmerman) Castetter *et al.*

C. pectinata (Englm.) B & R. = **?Coryphantha radians** (DC) B. & R.

C. pirtlei Werd. = **Escobaria emskoetteriana** (Quehl) Borg.

C. pseudoradians (Bravo) = **Coryphantha radians** (DC) B. & R.

C. sneedii (B. & R.) Berg. = **Escobaria sneedii** B. & R.

C. sneedii v. leei (Rose ex Boed.) Benson = **Escobaria leei** Boed.

C. vivipara (Nutt.) B. & R. = **Escobaria vivipara** (Nutt.) Bux.

'Delaetia woutersiana' Bkbg. = **Neoporteria neohankeana** (Ritt.) R.M. Ferryman.

Denmoza erythrocephala (Sch.) Berg. = **Denmoza rhodacantha** (S–D) B. & R.

Discocactus albispinus Buin. & Bred. = **Discocactus zehntneri** B. & R.

D. alteolens Lem. ex Dietr. = status doubtful.

D. araneispinus Buin. & Bred. = **Discocactus zehntneri** B. & R.

D. boliviensis Bkbg. = **Discocactus heptacanthus** (Rodr.) B. & R.

D. boomianus Buin. & Bred. = **Discocactus zehntneri** B. & R.

D. cangaensis Diers & Est. = **Discocactus heptacanthus** (Rodr.) B. & R.

D. catingicola Buin. & Bred. = **Discocactus heptacanthus** (Rodr.) B. & R.

D. cephaliaciculosus Buin. & Bred. = **Discocactus heptacanthus** (Rodr.) B. & R.

D. diersianus Est. = **Discocactus heptacanthus** (Rodr.) B. & R.

D. estevesii Diers = **Discocactus heptacanthus** (Rodr.) B. & R.

D. ferricola Buin. & Bred. = **Discocactus heptacanthus** (Rodr.) B. & R.

D. flavispinus Buin. & Bred. ex Buin. = **Discocactus heptacanthus** (Rodr.) B. & R.

D. goianus Diers & Est. = **Discocactus heptacanthus** (Rodr.) B. & R.

D. griseus Buin. & Bred. = **Discocactus heptacanthus** (Rodr.) B. & R.

D. latispinus Buin. & Bred. = **Discocactus placentiformis** (Lem.) Sch.

D. lindaianus Diers & Est. = **Discocactus heptacanthus** (Rodr.) B. & R.

D. magnimammus Buin. & Bred. = **Discocactus hartmannii** (Sch.) B. & R.

D. mamillosus Buin. & Bred. = **Discocactus hartmannii** (Sch.) B. & R.

D. melanochlorus Buin. & Bred. ex. Buin. = **Discocactus heptacanthus** (Rodr.) B. & R.

D. multicolorispinus Buin. & Bred. = **Discocactus placentiformis** (Lem.) Sch.

D. nigrisaetosus Buin. & Bred. ex Buin. = **Discocactus heptacanthus** (Rodr.) B. & R.

'D. paranaensis' Bkbg. = **Discocactus heptacanthus** (Rodr.) B. & R.

D. patulifolius Buin. & Bred. = **Discocactus hartmannii** (Sch.) B. & R.

D. pugionacanthus Buin. & Bred. ex Buin. = **Discocactus placentiformis** (Lem.) Sch.

D. pulvinicapitatus Buin. & Bred. ex Buin. = **Discocactus placentiformis** (Lem.) Sch.

D. rapirhizus Buin. & Bred. = **Discocactus heptacanthus** (Rodr.) B. & R.

D. semicampaniflorus Buin. & Bred. = **Discocactus heptacanthus** (Rodr.) B. & R.

D. silicicola Buin. & Bred. = **Discocactus heptacanthus** (Rodr.) B. & R.

D. silvaticus Buin. & Bred. ex Buin. = **Discocactus heptacanthus** (Rodr.) B. & R.

D. spinosior Buin. & Bred. ex Buin. = **Discocactus heptacanthus** (Rodr.) B. & R.

D. squamibaccatus Buin. & Bred. ex Buin. = **Discocactus heptacanthus** (Rodr.) B. & R.

D. subterraneo-proliferans Diers & Est. = **Discocactus heptacanthus** (Rodr.) B. & R.

D. subviridigriseus Buin. & Bred. ex Buin. = **Discocactus placentiformis** (Lem.) Sch.

D. tricornis Monv. ex Pfeiff. = **Discocactus placentiformis** (Lem.) Sch.

D. woutersianus Bred. & v.d. Broek = **Discocactus horstii** Buin. & Bred. ex Buin.

Dolichothele albescens (Tieg.) Bkbg. = **Mammillaria camptotricha** Dams.

D. baumii (Boed.) Werd. & Bux. = **Mammillaria baumii** Boed.

D. balsasoides (Craig) Bkbg. = **Mammillaria beneckei** Ehrenb.

D. beneckei (Ehrenb.) Bkbg. = **Mammillaria beneckei** Ehrenb.

D. camptotricha (Dams) Tieg. = **Mammillaria camptotricha** Dams.

D. decipiens (Scheidw.) Tieg. = **Mammillaria decipiens** Scheidw.

D. longimamma (DC) B. & R. = **Mammillaria longimamma** DC.

D. melaleuca (Karw.) Craig = **Mammillaria melaleuca** Karw.

D. nelsonii (B. & R.) Bkbg. = **Mammillaria beneckei** Ehrenb.

D. sphaerica (Dietr.) B. & R. = **Mammillaria sphaerica** Dietr.

D. surculosa (Boed.) Bux. = **Mammillaria surculosa** Boed.

D. uberiformis (Zucc.) B. & R. = **Mammillaria longimamma** DC.

D. zephyranthoides (Scheidw.) Bkbg. = **Mammillaria zephyranthoides** Scheidw.

Echinocactus grandis Rose = **Echinocactus platyacanthus** Link & Otto.

E. ingens Zucc. = **Echinocactus platyacanthus** Link & Otto.

E. palmeri Rose = **Echinocactus platyacanthus** Link & Otto.

E. visnaga Hook. = **Echinocactus platyacanthus** Link & Otto.

E. xeranthemoides (Coult.) Engelm. = **Echinocactus polycephalus v. xeranthemoides** Coult.

Echinocereus acifer (Otto ex salm-Dyck) Hort. F. A. Haage = **Echinocereus polyacanthus v. densus** (Regel) N.P. Taylor.

'E. albatus' Bkbg. = **Echinocereus nivosus** Glass & Foster.

E. amoenus (A. Dietr.) Sch. = **Echinocereus pulchellus v. amoenus** (A. Dietr.) Sch.

E. arizonicus Rose ex Orcutt = **Echinocereus triglochidiatus v. arizonicus** (Rose ex Orcutt) Benson.

E. armatus (Poselger) Berg. = **Echinocereus reichenbachii v. armatus** (Poselger) N.P. Taylor.

E. baileyi Rose = **Echinocereus reichenbachii v. baileyi** (Rose) N.P. Taylor.

E. blanckii (Poselger) Ruempler = **Echinocereus enneacanthus v. brevispinus** (W.O. Moore) Benson.

E. blanckii v. berlandieri (Engelm.) Bkbg. = **Echinocereus berlandieri** (Engelm.) Hort. F.A. Haage.

E. blanckii v. leonensis (Mathsson) Bkbg. = **Echinocereus pentalophus v. leonensis** (Mathsson) N.P. Taylor.

E. bonkerae Thornb. & Bonk. = **Echinocereus fendleri v. bonkerae** (Thornb. & Bonk.) Benson.

E. boyce-thompsonii (Orcutt) = Echinocereus fendleri v. boyce-thompsonii (Orcutt) Benson.

E. caespitosus (Engelm.) Engelm. = **Echinocereus reichenbachii** (Terscheck ex Walp.) Hort. F.A. Haage.

E. chlorophthalmus (Hook.) B. & R. = **Echinocereus cinerascens** (DC.) Lem.

E. coccineus Engelm. = **Echinocereus triglochidiatus v. melanacanthus** (Engelm.) Benson.

E. cucumis Werd. = **Echinocereus scheeri v. gentryi** (Clover) N.P. Taylor.

E. davisii A.D. Houghton = **Echinocereus viridiflorus v. davisii** (Houghton) W.T. Marsh.

E. dasyacanthus Engelm. = **Echinocereus pectinatus v. dasyacanthus** (Engelm.) N.P. Taylor.

E. dubius (Engelm.) Ruempler = **Echinocereus enneacanthus** Engelm.

E. durangensis Poselger ex Ruempler = **Echinocereus polyacanthus** Engelm.

E. ehrenbergii (Pfeiff.) Ruempler = **Echinocereus cinerascens v. ehrenbergii** (Pfeiff.) H. Bravo-H.

E. enneacanthus v. dubius (Engelm.) Benson = **Echinocereus enneacanthus** Engelm.

E. fasciculatus (Engelm. ex B.D. Jackson) Benson = **Echinocereus fendleri v. fasciculatus** (Engelm. ex B.D. Jackson) N.P. Taylor.

E. fasciculatus v. bonkerae (Thornber & Bonker) Benson = **Echinocereus fendleri v. bonkerae** (Thornber & Bonker) Benson.

E. fasciculatus v. boyce-thompsonii (Orcutt) Benson = **Echinocereus fendleri v. boyce-thompsonii** (Orcutt) Benson.

'*E. finnii*' = catalogue name = **Echinocereus chloranthus v. russanthus** (Wenig.) Lamb ex Rowley.

E. fitchii B. & R. = **Echinocereus reichenbachii v. fitchii** (B. & R.) Benson.

E. floresii Bkbg. = **Echinocereus sciurus v. floresii** (Bkbg). N.P. Taylor.

E. fobeanus Oehme = **Echinocereus chisoensis v. fobeanus** (Oehme) N.P. Taylor.

E. gentryi Clov. = **Echinocereus scheeri v. gentryi** (Clover) N.P. Taylor.

E. hempelii Fobe = **Echinocereus fendleri v. kuenzleri** (Castetter *et al*) Benson.

E. hexaedrus (Engelm.) Ruempler = **Echinocereus triglochidiatus v. melanacanthus** (Engelm.) Benson.

E. inermis hort. = a form of **Echinocereus triglochidiatus v. melanacanthus** (Engelm.) Benson.

E. knippelianus v. reyesii Lau = **Echinocereus knippelianus v. kruegeri** Glass & Foster.

E. kuenzleri Castetter *et al* = **Echinocereus fendleri v. kuenzleri** (Castetter *et al*) Benson.

E. ledingii Peebles = **Echinocereus fendleri v. ledingii** (Peebles) N.P. Taylor.

E. leeanus (Hook.) Lem. = **Echinocereus polyacanthus v. densus** (Regel) N.P. Taylor.

E. leonensis Mathsson = **Echinocereus pentalophus v. leonensis** (Mathsson) N.P. Taylor.

E. lindsayi Meyran = **Echinocereus ferreirianus v. lindsayi** (Meyran) N.P. Taylor.

'*E. melanocentrus*' Lowry = **Echinocereus reichenbachii v. fitchii** (B. & R.) Benson.

E. merkeri Hilm. ex Sch. = **Echinocereus enneacanthus** Engelm.

E. mojavensis (Englm. & Big.) Ruempl. = **Echinocereus triglochidiatus v. mojavensis** (Englm. & Big.) Benson.

E. morricalii = **Echinocereus viereckii v. morricalii** (Riha) N.P. Taylor.

E. ochoterenae = **Echinocereus subinermis v. ochoterenae** (J.G. Ortega) G. Unger.

E. pectinatus v. ctenoides (Engelm.) Weniger *nom. inv.* = **Echinocereus pectinatus v. dasyacanthus** (Engelm.) N.P. Taylor.

E. pectinatus v. minor (Englm.) Benson = **Echinocereus bristolii v. pseudopectinatus** N.P. Taylor.

E. pectinatus v. neomexicanus (J. Coulter) Benson = **Echinocereus pectinatus v. dasyacanthus** (Engelm.) N.P. Taylor.

E. pectinatus v. rigidissimus (Engelm.) Ruempler = **Echinocereus rigidissimus** (Engelm.) Hort. F.A. Haage.

E. pectinatus v. rubispinus Frank = **Echinocereus rigidissimus v. rubispinus** (Frank) N.P. Taylor.

E. pentalophus v. ehrenbergii (Pfeiff.) Bkbg. = **Echinocereus cinerascens v. ehrenbergii** (Pfeiff.) H. Bravo-H.

E. pentalophus v. procumbens (Engelm.) P. Fournier = **Echinocereus pentalophus v. pentalophus** (DC.) Lem.

E. perbellus B. & R. = **Echinocereus reichenbachii v. perbellus** (B. & R.) Benson.

E. poselgeri Lem. see under **Echinocereus leucanthus.**

E. procumbens (Engelm.) Lem. = **Echinocereus pentalophus v. pentalophus** (DC.) Lem.

E. purpureus Lahman = **Echinocereus reichenbachii** (Terscheck ex Walp) Hort. F.A. Haage.

E. radians Engelm. = **Echinocereus adustus v. adustus** Engelm.

E. reichenbachii v. albertii Benson = **Echinocereus reichenbachii v. fitchii** (B. & R.) Benson.

E. reichenbachii v. albispinus (Lahman) Benson = **Echinocercus reichenbachii v. baileyi** (Rose) N.P. Taylor.

E. reichenbachii v. chisoensis (W.T. Marsh) Benson = **Echinocereus chisoensis** W.T. Marsh.

E. roemeri Hort. F.A. Haage = **Echinocereus triglochidiatus v. melanacanthus** (Engelm.) Benson.

E. rosei Wooton & Standley = **Echinocereus triglochidiatus v. neomexicanus** (Standley) Benson.

E. russanthus = **Echinocereus chloranthus v. russanthus** (Weniger) Lamb ex G. Rowley.

E. salm-dyckianus Scheer = **Echinocereus scheeri** (S–D) Scheer.

E. salmianus Ruempler = **Echinocereus scheeri** (S–D) Scheer.

'*E. sanborgianus*' (J. Coulter) Bkbg. = **Echinocereus brandegeei** (J. Coulter) Sch.

E. schwarzii Lau = **Echinocereus adustus v. schwarzii** (Lau) N.P. Taylor.

'*E. spinibarbis*' Hort. F.A. Haage *sec.* Bkbg. = **Echinocereus cinerascens v. ehrenbergii** (Pfeiff.) H. Bravo-H.

E. standleyi B. & R. = **Echinocereus viridiflorus** Engelm.

E. steereae Clover = **Echinocereus pectinatus v. dasyacanthus** (Engelm.) N.P. Taylor.

E. stramineus v. conglomeratus (Foerster ex Sch.) H. Bravo-H. = **Echinocereus stramineus** (Engelm.) Ruempler.

E. subinermis v. aculeatus G. Unger = **Echinocereus subinermis** S–D ex Scheer.

E. subinermis v. luteus (B. & R.) Bkbg. = **Echinocereus subinermis** Salm-Dyck ex Scheer.

'*E. subterraneus*' Bkbg. = **Echinocereus sciurus** (K. Brandegee) Dams.

E. tayopensis W.T. Marsh = **Echinocereus stoloniferus v. tayopensis** (W.T. Marsh) N.P. Taylor.

E. viridiflorus v. chloranthus (Engelm.) Bkbg. = **Echinocereus chloranthus** (Engelm.) Hort. F.A. Haage.

E. viridiflorus v. cylindricus (Engelm.) Ruempler = **Echinocereus chloranthus v. cylindricus** (Engelm.) N.P. Taylor.

E. weinbergii Weingart = **Echinocereus pulchellus v. weinbergii** (Weingart) N.P. Taylor.

Echinofossulocactus albatus (Dietr.) B. & R. = **Stenocactus albatus** (Dietr.) A.W. Hill.

E. anfractuosus (Mart.) Lawr. = **Stenocactus crispatus** complex.

E. arrigens (Link ex Dietr.) B. & R. = **Stenocactus crispatus** complex.

E. boedekerianus (Berg.) Croiz. = status doubtful.

E. bustamentei (Bravo) Croiz. = **Stenocactus crispatus** complex.

E. caespitosus Bkbg. = status doubtful.

E. confusus B. & R. = status doubtful.

E. coptonogonus (Lem.) Lawr. = **Stenocactus coptonogonus** (Lem.) A.W. Hill.

E. crispatus (DC) Lawr. = **Stenocactus crispatus** (DC) A.W. Hill.

E. dichroacanthus (Mart. ex Pfeiff.) B. & R. = status doubtful.

'*E. erectocentrus*' Bkbg. = status doubtful.

E. gladiatus (Link & Otto) Lawr. = status doubtful.

E. grandicornis (Lem.) B. & R. = status doubtful.

E. guerraianus Bkbg. = **Stenocactus crispatus** complex.

E. hastatus (Hopff. ex Sch.) B. & R. = status doubtful.

E. heteracanthus (Muehlpf.) B. & R. = status doubtful.

E. kelleranus (Dietr.) B. & R. = ?**Stenocactus crispatus** complex.

E. lamellosus (Dietr.) B. & R. = **Stenocactus crispatus** complex.

E. lancifer (Dietr.) B. & R. = **Stenocactus crispatus** complex.

E. lexarzai (Bravo) Croiz. = **Stenocactus crispatus** complex.

E. lloydii B. & R. = **Stenocactus multicostatus 'lloydii'**.

E. multiareolatus (Bravo) = **Stenocactus crispatus** complex.

E. multicostatus (Hildm. ex Sch.) B. & R. = **Stenocactus multicostatus** (Hildm. ex Sch.) A.W. Hill.

E. ochoterenaus (Tieg.) Whitmore = **Stenocactus ochoterenaus** Tieg.

E. pentacanthus (Lem.) B. & R. = status doubtful.

E. phyllacanthus (Mart.) Lawr. = **Stenocactus phyllacanthus** (Mart.) A.W. Hill.

E. tetraxiphus (S–D ex Sch.) Oehme = status doubtful.

E. tricuspidatus (Scheidw.) B. & R. = **Stenocactus phyllacanthus** (Mart.) A.W. Hill.

E. vaupelianus (Werd.) Whitmore = **Stenocactus vaupelianus** (Werd.) A.W. Hill.

E. violaciflorus (Quehl) B. & R. = **Stenocactus crispatus** complex.

E. wippermannii (Muehlpf.) B. & R. = status doubtful.

E. xiphacanthus (Miq.) Bkbg. = status doubtful.

E. zacatecasensis B. & R. = **Stenocactus multicostatus 'zacatecasensis'**.

Encephalocarpus strobiliformis (Werd.) Berg. = **Pelecyphora strobiliformis** (Werd.) Kreuz.

Echinopsis aurantiaca Friedr. & Rowley = **Acanthocalycium thionanthum v. aurantiacum** (Rausch) Don.

E. brasiliensis Fric ex Pazout = **Echinopsis oxygona** (Link) Zucc.

E. calliantholilacina Card. = **Echinopsis obrepanda** (S–D) Sch.

E. callichroma Card. = **Echinopsis obrepanda** (S–D) Sch.

E. calorubra Card. = **Echinopsis obrepanda v. calorubra** (Card.) Rausch.

E. campylacantha Pfeiff. non R. Mey. = **Echinopsis leucantha** (Gill.) Walp.

'*E. carmineoflora*' = **Echinopsis obrepanda** (S–D) Sch.

E. cerdana Card. = **Lobivia ferox** B. & R.

E. cochabambensis Bkbg. see **Echinopsis bridgesii**.

E. cordobensis Speg. = **Echinopis leucantha** (Gill.) Walp.

E. coronata Card. = **Echinopsis obrepanda** (S–D) Sch.

E. cotacajesi Card. = **Echinopsis bridgesii** S–D.

E. eyriesii v. grandiflora R. Mey non Link = **Echinopsis oxygona fa. brevispina** Ritt.

E. fallax (Oehme) Friedr. = **Lobivia aurea v. fallax** (Oehme) Rausch.

E. fiebrigii Guerke = **Echinopsis obrepanda** (S–D) Sch.

E. glaucina Friedr. & Rowley = **Acanthocalycium thionanthum v. glaucum** (Ritt.) Don. ex Rausch.

E. hamatacantha Bkbg. = **Echinopsis ancistrophora** Speg.

E. herbasii Card. = **Echinopsis mamillosa** Guerke.

E. hystrichoides Ritt. = **Echinopsis mamillosa v. hystrichoides** (Ritt.) Rausch.

E. ibicuatensis Card. = **Echinopsis bridgesii** S–D.

E. intricatissima Speg. = **Echinopsis leucantha** (Gill.) Walp.

'*E. kermesina*' = catalogue name = **Echinopsis mamillosa v. kermesina** (Krainz) Fried.

E. kratochviliana Bkbg. = **Echinopsis ancistrophora** Speg.

E. lecoriensis Card. = **Lobivia ferox** B. & R.

E. leucorhodantha Bkbg. = **Echinopsis ancistrophora** Speg.

E. mataranensis Card. = **Echinopsis obrepanda** (S–D) Sch.

E. multiplex (Pfeiff.) Zucc. = **Echinopsis oxygona** (Link) Zucc.

E. orozasana Ritt. = **Echinopsis mamillosa** Guerke.

E. pamparuizii Card. = **Echinopsis semidenudata** Card.

'*E. paraguayensis*' Knebel = **Echinopsis dehrenbergii** Fric.

E. pelecyrhachis Bkbg. = **Echinopsis ancistrophora** Speg.

E. pojoensis Card. = **Echinopsis bridgesii** S–D.

E. polyancistra Bkbg. = **Echinopsis ancistrophora** Speg.

E. potosina Werd. = **Lobivia ferox** B. & R.

E. pseudomamillosa Card. = **Echinopsis obrepanda** (S–D) Sch.

E. riviere-de-caraltii Card. = **Echinopsis obrepanda** (S–D) Sch.

E. robinsoniana Werd. = **Echinopsis minuana** Speg.

E. rojasii Card. = **Echinopsis obrepanda** (S–D) Sch.

E. roseo-lilacina Card. = **Echinopsis obrepanda** (S–D) Sch.

'*E. seminuda*' = **Echinopsis semidenudata** Card.

E. spegazziniana B. & R. = **Echinopsis leucantha** (Gill.) Walp.

E. toralapana Card. = **Echinopsis obrepanda** (S–D) Sch.

E. turbinata (Pfeiff.) Zucc. = **Echinopsis eyriesii** (Turp.) Zucc.

E. vallegrandensis Card. = **Echinopsis bridgesii** S–D.

E. werdermannii Fric ex Fleischer = **Echinopsis oxygona** (Link) Zucc.

Eriocactus claviceps Ritt. = **Notocactus schumannianus** (Sch.) Berg. emend Buin.

E. grossei (Sch.) Bkbg. = **Notocactus schumannianus** (Sch.) Berg. emend. Buin. jr.

E. leninghausii (Haage jr.) Bkbg. = **Notocactus leninghausii** Haage jr.

E. magnificus Ritt. = **Notocactus magnificus** (Ritt.) Krainz.

Eriosyce algarrobensis Ritt. = **Eriosyce sandillon** (Remy) Phil.

E. aurata Bkbg. = **Eriosyce sandillon** (Remy) Phil.

E. ausseliana Ritt. *n.n.* = **Eriosyce sandillon** (Remy) Phil.

E. ceratistes B. & R. = **Eriosyce sandillon** (Remy) Phil.

E. ihotzkyanae Ritt. = **Eriosyce sandillon** (Remy) Phil.

E. lapampaensis Ritt. = **Eriosyce sandillon** (Remy) Phil.

E. rodentiophila Ritt. = **Eriosyce megacarpa** Ritt.

E. spinibarbis Ritt. = **Eriosyce sandillon** (Remy) Phil.

Escobaria aggregata = a name mis-applied to **Escobaria vivipara**.

E. asperispina (Boed.) D. Hunt = **Escobaria missouriensis v. asperispina** (Boed.) N.P. Taylor.

E. bella B. & R. = status doubtful.

E. chaffeyi B. & R. = **Escobaria dasyacantha v. chaffeyi** (B. & R.) N.P. Taylor.

E. duncanii (Hester) Bkbg. = **Escobaria dasyacantha** (Engelm.) B. & R.

E. guadalupensis see under **Escobaria sneedii**.

E. lloydii B. & R. = status doubtful.

E. muehlbaueriana (Boed.) Knuth = **Escobaria emskoetteriana** (Quehl) Borg.

E. nellieae (Croiz.) Bkbg. = **Escobaria minima** (Baird) D. Hunt.

E. orcuttii & vars see under **Escobaria villardii**.

'*E. rigida*' Bkbg. = **Escobaria laredoi** (Glass & Foster) N.P. Taylor.

E. runyonii B. & R. = **Escobaria emskoetteriana** (Quehl) Borg.

E. sandbergii see under **Escobaria villardii**.

E. sneedii v. leei (Boed.) D. Hunt = **Escobaria leei** Boed.

E. tuberculosa (Engelm.) B. & R. = **Escobaria strobiliformis** (Poselg.) Boed.

E. variicolor Tieg. = **Escobaria strobiliformis** (Poselg.) Boed.

Ferocactus acanthodes sensu B. & R. = **Ferocactus cylindraceus** (Engelm.) Orcutt.

F. acanthodes v. eastwoodiae Benson = **Ferocactus cylindraceus v. eastwoodiae** (Benson) N.P. Taylor.

F. acanthodes v. lecontei (Engelm.) G. Lindsay = **Ferocactus cylindraceus v. lecontei** (Engelm.) H. Bravo-H.

F. acanthodes v. tortulispinus (H. Gates) G. Lindsay = **Ferocactus cylindraceus** (Engelm.) Orcutt.

F. alamosanus (B. & R.) B. & R. = **Ferocactus pottsii v. alamosanus** (B. & R.) G. Unger.

F. bicolor (Gal. ex Pfeiff.) N.P. Taylor = **Thelocactus bicolor** (Gal. ex Pfeiff.) B. & R.

F. bicolor v. bolaensis (Runge) N.P. Taylor = **Thelocactus bicolor v. bolaensis** (Runge) Berg.

F. bicolor v. flavidispinus (Bkbg.) N.P. Taylor = **Thelocactus bicolor** (Gal. ex Pfeiff.) B. & R.

F. bicolor v. schwarzii (Bkbg.) N.P. Taylor = **Thelocactus bicolor v. schwarzii** (Bkbg.) E.F. Anderson.

F. coloratus H. Gates = **Ferocactus gracilis v. coloratus** (H. Gates) G. Lindsay.

F. covillei B. & R. = **Ferocactus emoryi** (Engelm.) Orcutt.

F. echidne v. victoriensis (Rose) G. Lindsay = **Ferocactus echidne** (DC) B. & R.

'*F. electracanthus*' hort. = **Ferocactus histrix** (DC) G. Lindsay.

'*F. guirocobensis*' F. Schwarz n.n. = **Ferocactus pottsii** (Salm-Dyck) Bkbg.

F. hamatacanthus v. crassispinus (Engelm.) Benson = **Ferocactus hamatacanthus** (Muehlenpf.) B. & R.

F. hastifer (Werd. & Boed.) N.P. Taylor = **Thelocactus hastifer** (Werd. & Boed.) Knuth.

F. heterochromus (Weber) N.P. Taylor = **Thelocactus heterochromus** (Weber) van Oosten.

F. leucacanthus (Zucc. ex Pfeiff.) N.P. Taylor = **Thelocactus leucacanthus** (Zucc. ex Pfeiff.) B. & R.

F. mathssonii = **Ancistrocactus crassihamatus** (Web.) Benson.

F. orcuttii (Engelm.) B. & R. = **Ferocactus viridescens** (Torrey & A. Gray) B. & R.

F. peninsulae v. viscainensis (H. Gates) G. Lindsay = **Ferocactus gracilis v. coloratus** (H. Gates) G. Lindsay.

F. rafaelensis (Purpus) Borg = **Ferocactus echidne** (DC) B. & R.

F. rectispinus (Engelm.) B. & R. = **Ferocactus emoryi v. rectispinus** (Engelm.) N.P. Taylor.

F. recurvus Borg = **Ferocactus macrodiscus v. spiralis** (Karw. ex Pfeiff.) N.P. Taylor.

F. setispinus (Engelm.) Benson = **Thelocactus setispinus** (Engelm.) E.F. Anderson.

'*F. stainesii*' = **Ferocactus pilosus** (Gal. ex S–D) Werd.

F. townsendianus B. & R. = **Ferocactus peninsulae v. townsendianus** (B. & R.) N.P. Taylor.

F. townsendianus v. santa-maria (B. & R.) G. Lindsay = **Ferocactus peninsulae v. santa-maria** (B. & R.) N.P. Taylor.

F. victoriensis (Rose) Bkbg. = **Ferocactus echidne** (DC) B. & R.

F. viscainensis H. Gates = **Ferocactus gracilis v. coloratus** (H. Gates) G. Lindsay.

Frailea albiareolata Buin. & Bred. = **Frailea pumila** (Lem.) B. & R.

F. asterioides Werd. = **Frailea castanea** Bkbg.

F. carmenifilamentosa Kilian = **Frailea pumila** (Lem.) B. & R.

F. friedrichii Buin. & Moser. = **Frailea pumila** (Lem.) B. & R.

F. perbella Prestle = **Frailea phaeodisca** Speg.

F. pygmaea v. phaeodisca (Speg.) Ito = **Frailea phaeodisca** Speg.

Glandulicactus crassihamatus (Web.) Bkbg. = **Ancistrocactus crassihamatus** (Web.) Benson.

G. uncinatus (Gal.) Bkbg. = **Ancistrocactus uncinatus** (Gal.) L. Benson.

Gymnocalycium acorrugatum Lambert = **Gymnocalycium castellanosii** Bkbg.

G. albispinum Bkbg. = **Gymnocalycium bruchii** (Speg.) Hoss.

G. artigas Hert. = **Gymnocalycium uruguayense** (Arech.) B. & R.

G. asterium Ito = **Gymnocalycium stellatum** Speg.

G. bayensis n.n. = **Gymnocalycium schroederianum v. bayense** Kiesling.

G. bodenbenderianum (Hoss.) Berg. = **Gymnocalycium stellatum** Speg.

G. brachyanthum (Guerke) B. & R. = **Gymnocalycium monvillei** (Lem.) B. & R.

G. brachypetalum Speg. = **Gymnocalycium gibbosum** (Haw.) Pfeiff.

G. chubutense (Speg.) Speg. = **Gymnocalycium gibbosum** (Haw.) Pfeiff.

G. chuquisacanum Card. = **Gymnocalycium pflanzii** (Vpl.) Werd.

G. comarapense Bkbg. *n.n.* = **Gymnocalycium pflanzii v. zegarrae** (Card.) Don.

G. deeszianum Doeltz = status doubtful.

G. delaetii = **Gymnocalycium schickendantzii v. delaetii** (Sch.) Bkbg.

'*G. eluhilton*' = catalogue name = **Gymnocalycium hybopleurum** (Sch.) Bkbg.

'*G. esposteo*' = catalogue name.

G. euchlorum Bkbg. *nom. prov.* = **Gymnocalycium hybopleurum** (Sch.) Bkbg.

G. eytianum Card. = **Gymnocalycium pflanzii** (Vpl.) Werd.

G. fricianum Plesnik = **Gymnocalycium tudae** Ito.

'*G. gerardii*' = catalogue name = **Gymnocalycium gibbosum** (Haw.) Pfeiff.

G. grandiflorum Bkbg. = status doubtful.

G. guanchinense Schuetz = **Gymnocalycium mazanense** Bkbg.

G. guerkeanum (Heese) B. & R. = **Gymnocalycium uruguayense** (Arech.) B. & R.

'*G. hammerschmidii*' Bkbg. = **Gymnocalycium chiquitanum** Card.

'*G. hennisii*' = hort. hybrid.

G. horstii v. buenekeri Buin. = **Gymnocalycium buenekeri** Smales.

G. hossei (Haage jr.) Berg. = status doubtful.

G. hyptiacanthum (Lem.) B. & R. = status doubtful.

G. izozogsii Card. = **Gymnocalycium tudae v. 'izozogsii'**.

G. joossensianum (Berg.) B. & R. = status doubtful.

G. kozelskyanum Schuetz = **Gymnocalycium stellatum** Speg.

G. kurtzianum (Guerke) B. & R. = **Gymnocalycium mostii** (Guerke) B. & R.

G. lafaldense Vpl. = **Gymnocalycium bruchii** (Speg) Hoss.

G. lagunillasense Card. = **Gymnocalycium pflanzii v. lagunillasense** (Card.) Don.

G. leptanthum (Speg.) Speg. = status doubtful.

G. marquezii Card. = **Gymnocalycium pflanzii** (Vpl.) Werd.

G. matoense Buin. & Bred. = **Gymnocalycium tudae** Ito.

G. meglothelos (Sencke) B. & R. = status doubtful.

G. megatae Ito = **Gymnocalycium tudae** Ito.

G. melanocarpum (Ar.) B. & R. = **Gymnocalycium uruguayense** (Arech.) B. & R.

G. michoga (Fric) Ito = **Gymnocalcium schickendantzii** (Web.) B. & R.

G. mihanovichii v. friedrichii Werd. = **Gymnocalycium friedrichii** Pazout.

G. millaresii Card. = **Gymnocalycium pflanzii v. millaresii** (Card.) Don.

G. mucidum Oehme = **Gymnocalycium mazanense** Bkbg.

G. netrelianum (Monv.) B. & R. = **Gymnocalycium leeanum** (Hook.) B. & R.

G. ochoterenai Bkbg. = **Gymnocalycium stellatum** Speg.

G. oenanthemum Bkbg. = status doubtful.

G. onychacanthum Ito = *Gymnocalycium tudae* Ito.

'*G. ourselianum*' = **Gymnocalycium multiflorum** (Hook.) B. & R.

G. paraguayense (Sch.) Schuetz = **Gymnocalycium denudatum** (Link & Otto) Pfeiff.

G. parvulum (Speg.) Speg. = **Gymnocalycium quehlianum** (Haage jr.) Berg.

G. pflanzii v. izozogsii (Card.) Don. = **Gymnocalycium tudae v. 'izozogsii'**.

G. platense (Speg.) B. & R. = status doubtful.

'*G. pseudomalacocarpus*' Bkbg. = '**Gymnocalycium tudae v. pseudomalacocarpus**' (Bkbg.) Don.

'*G. pseudonobile*' = catalogue name.

G. pseudoragonesii n.n. = **Gymnocalycium obductum n.n.**

G. pugionacanthum Bkbg. = **Gymnocalycium hybopleurum** (Sch.) Bkbg.

G. pungens Fleischer = **Gymnocalycium schickendantzii** (Web.) B. & R.

G. riograndense Card. = **Gymnocalycium pflanzii v. riograndense** (Card.) Don.

G. riojense Fric ex Pazout = **Gymnocalycium stellatum** Speg.

G. stuckertii (Speg.) B. & R. = status doubtful.

'*G. tortuga*' hort. = **Gymnocalycium tudae** Ito.

G. triacanthum Bkbg. = **Gymnocalycium stellatum** Speg.

G. venturianum Fric = **Gymnocalycium baldianum** (Speg) Speg.

G. zegarrae Card. = **Gymnocalycium pflanzii v. zegarrae** (Card.) Don.

Hamatocactus hamatacanthus (Muehlenpf.) Knuth = **Ferocactus hamatacanthus** (Muehlenpf.) B. & R.

H. setispinus (Engelm.) B. & R. = **Thelocactus setispinus** (Engelm.) E.F. Anderson.

H. sinuatus (Dietr.) Orcutt = **Ferocactus hamatacanthus v. sinuatus** (Dietr.) Benson.

Helianthocereus crassicaulis Bkbg. = **Lobivia grandiflora v. crassicaulis** (Bkbg.) Rausch.

H. grandiflorus Bkbg. = **Lobivia grandiflora** B. & R.

Horridocactus aconcaguensis (Ritt.) Bkbg. = **Neoporteria horrida** (Remy ex Gay) D. Hunt.

H. andicolus Ritt.
H. andicolus v. *descendens* Ritt.
H. andicolus v. *mollensis* Ritt. } = **Neoporteria curvispina** (Bert.) Don. & Rowley
H. andicolus v. *robustus* Ritt.

H. armatus (Ritt.) Bkbg. = **Neoporteria horrida** (Remy ex Gay) D. Hunt.

H. atroviridis (Ritt.) Bkbg. = **Neoporteria atroviridis** (Ritt.) R.M. Ferryman.

H. carrizalensis (Ritt.) Bkbg. = **Neoporteria totoralensis v. carrizalensis** (Ritt.) R.M. Ferryman.

H. choapensis (Ritt.) Bkbg. = **Neoporteria horrida** (Remy ex Gay) D. Hunt.

H. crispus (Ritt.) Bkbg. = **Neoporteria crispa** (Ritt.) Don. & Rowley.

H. curvispinus (Bert.) Bkbg. = **Neoporteria curvispina** (Bert.) Don. & Rowley.

H. echinus (Ritt.) Bkbg. = **Neoporteria echinus** (Ritt.) R.M. Ferryman.

H. eriosyzoides Ritt. = **Neoporteria eriosyzoides** (Ritt.) Don. & Rowley.

H. froehlichianus (Sch.) Bkbg. = status doubtful.

H. garaventai Ritt. = **Neoporteria garaventai** (Ritt.) R.M. Ferryman.

H. geissei (Pos.) Doelz = status doubtful.

H. grandiflorus (Ritt.) Bkbg. = **Neoporteria curvispina v. grandiflora** (Ritt.) Don. & Rowley.

H. heinrichianus Bkbg. = **Neoporteria heinrichiana** (Bkbg.) R.M. Ferryman.

H. horridus (Remy ex Gay) Bkbg. = **Neoporteria horrida** (Remy ex Gay) D. Hunt.

H. kesselringianus Doelz = status doubtful.

H. lissocarpus & v. *gracilis* (Ritt.) Bkbg. = **Neoporteria curvispina** (Bert.) Don. & Rowley.

H. marksianus & v. *tunensis* (Ritt.) Bkbg. = **Neoporteria marksiana** (Ritt.) Don. & Rowley.

H. nigricans (Dietr.) Bkbg. & Doelz = status doubtful.

H. paucicostatus & v. *viridis* (Ritt.) = **Neoporteria paucicostata** (Ritt.) Don. & Rowley.

H. scoparius n.n. Ritt. = **Neoporteria calderana** (Ritt.) Don. & Rowley.

H. tuberisulcatus (Jac.) Ito. = **Neoporteria horrida** (Remy ex Gay) D. Hunt.

H. vallenarensis (Ritt.) Bkbg. = **Neoporteria vallenarensis** (Ritt.) Hoffmann.

Islaya chalaensis Ritt. n.n. = **Neoporteria islayensis** (Foerst.) Don & Rowley.

I. copiapoides Rauh & Bkbg. = **Neoporteria islayensis** (Foerst.) Don. & Rowley.

I. divaricatiflora Ritt. = **Neoporteria islayensis v. divaricatiflora** (Ritt.) Don. & Rowley.

I. flavida Ritt. n.n. = **Neoporteria islayensis** (Foerst.) Don. & Rowley.

I. grandiflorens Rauh & Bkbg. = **Neoporteria islayensis** (Foerst.) Don. & Rowley.

I. grandis & v. *brevispina* Rauh & Bkbg. = **Neoporteria islayensis v. grandis** (Rauh & Bkbg.) Don. & Rowley.

I. islayensis (Foerst.) Bkbg. = **Neoporteria islayensis** (Foerst.) Don. & Rowley.

I. krainziana Ritt. = **Neoporteria krainziana** (Ritt.) Don. & Rowley.

'*I. longicarpa*' = **Neoporteria islayensis** (Foerst.) Don. & Rowley.

I. maritima Ritt. n.n. = **Neoporteria islayensis** (Foerst.) Don. & Rowley.

I. minor Bkbg. = **Neoporteria islayensis** (Foerst.) Don. & Rowley.

I. minuscula Ritt. n.n. = **Neoporteria islayensis** (Foerst.) Don. & Rowley.

I. mollendensis (Vpl.) Bkbg. = **Neoporteria islayensis** (Foerst.) Don. & Rowley.

I. omasensis Ostolaza & Mischler = **Neoporteria omasensis** (Ostolaza & Mischler) R.M. Ferryman.

I. paucispina Rauh & Bkbg. = **Neoporteria islayensis** (Foerst.) Don. & Rowley.

I. paucispinosa Rauh & Bkbg. = **Neoporteria islayensis** (Foerst.) Don. & Rowley.

Krainzia guelzowiana (Werd.) Bkbg. = **Mammillaria guelzowiana** Werd.

K. longiflora (B. & R.) Bkbg. = **Mammillaria longiflora** (B. & R.) Berg.

Lepidocoryphantha macromeris (Englm.) Bkbg. = **Coryphantha macromeris** Engelm.

L. runyonii (B. & R.) Bkbg. = **Coryphantha macromeris v. runyonii** (B. & R.) Benson.

Lobivia aculeata Buin. = **Lobivia pentlandii** (Hook.) B. & R.

L. adpressispina Ritt. = **Lobivia pugionacantha v. cornuta** (Rausch) Rausch.

L. aguilari Vasq. = **Echinopsis obrepanda v. aguilari** (Vasq.) Rausch.

L. akersii Rausch = **Lobivia tegeleriana v. akersii** (Rausch) Rausch.

L. allegraiana Bkbg. = **Lobivia hertrichiana** Bkbg.

L. amblayensis & v. *albispina* Rausch = **Lobivia haematantha v. amblayensis** (Rausch) Rausch.

L. andalgalensis B. & R. *non* Web. = **Lobivia grandiflora v. crassicaulis** (Bkbg.) Rausch.

L. argentea Bkbg. = **Lobivia pentlandii** (Hook.) B. & R.

L. atrovirens v. *raulii* (Rausch) Rausch = **Rebutia raulii** Rausch.

L. atrovirens v. *ritteri* (Wessn.) Rausch = **Rebutia ritteri** (Wessn.) Don.

L. atrovirens v. *yuquinensis* (Rausch) Rausch = **Rebutia yuquinensis** Rausch.

L. aurantiaca Bkbg. = **Lobivia pentlandii** (Hook.) B. & R.

L. aureolilacina Card. = **Lobivia ferox v. longispina** (B. & R.) Rausch.

L. aureosenilis Knize = **Lobivia pampana** B. & R.

L. ayacuchoensis Ito = **Lobivia tegeleriana** Bkbg.

L. backebergii subsp. wrightiana (Bkbg.) Rausch = **Lobivia wrightiana** Bkbg.

L. backebergii subsp. zecheri (Rausch) Rausch = **Lobivia zecheri** Rausch.

L. backebergii v. *larae* (Card.) Rausch = **Lobivia larae** Card.

L. backbergii v. oxyalabastra (Card. & Rausch) Rausch = **Lobvia oxyalabastra** Card. & Rausch.

L. binghamiana Bkbg. = **Lobiva hertrichiana** Bkbg.

L. boliviensis B. & R. = **Lobivia pentlandii** (Hook.) B. & R.

L. breviflora Bkbg. = **Lobivia sanguiniflora** Bkbg.

L. brunneo-rosea Bkbg. = **Lobivia pentlandii** (Hook.) B. & R.

L. buiningiana Ritt. = **Lobivia jajoiana** Bkbg.

L. caespitosa (Purp.) B. & R. = **Lobivia maximiliana v. caespitosa** (Purp.) Rausch.

L. caespitosa v. rinconadensis Ritt. = **Lobivia maximiliana v. hermanniana** (Bkbg.) Rausch.

'L. callochrysea' = **Lobivia aurea v. callochrysea** (Ritt.) Rausch.

L. camataquiensis Card. = **Lobivia lateritia** (Guerke) B. & R.

L. campicola Ritt. = **Lobivia pugionacantha v. culpinensis** (Ritt.) Rausch.

L. cariquinensis Card. = **Lobivia maximiliana** (Heyder) Bkbg.

L. carminantha Bkbg. = **Lobivia pentlandii** (Hook.) B. & R.

L. capinotensis Rausch *n.n.* = **Lobivia pentlandii** (Hook.) B. & R.

L. cardenasiana Rausch = **'Echinopsis cardensiana'**

L. caespitosa v. rinconadensis Ritt. = **Lobivia maximiliana v. hermanniana** (Bkbg.) Rausch.

L. charcasina Card. = **Lobivia cinnabarina** (Hook.) B. & R.

L. chilensis Knize *n.n.* = **Lobivia wrightiana** Bkbg.

L. chlorogona Wessn. = **Lobivia haematantha v. rebutioides** (Bkbg.) Rausch.

L. chorrillosensis Rausch = **Lobivia haematantha v. chorrillosensis** (Rausch) Rausch.

L. churinensis Johns. *n.n.* = **Lobivia tegeleriana v. akersii** (Rausch) Rausch.

L. cintiensis Card. = **Lobivia lateritia** (Guerke) B. & R.

L. claeysiana Bkbg. = **Lobivia ferox v. longispina** (B. & R.) Rausch.

L. corbula (Herrera) B. & R. = **Lobivia maximiliana v. corbula** (Herrera) Rausch.

L. corbula B. & R. (non Herrera) = **Lobivia maximilliana** (Heyder) Bkbg.

L. cornuta Rausch = **Lobivia pugionacantha v. cornuta** (Rausch) Rausch.

L. crassicaulis Bkbg. = **Lobivia grandiflora v. crassicaulis** (Bkbg.) Rausch.

L. cruciaureispina Knize = **Lobivia maximiliana v. westii** (Hutch.) Rausch.

L. culpinensis Ritt. = **Lobivia pugionacantha v. culpinensis** (Ritt.) Rausch.

L. cylindracea Bkbg. = **Lobivia aurea v. shaferi** (B. & R.) Rausch.

L. cylindrica Bkbg. = **Lobivia aurea** (B. & R.) Bkbg.

L. densispina Werd. = **Lobivia haematantha v. densispina** (Werd.) Rausch.

'L. densispina v. leucomalla' = **Lobivia aurea v. leucomalla** (Wessn.) Rausch.

L. digitiformis Bkbg. = **Rebutia pygmaea** (Fries) B. & R.

L. dobeana Doelz = **Lobivia aurea v. dobeana** (Doelz) Rausch.

L. dragae Fric *n.n.* = **Lobivia chrysantha** (Werd.) Bkbg.

L. draxleriana Rausch = **Lobivia cinnabarina v. draxleriana** (Rausch) Rausch.

L. drijveriana & vars. Bkbg. = **Lobivia haematantha v. kuehnrichii** (Fric) Rausch.

L. ducis pauli Fric = **Lobivia ferox** B. & R.

L. ducis pauli v. rubriflora Schuetz = **Lobivia ferox v. longispina** (B. & R.) Rausch.

L. duursmaiana Bkbg. = **Lobivia sanguiniflora** Bkbg.

L. echinata Rausch = **Lobivia hertrichiana** Bkbg.

L. einsteinii v. aureiflora (Bkbg.) Rausch = **'Rebutia einsteinii v. aureiflora'**.

L. einsteinii v. gonjianii (Kies.) Don. = **'Rebutia einsteinii v. gonjianii'**.

L. elongata Bkbg. = **Lobivia haematantha v. elongata** (Bkbg.) Rausch.

L. euanthema Bkbg. = **'Rebutia euanthema'**.

L. fallax Oehme = **Lobivia aurea v. fallax** (Oehme) Rausch.

'L. famatimensis' hort. = **Lobivia haematantha v. densispina** (Werd.) Rausch.

L. famatimensis sensu Bkbg. = **Lobivia haematantha v. rebutioides** (Bkbg.) Rausch.

L. famatimensis v. leucomalla (Wessn.) Bkbg. = **Lobivia aurea v. leucomalla** (Wessn.) Rausch.

L. formosa v. bruchii (B. & R.) Rausch = **Lobivia bruchii** B. & R.

L. formosa v. kieslingii (Rausch) Rausch = **Lobivia kieslingii** Rausch.

L. formosa v. rosarioana (Rausch) Rausch = **Lobivia rosarioana** Rausch.

L. fricii Rausch = **Lobivia tiegeliana v. cinnabarina** (Fric) Rowley.

L. glauca & v. paucicostata Rausch = **Lobivia jajoiana v. paucicostata** (Rausch) Rausch.

L. glaucescens Ritt. = **Lobivia pampana** B. & R.

'L. grandis v. aureiflora' = catalogue name = **Lobivia rosarioana** Rausch.

L. graulichii v. cinnabarina Fric = **Lobivia tiegeliana v. cinnabarina** (Fric) Rowley.

L. haageana Bkbg. = **Lobivia marsoneri** (Werd.) Bkbg.

L. haagei (Fric & Schelle) Wessn. = **Rebutia pygmaea v. haagei** Fric & Schelle.

L. haagei v. canacruzensis (Rausch) Rausch = **'Rebutia pygmaea v. canacruzensis'**.

L. haagei v. crassa Rausch = **'Rebutia pygmaea v. crassa'**.

L. haagei v. eos (Rausch) Rausch = **'Rebutia pygmaea v. eos'**

L. haagei v. elegantula Rausch = **'Rebutia pygmaea v. elegantula'**

L. haagei v. mudanensis (Rausch) Rausch = **'Rebutia pygmaea v. mudanensis'**.

L. haagei v. nazarenoensis (Rausch) Rausch = **'Rebutia pygmaea v. nazarenoensis'**.

L. haagei v. pallida (Rausch) Rausch = **'Rebutia pygmaea v. pallida'**.

L. haagei v. pelzliana Rausch = **'Rebutia pygmaea v. pelzliana'**.

L. haagei v. violascens (Ritt.) Rausch = **Rebutia violascens** Ritt.

L. hastifera Werd. = **Lobivia ferox v. longispina** (B. & R.) Rausch.

L. hermanniana Bkbg. = **Lobivia maximiliana v. hermanniana** (Bkbg.) Rausch.

L. higginsiana Bkbg. = **Lobivia pentlandii** (Hook.) B. & R.

L. horrida Ritt. = **Lobivia ferox v. longispina** (B. & R.) Rausch.

L. hualfinensis & v. fechseri Rausch = **Lobivia haematantha v. hualfinensis** (Rausch) Rausch.

L. huilcanota Rauh & Bkbg. = **Lobivia hertrichiana** Bkbg.

L. imporana Ritt. *n.n.* = **Lobivia lateritia** (Guerke) B. & R.

L. incaica Bkbg. = **Lobivia hertrichiana** Bkbg.

L. incuiensis Rauh & Bkbg. = **Lobivia tegeleriana v. incuiensis** (Rauh & Bkbg.) Rausch.

L. intermedia Rausch = **Lobivia maximiliana v. intermedia** (Rausch) Rausch.

L. iridescens Bkbg. = **Lobivia marsoneri v. iridescens** (Bkbg.) Rausch.

L. janseniana Bkbg. = **Lobivia chrysantha** (Werd.) Bkbg.

L. johnsoniana Bkbg. = **Lobivia pentlandii** (Hook.) B. & R.

L. klusacekii Fric = **Lobiva chrysantha** (Werd.) Bkbg.

L. kuehnrichii Fric = **Lobivia haemantha v. kuehnrichii** (Fric) Rausch.

L. kupperiana Bkbg. = **Lobivia lateritia v. kupperiana** (Bkbg.) Rausch.

L. kupperiana v. rubriflora Bkbg. = **Lobivia lateritia v. rubriflora** (Bkbg.) Rausch.

L. lauramarca Rauh & Bkbg. = **Lobivia maximiliana v. corbula** (Herrera) Rausch.

L. lauii Don. = **Lobivia hertrichiana** Bkbg.

L. leptacantha Rausch = **Lobivia schieliana v. leptacantha** (Rausch) Rausch.

L. leucomalla Wessn. = **Lobivia aurea v. leucomalla** (Wessn.) Rausch.

L. leucorhodon Bkbg. = **Lobivia pentlandii** (Hook.) B. & R.

L. leucoviolacea Bkbg. = **Lobivia pentlandii** (Hook.) B. & R.

L. longiflora Ito = **Lobivia maximiliana v. caespitosa** (Purp.) Rausch.

L. longispina B. & R. = **Lobivia ferox v. longispina** (B. & R.) Rausch.

L. markusii Rausch = **Lobivia chrysochete v. markusii** (Rausch) Rausch.

L. megacarpa Ritt. *n.n.* = **Echinopsis ayopayana** (Ritt.) Rausch.

L. miniatiflora Ritt. = **Lobivia maximiliana v. miniatiflora** (Ritt.) Rausch.

L. minuta Ritt. = **Lobivia hertrichiana** Bkbg.

L. mistiensis Bkbg. = **Lobivia pampana** B. & R.

L. mizquensis Rausch = **Echinopsis obrepanda v. mizquensis** (Rausch) Rausch.

L. muhriae Bkbg. = **Lobivia marsoneri v. iridescens** (Bkbg.) Rausch.

'*L. napina*' Pazout = **Lobivia haemantha v. rebutioides** (Bkbg.) Rausch.

L. neocinnabarina Bkbg. = **Lobivia acanthoplegma v. oligotricha** (Card.) Rausch.

L. nigrispina Bkbg. = **Lobivia haemantha v. kuehnrichii** (Fric) Rausch.

L. nigristoma Buin. = **Lobivia jajoiana v. nigristoma** (Buin.) Bkbg.

L. oligotricha Card. = **Lobivia acanthoplegma v. oligotricha** (Card.) Rausch.

L. omasuyana Card. = **Lobivia pentlandii** (Hook.) B. & R.

L. oyonica Akers *n.n.* = **Lobivia tegeleriana v. akersii** (Rausch) Rausch.

L. peclardiana Krainz = **Lobivia tiegeliana** Wessn.

L. pectinifera Wessn. = **Lobivia haemantha v. rebutioides** (Bkbg.) Rausch.

L. penca poma Blossf. *n.n.* = **Lobivia haemantha v. kuehnrichii** (Fric) Rausch.

L. pentlandii v. larae (Card.) Rausch = **Lobivia larae** Card.

L. pentlandii v. maximiliana (Heyder) Rausch = **Lobivia maximiliana** (Heyder) Bkbg.

L. pictiflorea Ritt. = **Lobivia ferox v. longispina** (B. & R.) Rausch.

L. planiceps Bkbg. = **Lobivia hertrichiana** Bkbg.

L. pojoensis Rausch = **Echinopsis rauschii** Friedm.

L. polaskiana Bkbg. = **Lobivia chrysantha** (Werd.) Bkbg.

L. polycephala Bkbg. = **Lobivia sanguiniflora** Bkbg.

'*L. potosina*' = **Lobivia ferox** B. & R.

L. prestoana Card. = **Lobivia cinnabarina** (Hook.) B. & R.

L. pseudocachensis Bkbg. = **Lobivia saltensis v. pseudocachensis** (Bkbg.) Rausch.

L. pseudocariquinensis Card. = **Lobivia maximiliana** (Heyder) Bkbg.

L. pseudocinnabarina Bkbg. = **Lobivia acanthoplegma v. oligotricha** (Card.) Rausch.

L. pugionacantha v. rossii (Boed.) Rausch = **Lobivia rossii** Boed.

L. pugionacantha v. versicolor (Rausch) Rausch = **Lobivia versicolor** Rausch.

L. pusilla Ritt. = **Lobivia tiegeliana v. pusilla** (Ritt.) Rausch.

L. pusilla fa. flaviflora Ritt. = **Lobivia tiegeliana v. flaviflora** (Ritt.) Rausch.

L. pygmaea (Fries) Bkbg. = **Rebutia pygmaea** (Fries) B. & R.

L. pygmaea v. colorea (Ritt.) Rausch = **'Rebutia pygmaea v. colorea'**.

L. pygmaea v. diersiana (Rausch) Rausch = **'Rebutia pygmaea v. diersiana'**.

L. pygmaea v. friedrichiana (Rausch) Rausch = **'Rebutia pygmaea v. friedrichiana'**.

L. pygmaea v. iscayachensis (Rausch) Rausch = **'Rebutia pygmaea v. iscayachensis'**.

L. quiabayensis Rausch = **Lobivia schieliana v. quiabayensis** (Rausch) Rausch.

L. raphidacantha Bkbg. = **Lobivia pentlandii** (Hook.) B. & R.

L. rebutioides & vars. Bkbg. = **Lobivia haemantha v. rebutioides** (Bkbg.) Rausch.

L. rubescens Bkbg. = **Lobivia marsoneri** (Werd.) Bkbg.

L. salitrensis Rausch = **Lobivia pugionacantha v. salitrensis** (Rausch) Rausch.

L. saltensis v. stilowiana (Bkbg.) Rausch = **Lobivia schreiteri v. stilowiana** (Bkbg.) Rausch.

L. schneideriana Bkbg. = **Lobivia pentlandii** (Hook.) B. & R.

L. scopulina Bkbg. = **Lobivia lateritia** (Guerke) B. & R.

L. shaferi B. & R. = **Lobivia aurea v. shaferi** (B. & R.) Rausch.

L. sicuaniensis Rausch = **Lobivia maximiliana v. sicuaniensis** (Rausch) Rausch.

L. simplex Rausch = **Lobivia hertrichiana v. simplex** (Rausch) Rausch.

L. spiniflora (Sch.) Rausch = **Acanthocalycium spiniflorum** (Sch.) Bkbg.

L. spiniflora v. klimpeliana (Weidl. & Werd.) Rausch = **Acanthocalycium spiniflorum v. klimpelianum** (Weidl. & Werd.) Don.

L. spiniflora v. violacea (Werd.) Rausch = **Acanthocalycium spiniflorum fa. violaceum** (Werd.) Don.

L. staffenii Fric = **Lobivia chrysantha** (Werd.) Bkbg.

L. steinmannii v. applanata Rausch = **'Rebutia steinmannii v. applanata'**.

L. steinmannii v. cincinnata (Rausch) Rausch = **'Rebutia steinmannii v. cincinnata'.**

L. steinmannii v. costata (Werd.) Rausch = **'Rebutia steinmannii v. costata'.**

L. steinmannii v. major Rausch = **'Rebutia steinmannii v. major'.**

L. steinmannii v. rauschii (Zech.) Rausch = **'Rebutia steinmannii v. rauschii'.**

L. stilowiana Bkbg. = **Lobivia schreiteri v. stilowiana** (Bkbg.) Rausch.

L. sublimiflora Bkbg. = **Lobivia haematantha v. rebutioides** (Bkbg.) Rausch.

L. taratensis Card. = **Lobivia acanthoplegma** (Bkbg.) Bkbg.

L. tenuispina Ritt. = **Lobivia chrysochete v. tenuispina** (Ritt.) Rausch.

L. thionantha v. aurantiaca (Rausch) Rausch = **Acanthocalycium thionanthum v. aurantiacum** (Rausch) Don.

L. thionantha v. brevispina (Ritt.) Rausch = **Acanthocalycium thionanthum v. brevispinum** (Ritt.) Don.

L. thionantha v. catamarcensis (Ritt.) Rausch = **Acanthocalycium thionanthum** (Speg.) Bkbg.

L. thionantha v. chionantha (Speg.) Rausch = **Acanthocalycium thionanthum v. chionanthum** (Speg.) Hoss.

L. thionantha v. ferrarii (Rausch) Rausch = **'Acanthocalycium thionanthum v. ferrarii'**

L. thionantha v. glauca (Ritt.) Rausch = **Acanthocalycium thioanthum v. glaucum** (Ritt.) Don.

L. thionantha v. variiflora (Bkbg.) Rausch = **Acanthocalycium thionanthum v. variiflorum** (Bkbg.) Don.

L. tiegeliana v. fricii Rausch = **Lobivia tiegeliana v. cinnabarina** (Fric) Rowley.

L. titicacensis Card. = **Lobivia pentlandii** (Hook.) B. & R.

L. uitewaaleana Buin. = **Lobivia marsoneri v. iridescens** (Bkbg.) Rausch.

L. varians Bkbg. = **Lobivia pentlandii** (Hook.) B. & R.

L. variispina Ritt. = **Lobivia ferox v. longispina** (B. & R.) Rausch.

L. vatteri Krainz = **Lobivia jajoiana v. nigristoma** (Buin.) Bkbg.

L. wegheiana Bkbg. = **Lobivia pentlandii** (Hook.) B. & R.

'L. wegneriana' Grunert & Kluegl. = **Lobivia hertrichiana** Bkbg.

L. wessneriana Fritz. = **Lobivia haematantha v. rebutioides** (Bkbg.) Rausch.

L. westii Hutch. = **Lobivia maximiliana v. westii** (Hutch.) Rausch.

L. winteriana Ritt. = **Lobivia wrightiana v. winteriana** (Ritt.) Rausch.

L. zudanensis Card. = **Lobivia cinnabarina** (Hook.) B. & R.

Lophophora echinata Croiz = **Lophophora williamsii** (Lem. ex S–D) Coult.

L. echinata v. diffusa Croiz = **Lophophora diffusa** (Croiz) Bravo.

'L. jordaniana' (Rebut) Kreuz. = **Lophophora williamsii** (Lem. ex S–D) Coult.

L. lutea (Rouh.) Bkbg. = status doubtful.

'L. ziegleri' Schmoll = status doubtful.

Malacocarpus see under *Wigginsia*.

Mamillopsis diguetii (Web.) B. & R. = status uncertain.

M. senilis (S–D) B. & R. = **Mammillaria senilis** [attrib. to Lodd. by] S–D.

Mammillaria acanthoplegma Lem. = status doubtful.

M. affinis DC = **Mammillaria polythele** Mart.

M. albescens Tiegel = **Mammillaria decipiens** Scheidw. with white spines.

M. albiarmata Boed. = **Mammillaria coahuilensis** (Boed.) Moran.

M. albida Haage ex Pfeiff. = **Mammillaria discolor** Haw.

'M. albidula' Bkbg. = **Mammillaria conspicua** Purpus.

'M. aljibensis' = catalogue name = ?**Mammillaria perbella** Hildm. ex Sch.

M. ancistroides Lem. = status doubtful.

'M. alpina' hort. = catalogue name = **Mammillaria kraehenbuehlii** (Krainz) Krainz.

M. amoena Hopfer ex S–D = **Mammillaria discolor** Haw.

M. angularis Link & Otto = **Mammillaria compressa** DC.

M. applanata Engelm. = **Mammillaria heyderi** *Muehl.*

M. armatissima Craig = **Mammillaria gigantea** Hildm. ex Sch.

M. ascensionis Repp. = **Mammillaria glassii v. ascensionis** Glass & Foster.

M. atroflorens Bkbg. = **Mammillaria mystax** Mart.

M. aureiceps Lem. = **Mammillaria rhodantha** Link & Otto.

M. aureoviridis Heinr. = status doubtful.

M. auriareolis Tiegel = **Mammillaria parkinsonii** Ehrenb.

M. auricantha Craig = **Mammillaria canelensis** Craig.

M. auricoma Dietr. = **Mammillaria spinosissima** Lem.

M. aurisaeta Bkbg. = **Mammillaria picta** Meins.

M. auritricha Craig = **Mammillaria canelensis** Craig.

M. avila-camachoi Shurly n.n. = **Mammillaria parkinsonii** Ehrenb.

M. aylostera Werd. = **Mammillaria beneckei** Ehrenb.

M. bachmannii Boed. = status doubtful.

M. balsasensis Boed. = **Mammillaria beneckei** Ehrenb.

M. balsasoides Craig = **Mammillaria beneckei** Ehrenb.

M. barkeri Shurly n.n. = **Mammillaria beneckei** Ehrenb.

M. bellacantha Craig = **Mammillaria canelensis** Craig.

M. bellisiana Craig = **Mammillaria sonorensis** Craig.

M. bicornuta Tiegel n.n. = **Mammillaria bucareliensis** Craig.

M. boedekeriana Quehl = status doubtful.

M. bogotensis Werd. = **Mammillaria columbiana** S–D.

M. bonavitii Schmoll = ?**Mammillaria discolor** form.

M. bravoae Craig = **Mammillaria hahniana** Werd.

M. buchenauii Bkbg. = **Mammillaria crucigera** Mart.

M. bullardiana (Gates) Boed. = **Mammillaria hutchisoniana** (Gates) Boed.

'M. cadereytana' = catalogue name = **Mammillaria pygmaea** (B. & R.) Berg.

M. caerulea Craig = **Mammillaria chionocephala** Purpus.

M. calleana Bkbg. = **Mammillaria wildii** Dietr.

M. casoi H. Bravo = **Mammillaria mystax** Mart.

M. celsiana Lem. = *nom. dub.*, plants supplied under this name are invariably **Mammillaria muehlenpfordtii**.

M. centricirrha Lem. = **Mammillaria magnimamma** Haw.

M. chavezii Cowper = **Mammillaria viridiflora** (B. & R.) Boed.

M. cirrhifera Mart. = **Mammillaria compressa** DC.

M. collina Purpus = **Mammillaria haageana** Pfeiff.

M. collinsii (B. & R.) Orcutt = **Mammillaria voburnensis v. collinsii** (B. & R.) Repp.

M. colonensis Craig = **Mammillaria beneckei** Ehrenbg.

M. confusa (B. & R.) Orcutt = **Mammillaria karwinskiana** Mart.

M. conzattii (B. & R.) Orcutt = **Mammillaria karwinskiana** Mart.

M. coronaria Sch. = status doubtful.

M. cowperae Shurly = **Mammillaria moellerana** Boed.

M. criniformis DC = ?**Mammillaria crinita** DC.

M. crispiseta Craig = **Mammillaria mystax** Mart.

M. crocidata Lem. = status doubtful.

M. dawsonii (Houghton) Craig = **Mammillaria glareosa** Boed.

M. dealbata Dietr. = **Mammillaria haageana** Pfeiff.

M. deliusiana Shurly = **Mammillaria bella** Bkbg.

M. denudata (Engelm.) Berg = **Mammillaria lasiacantha** Engelm.

M. diacentra Jac. = status doubtful.

M. diguetii (Weber) D. Hunt = **Mammillaria senilis** [Att. to Lodd] by S–D

M. dodsonii Bravo = **Mammillaria deherdtiana v. dodsonii** (Bravo) Glass & Foster.

M. dolichocentra Lem. = **Mammillaria obconella** Scheidw.

M. donatii Berg. ex Sch. = status doubtful.

M. dyckiana Zucc. = **Mammillaria haageana** Pfeiff.

M. ebenacantha Schmoll = **Mammillaria karwinskiana** Mart.

M. echinaria DC = **Mammillaria elongata** DC.

M. egregia Bkbg. = **Mammillaria lasiacantha** Engelm.

M. eichlamii Quehl = **Mammillaria voburnensis v. eichlamii** (Quehl) Repp.

M. ekmanii Werd. = ?**Mammillaria mammillaris** (L.) Karst.

M. elegans v. schmollii Craig = **Mammillaria meissneri** Ehrenb.

M. erectohamata Boed. = status doubtful.

M. ernestii Fittkau = **Mammillaria backebergiana v. ernestii** (Fitt.) Glass & Foster.

M. esperanzaensis Boed. = **Mammillaria discolor** Haw.

'*M. essaussieri*' = catalogue name = **Mammillaria densispina** (Coulter) Orcutt.

M. esseriana Boed. = status doubtful.

M. estanzuelensis Moeller = **Mammillaria candida** Scheid.

M. estebanensis Lindsay = **Mammillaria angelensis v. estebanensis** (Lindsay) Repp.

M. euthele Bkbg. *n.n.* = **Mammillaria melanocentra** Poselg.

M. fasciculata Englm. = **Mammillaria thornberi** Orcutt.

M. fertilis Hildm. = **Mammillaria backebergiana** Buchenau.

M. fischeri Pfeiff. = **Mammillaria karwinskiana** Mart.

M. flavescens Haw. = **Mammillaria nivosa** Link ex Pfeiff.

M. flavescens v. nivosa (Link) Bkbg. = **Mammillaria nivosa** Link ex Pfeiff.

M. flavicentra Bkbg. = **M. dixanthocentron v. flavicentra** (Bkbg.) Repp.

M. flavihamata Bkbg. = **Mammillaria jaliscana** (B. & R.) Boed.

M. flavovirens S–D = **Mammillaria magnimamma** Haw.

M. floresii Bkbg. = **Mammillaria canelensis** Craig.

M. fragilis S–D = **Mammillaria gracilis** Pfeiff.

M. fuliginosa S–D = status doubtful.

M. fuscata Link & Otto = **Mammillaria rhodantha** Link & Otto.

M. garessii Cowper = **Mammillaria barbata** Engelm.

'*M. ginsaumae*' = hort. var. = **Mammillaria discolor** Haw.

M. gladiata Mart. = **Mammillaria magnimamma** Haw.

M. glochidiata Mart. = status doubtful.

M. goldii Glass & Foster = **Mammillaria saboae v. goldii** (G. & F.) Glass & Foster.

M. goodridgii v. rectispina Dawson = **Mammillaria rectispina** (Dawson) Repp.

M. graessneriana Boed. = status doubtful.

M. gueldemanniana Bkbg. = ?**Mammillaria sheldonii** (B. & R.) Boed.

M. guiengolensis Bravo = **Mammillaria beneckei** Ehrenbg.

M. guillauminiana Bkbg. = **Mammillaria mercadensis v. guillauminiana** (Bkbg.) Repp.

M. guirocobensis Craig = ?**Mammillaria sheldonii** (B. & R.) Boed.

M. gummifera v. macdougalii (Rose) Benson = **Mammillaria macdougalii** Rose.

M. gummifera v. meiacantha (Engelm.) Benson = **Mammillaria meiacantha** Engelm.

'*M. haasii*' = catalogue name = **Mammillaria virginis** Fitt. & Kladiwa.

M. haehneliana Boed. = **Mammillaria knebeliana** Boed.

M. halbingeri Boed. = status doubtful.

M. hamata Lehmann ex Pfeiff. = *nom. dub.*, plants currently supplied as this are similar to **Mammillaria duoformis** Craig & Dawson.

M. hamiltonhoytea (Bravo) Werd. = **Mammillaria gigantea** Hildm. ex Sch.

M. hastifera Krainz & Keller = **Mammillaria gigantea** Hildm. ex Sch.

M. haudeana Lau & Wagner = **Mammillaria saboae fa. haudeana** (Lau & Wagner) D. Hunt.

M. haynei Ehrenb. = status doubtful.

M. heeriana Bkbg. *n.n.* = status doubtful., plants supplied as this are similar to **Mammillaria duoformis** Craig & Dawson.

M. hemisphaerica Engelm. = **Mammillaria heyderi v. hemisphaerica** (Engelm.) Engelm.

M. hennisii Boed. = **Mammillaria columbiana** S–D.

M. heyderi v. macdougalii (Rose) Benson = **Mammillaria macdougalii** Rose.

M. heyderi v. meiacantha (Engelm.) Benson = **Mammillaria meiacantha** Engelm.

M. hidalgensis Purpus = **Mammillaria polythele** Mart.

'*M. hildmannii*' = catalogue name.

M. hoffmanniana (Tiegel) Bravo = **Mammillaria polythele** Mart.

'*M. huriana*' = catalogue name.

M. icamolensis Boed. = status doubtful.

M. inaiae Craig = **Mammillaria sheldonii** (B. & R.) Boed.

M. infernillensis Craig = **Mammillaria parkinsonii** Ehrenb.

M. ingens Bkbg. = **Mammillaria polythele** Mart.

M. kelleriana Schmoll ex Craig = **Mammillaria polythele** Mart.

M. kewensis S–D = **Mammillaria polythele** Mart.

'*M. kladiwae*' = hort. = ?**Mammillaria spinosissima** Lem.

M. kuentziana P. & B. Fearn = **Mammillaria vetula** Mart.

M. kunthii Ehrenb. = **Mammillaria haageana** Pfeiff.

M. kunzeana Boed. & Quehl = status doubtful., plants supplied as this are usually **Mammillaria bocasana** Poselg.

M. lanata (B. & R.) Orcutt = **Mammillaria supertexta** Mart. ex Pfeiff.

M laneusumma Craig = **Mammillaria canelensis** Craig.

M. lauii fa. subducta D. Hunt = **Mammillaria subducta** (D. Hunt) Repp.

M. lengdobleriana Boed. = status doubtful.

M. leona Poselg. = **Mammillaria pottsii** Scheer ex S−D.

M. lesaunieri (Rebut) Sch. = status doubtful.

M. leucocentra Berg. = ?**Mammillaria geminispina** Haw.

M. macracantha DC = **Mammillaria magnimamma** Haw.

M. magneticola Meyran = **Mammillaria vetula** Mart.

M. marneriana Bkbg. = **Mammillaria grahamii v. oliviae** (Orcutt) Benson.

M. marshalliana (Gates) Boed. ex Bkbg. = **Mammillaria baxteriana** (Gates) Boed.

M. martinezii Bkbg. = **Mammillaria supertexta** Mart.

M. mayensis Craig = **Mammillaria canelensis** Craig.

M. melispina Werd. = status doubtful.

M. mendeliana (Bravo) Werd. = **Mammillaria hahniana** Werd.

M. meridiorosei Castetter *et al* = **Mammillaria wrightii v. wilcoxii** (Toumey ex Sch.) Marshall.

M. mexicensis Craig = status doubtful.

'*M. michoacanensis*' = catalogue name = ?**Mammillaria meyranii** Bravo.

M. microcarpa Engelm. = **Mammillaria milleri** (B. & R.) Boed.

M. microcarpa v. grahamii Engelm. = **Mammillaria grahamii** Engelm.

M. microheliopsis Werd. = **Mammillaria microhelia** Werd.

M. mitlensis Bravo = **Mammillaria rekoi** (B. & R.) Vpl.

M. mixtecensis Bravo = **Mammillaria casoi** Bravo.

M. mollihamata Shurly = **Mammillaria pygmaea** (B. & R.) Berg.

M. monancistracantha Bkbg. = **Mammillaria nana** Bkbg. ex Mottram.

M. monocentra Jac. = status doubtful.

M. montensis Craig = ?**Mammillaria canelensis** Craig.

M. morricalii Cowper = **Mammillaria barbata** Engelm.

M. movensis Craig = **Mammillaria standleyi** (B. & R.) Orcutt

M. multicentralis Craig = status doubtful.

M. multiceps S−D = **Mammillaria prolifera** (Miller) Haw.

M. multiformis (B. & R) Boed. = **Mammillaria erythrosperma** Boed.

M. multihamata Boed. = status doubtful.

M. multiseta Ehrenb. = **Mammillaria karwinskiana** Mart.

M. mutabilis Scheidw. = **Mammillaria mystax** Mart.

M. nelsonii (B. & R.) Boed. = **Mammillaria beneckei** Ehrenb.

M. neobertrandiana Bkbg. = **Mammillaria magallanii** Schmoll.

M. neocoronaria Knuth = status doubtful.

M. neocrucigera Bkbg. = status doubtful.

M. neomystax Bkbg. = **Mammillaria mystax** Mart.

M. neophaeacantha Bkbg. = **Mammillaria polythele** Mart.

M. neopotosina Craig = **Mammillaria muehlenpfordtii** Foerst.

M. neoschwarzeana Bkbg. = **Mammillaria bocensis** Craig.

M. obscura Hildm. = ?**Mammillaria petterssonii** Hildm.

M. obvallata Otto ex Dietr. = status doubtful.

M. ocamponis Ochot. = **Mammillaria mercadensis v. guillauminiana** (Bkbg.) Repp.

M. ochoterenae (Bravo) Werd. = **Mammillaria discolor** Haw.

M. ocotillensis Craig = **Mammillaria gigantea** Hildm.

M. oliviae Orcutt = **Mammillaria grahamii v. oliviae** (Orcutt) Benson.

M. orestera Benson = **Mammillaria viridiflora** (B. & R.) Boed.

M. ortegae (B. & R.) Orcutt = **Mammillaria scrippsiana** (B. & R.) Orcutt.

'*M. ortiz-rubiona*' (Bravo) Weid. = **Mammillaria candida** Scheid.

M. pachyrhiza Bkbg. = **Mammillaria discolor** Haw.

M. painteri Rose ex Quehl see under **Mammillaria pygmaea**.

M. palmeri Jac. non Boed. = status doubtful.

M. parensis Craig = **Mammillaria pringlei** (Coulter) K. Brandegee.

M. patonii (Bravo) Boed. = **Mammillaria mazatlanensis** Sch.

M. pectinifera fa. solisoides (Bkbg.) S.-Mejorada = **Mammillaria solisioides** Bkbg.

M. pennispinosa v. nazasensis Glass & Foster = **Mammillaria nazasensis** (Glass & Foster) Repp.

M. pentacantha Pfeiff. = status doubtful.

M. phaeacantha Lem. = status doubtful.

M. phymatothele Berg. = status doubtful.

M. pilensis Shurly = **Mammillaria petterssonii** Hildm.

M. pitcayensis = incorrect spelling of **Mammillaria pilcayensis** Bravo.

M. polygona S−D = status doubtful.

M. posseltiana Boed. = **Mammillaria rettigiana** Boed.

M. praelii Muehlpf. = status doubtful.

M. pseudoalamensis Bkbg. = **Mammillaria grahamii v. oliviae** (Orcutt) Benson.

M. pseudorekoi [attrib. to (Rose) Boed. (1931) by] Boed. = *nom. dub.*

'*M. pseudoschiedeana*' hort. = **Mammillaria dumetorum** Purpus.

M. pseudoscrippsiana Bkbg. = **Mammillarian scrippsiana** (B. & R.) Orcutt.

M. pseudosimplex W. Haage & Bkbg. = **Mammillaria mammillaris** (L.) Karsten.

'*M. pseudosupertexta*' = catalogue name.

M. pubispina Boed. =**Mammillaria pygmaea** (B. & R) Berg.

M. pusilla (DC) Sweet = **Mammillaria prolifera** (Miller) Haw.

M. pyrrhocephala Scheidw. = **Mammillaria karwinskiana** Mart.

M. queretarica Craig = **Mammillaria parkinsonii** Ehrenb.

'*M. quevedoi*' = catalogue name = **Mammillaria hahniana** Craig.

M. radiaissima Lindsay = **Mammillaria baumii** Boed.

'*M. rawlii*' = catalogue name = **Mammillaria nana** Bkbg.

M. rekoi v. aurispina Lau = **Mammillaria aurispina** (Lau) Repp.

M. rekoi v. leptacantha Lau = **Mammillaria leptacantha** (Lau) Repp.

'*M. rekoiana*' Craig = **Mammillaria rekoi** (B. & R) Vpl.

M. rosensis Craig = **Mammillaria parkinsonii** Ehrenb.

M. roseocentra Boed. & Ritt. = **Mammillaria magallanii** Schmoll ex Craig.

M. rossiana Heinr. = ?**Mammillaria duoformis** Craig & Dawson.

M. rubida Schwarz = **Mammillaria bocensis v. rubida** Repp.

M. runyonii (B. & R.) Boed. = **Mammillaria melanocentra** Poselg.

N. rutila Zucc. ex Pfeiff. = status doubtful.

M. saboae v. theresae (Cutak) Rowley = **Mammillaria theresae** Cutak.

M. saffordii (B. & R.) Bravo = **Mammillaria carretii** Rebut ex Sch.

M. sanluisensis Shurly = **Mammillaria pilispina** Purpus.

M. santaclarensis Cowper = **Mammillaria barbata** Engelm.

M. scheidweilerana Otto ex A. Dietr. = **Mammillaria erythrosperma** Boed.

M. schelhasii Pfeiff. = status doubtful, plants supplied as this are usually **Mammillaria bocasana**.

M. schieliana Schick. = **Mammillaria picta** Meins.

M. schmollii (Bravo) Werd. = **Mammillaria discolor** Haw.

'*M. schmuckeri*' hort. Schmoll = status doubtful.

M. schwartzii (Boed.) Buxb. = **Mammillaria coahuilensis** (Boed.) Moran.

M. seideliana Quehl = status doubtful.

M. seitziana Mart. ex Pfeiff. = status doubtful.

M. shurliana Gates ex Shurly = **Mammillaria blossfeldiana v. shurliana** (Gates) Wiggins.

M. simplex Haw. = **Mammillaria mammillaris** (L.) Karsten.

M. sinaloensis (Rose ex Ortega) Mottram = **Mammillaria mazatlanensis** Sch.

M. slevinii (B. & R.) Boed. = **Mammillaria albicans** (B. & R.) Berg.

M. soehlemannii W. Haage & Bkbg. = **Mammillaria columbiana** Salm-Dyck.

M. solisii (B. & R.) Boed. = **Mammillaria nunezii** (B. & R.) Orcutt.

M. stampferi Repp. = **Mammillaria longiflora fa. stampferi** (Repp.) D. Hunt.

M. stella-de-tacubaya Heese = identification uncertain.

M. subdurispina Bkbg. = **Mammillaria polythele** Mart.

M. subtilis Bkbg. = **Mammillaria pilispina** J.A. Purpus

M. tamayonis Killip ex L. Schnee = **Mammillaria columbiana** Salm-Dyck.

M. tenampensis (B. & R.) Berg. = **Mammillaria sartorii** Purpus

M. tetracantha S–D = **Mammillaria obconella** Scheidw.

M. tetracentra [attrib. to Otto by] Foerst. = status doubtful.

M. tiegeliana Bkbg. = **Mammillaria parkinsonii** Ehrenb.

M. tricacantha Sch. = status doubtful.

M. trohartii Hildm. ex Sch. = **Mammillaria magnimamma** Haw.

M. umbrina Ehrenbg. = status doubtful.

M. unihamata Boed. = **Mammillaria weingartiana** Boed.

M. vagaspina Craig = **Mammillaria magnimamma** Haw.

M. vaupelii Tiegel = **Mammillaria haageana** Pfeiff.

M. verhaertiana Boed. = status doubtful.

'*M. viescensis*' = catalogue name = **Mammillaria chica** Repp.

M. vonwyssiana Krainz = **Mammillaria parkinsonii** Ehrenb.

M. wilcoxii v. viridiflora (B. & R.) Marshall & Bock = **Mammillaria viridiflora** (B. & R.) Boed.

M. woodsii Craig = **Mammillaria hahniana** Werd.

M. wrightii v. viridiflora (B. & R.) Marshall = **Mammillaria viridiflora** (B. & R.) Marshall.

M. wrightii v. wilcoxii (Toumey) Marshall = **Mammillaria wilcoxii** Toumey ex Sch.

'*M. wolfii*' = **Mammillaria wrightii v. wolfii** (D. Hunt) Repp.

M. wuthenauiana Bkbg. = **Mammillaria nunezii** (B. & R.) Orcutt.

M. xanthina (B. & R.) Boed. = status doubtful.

M. zahniana Boed. = **Mammillaria winterae** Boed.

M. zapilotensis Craig = **Mammillaria guerreronis** (Bravo) [attrib. to Boed. by] Bkbg. & Knuth.

'*Matucana armillata*' = **Matucana haynei** (Otto) B. & R.

M. blancii Bkbg. = **Matucana haynei** (Otto) B. & R.

M. breviflora Rauh & Bkbg. = '**Matucana haynei v. breviflora**'.

'*M. caespitosa*' = **Matucana paucicostata** Ritt.

M. calliantha Ritt. = **Matucana krahnii** (Don.) Bregman.

M. calocephala Skarupke = **Matucana myriacantha** (Vpl). Bux.

M. calvescens (Kim. & Hutch.) Bux. = **Matucana aurantiaca** (Vpl.) Bux.

M. celendinensis Ritt. = **Matucana intertexta v. celendinensis** (Ritt.) Bregman.

M. cereoides Rauh & Bkbg. = **Matucana haynei** (Otto) B. & R.

'*M. clavispina*' = **Matucana haynei** (Otto) B. & R.

M. currundayensis Ritt. = **Matucana aurantiaca** (Vpl.) Bux.

M. elongata Rauh & Bkbg. = **Matucana haynei** (Otto) B. & R.

'*M. eriodisca*' = **Matucana paucicostata** Ritt.

M. herzogiana Bkbg. = **Matucana haynei** (Otto) B. & R.

'*M. huaricensis*' = **Matucana paucicostata** Ritt.

M. huarinensis Knize *n.n.* = **Matucana myriacantha** (Vpl.) Bux.

M. hystrix Rauh & Bkbg. = **Matucana haynei** (Otto) B. & R.

M. multicolor Rauh & Bkbg. = **Matucana haynei** (Otto) B. & R.

'*M. paucispina*' = **Matucana paucicostata** Ritt.

M. purpureoalba Ritt. = **Matucana myriacantha** (Vpl.) Bux.

M. roseoalba Ritt. *n.n.* = **Matucana myriacantha** (Vpl.) Bux.

'*M. senile*' = **Matucana paucicostata** Ritt.

'*M. senilis*' = **Matucana paucicostata** Ritt.

M. supertexta Ritt. = **Matucana haynei** (Otto) B. & R.

'*M. turbiniformis*' = **Matucana paucicostata** Ritt.

M. variabilis Rauh & Bkbg. = **Matucana haynei** (Otto) B. & R.

'*M. villarica*' = **Matucana haynei** (Otto) B. & R.

M. winteri Ritt. = **Matucana myriacantha** (Vpl.) Bux.

M. yanganucensis Rauh & Bkbg. = **Matucana haynei** (Otto) B. & R.

Mediolobivia Not included below are a number of invalid combinations, (originally published as *nomena nuda* in this genus), from seed and plant merchants' catalogues. If not listed, these names should be sought under *Rebutia*.

Mediolobivia albopectinata Rausch = **Rebutia albopectinata** Rausch.

M. auranitida (Wessn.) Krainz = **Rebutia einsteinii** Fric.

M. aureiflora (Bkbg.) Bkbg. and *vars.* = '**Rebutia einsteinii v. aureiflora**'

M. brunescens Rausch = **Rebutia brunescens** Rausch.

M. conoidea (Wessn.) Krainz = **Rebutia einsteinii** Fric.

M. costata (Werd.) Krainz = '**Rebutia steinmannii v. costata**'.

M. duursmaiana Bkbg. = '**Rebutia einsteinii v. aureiflora**'.

M. elegans Bkbg. = **Rebutia einsteinii** Fric.

M. euanthema (Bkbg.) Krainz. = **Rebutia euanthema** (Bkbg.) Buin. & Don.

M. eucaliptana (Bkbg.) Krainz = **Rebutia steinmannii** (Solms-Laub.) B. & R.

M. fuauxiana Bkbg. = status doubtful.

M. haefneriana Cullm. = ?**Rebutia pygmaea** (Fries.) B. & R.

M. ithyacantha Card. = **Rebutia ithyacantha** (Card.) Diers.

M. nigricans (Wessn.) Krainz = **Rebutia ritteri** (Wessn.) Buin. & Don.

M. orurensis Bkbg. = '**Rebutia pygmaea v. orurensis**'.

M. pectinata (Bkbg.) Bkbg. non Fric = **Rebutia pygmaea** (Fries.) B. & R.

M. pectinata v. orurensis (Bkbg.) Bkbg. = '**Rebutia pygmaea v. orurensis**'.

M. pygmaea Bkbg. = '**Rebutia pygmaea v. haagei**'.

M. ritteri (Wessn.) Krainz = **Rebutia ritteri** (Wessn.) Don.

M. rubelliflora Bkbg. = '**Rebutia einsteinii v. aureiflora**'.

M. rubriflora Bkbg. = **'Rebutia einsteinii v. aureiflora'**.

M. schmiedcheniana (Koehl.) Krainz and *vars.* = **Rebutia einsteinii** Fric.

M. spiralisepala Jajo = status doubtful.

'Melocactus alpestris' = **Melocactus peruvianus** Vpl.

M. amstutziae Rauh & Bkbg. = **Melocactus peruvianus** Vpl.

M. azulensis Buin. *et. al.* = **Melocactus oreas subsp. ernestii** (Vpl.) Braun.

'M. chalensis' = **Melocactus peruvianus** Vpl.

M. cremnophilus Buin. & Bred. = **Melocactus oreas** Miqu.

M. ernestii Vpl. = **Melocactus oreas subsp. ernestii** (Vpl.) Braun.

M. erythracanthus Buin. & Bred. = **Melocactus oreas** Miqu.

M. huallancaensis Rauh & Bkbg. = **Melocactus peruvianus** Vpl.

M. jansenianus Bkbg. = **Melocactus peruvianus** Vpl.

M. longispinus Buin. *et. al.* = **Melocactus oreas** Miqu.

M. nitidus Ritt. = **Melocactus oreas subsp. ernestii** (Vpl.) Braun.

M. rubrisaetosus Buin. *et. al.* = **Melocactus oreas** Miqu.

M. trujilloensis Rauh & Bkbg. = **Melocactus peruvianus** (Vpl.)

M. unguispinus Bkbg. = **Melocactus peruvianus** Vpl.

Mila: for all published names see **Mila caespitosa** B. & R.

Navajoa sp. see under **Pediocactus peeblesianus** (Croiz.) Benson.

Neobesseya asperispina (Boed.) Boed. = **Escobaria missouriensis v. asperispina** (Boed.) N.P. Taylor.

N. missouriensis (Sweet) B. & R. = **Escobaria missouriensis** (Sweet) D. Hunt.

N. notesteinii (Brit.) B. & R. = **Escobaria missouriensis v. similis** (Engelm.) N.P. Taylor.

N. rosiflora Lahm. = **Escobaria missouriensis v. similis** (Engelm.) N.P. Taylor.

N. similis (Engelm.) B. & R. = **Escobaria missouriensis v. similis** (Engelm.) N.P. Taylor.

N. wissmannii (Hildm.) B. & R. = **Escobaria missouriensis** (Sweet) D. Hunt.

Neochilenia aerocarpa (Ritt.) Bkbg. = **Neoporteria iquiquensis** (Ritt.) Don. & Rowley.

N. andreaeana Bkbg. = **Pyrrhocactus andreaeanus** (Bkbg.) Ritt.

N. aricensis (Ritt.) Bkbg. = **Neoporteria iquiquensis** (Ritt.) Don. & Rowley.

N. aspillagai (Soehr.) Bkbg. = **Neoporteria aspillagai** (Soehr.) Bkbg.

'N. atra' Bkbg. = **Neoporteria reichei** (Sch.) Bkbg.

N. calderana (Ritt.) Bkbg. = **Neoporteria calderana** (Ritt.) Don. & Rowley.

N. carneoflora Kilian = probable hybrid.

N. chilensis (Hildm.) Bkbg. = **Neoporteria chilensis** (Hildm.) Don. & Rowley.

N. chorosensis (Ritt.) Bkbg. = **Neoporteria chorosensis** (Ritt.) Don. & Rowley.

N. confinis (Ritt.) Bkbg. = **Neoporteria confinis** (Ritt.) Don. & Rowley.

'N. deherdtiana' Bkbg. = **Neoporteria chorosensis** (Ritt.) Don. & Rowley.

N. dimorpha (Ritt.) Bkbg. = **Neoporteria jussieui v. dimorpha** (Ritt.) Hoffmann.

N. duripulpa (Ritt.) Bkbg. = **Neoporteria reichei** (Sch.) Bkbg.

N. eriocephala Bkbg. = status doubtful.

N. eriosyzoides (Ritt.) Bkbg. = **Neoporteria eriosyzoides** (Ritt.) Don. & Rowley.

'N. esmeraldana' (Ritt.) Bkbg. = **Neoporteria esmeraldana** (Ritt.) Don. & Rowley.

N. floccosa (Ritt.) Bkbg. = **Neoporteria echinus v. floccosa** (Ritt.) R.M. Ferryman.

N. fobeana (Mieckl.) Bkbg. = status doubtful.

N. fusca (Muehlpf.) B. & R. = status doubtful.

N. glabrescens Ritt. = **Neoporteria napina** (Phil.) Bkbg.

N. glaucescens (Ritt.) Bkbg. = **Neoporteria echinus** (Ritt.) R.M. Ferryman.

N. gracilis (Ritt.) Bkbg. = **Neoporteria calderana** (Ritt.) Don. & Rowley.

N. hankeana & vars. = status doubtful.

N. huascensis (Ritt.) Bkbg. = **Neoporteria huascensis** (Ritt.) Don. & Rowley.

N. imitans Bkbg. = **Neoporteria odieri** (Lem.) Berg.

N. intermedia (Ritt.) Bkbg. = **Neoporteria calderana** (Ritt.) Don. & Rowley.

N. iquiquensis (Ritt.) Bkbg. = **Neoporteria iquiquensis** (Ritt.) Don. & Rowley.

N. jussieui (Monv.) Bkbg. = **Neoporteria jussieui** (Monv.) B. & R.

N. kunzei (Foerst.) Bkbg. = **Neoporteria kunzei** (Foerst.) Bkbg.

'N. krausii' (Ritt.) Bkbg. = **Neoporteria odieri v. malleolata** (Ritt.) R.M. Ferryman.

'N. lembckei' Bkbg. = **Neoporteria reichei** (Sch.) Bkbg.

N. malleolata (Ritt.) Bkbg. = **Neoporteria odieri v. malleolata** (Ritt.) R.M. Ferryman.

N. malleolata v. solitaria Ritt. = **Neoporteria odieri v. malleolata** (Ritt.) R.M. Ferryman.

N. mebbesii (Hildm.) Bkbg. = status doubtful.

N. minima n.n. = **Neoporteria chorosensis** (Ritt.) Don. & Rowley.

N. mitis (Phil.) Bkbg. = **Neoporteria napina** (Phil.) Bkbg.

N. monte-amargensis' Bkbg. = **Neoporteria odieri v. monte-amargensis** (Bkbg.) R.M. Ferryman comb. nov.

N. napina (Phil.) Bkbg. = **Neoporteria napina** (Phil.) Bkbg.

N. napina v. spinosior (Bkbg.) Bkbg. = **Neoporteria napina** (Phil.) Bkbg.

N. neofusca Bkbg. = **Neoporteria jussieui** (Monv.) B. & R.

'N. neoreichei' Bkbg. = **Neoporteria reichei** (Sch.) Bkbg.

'N. nigriscoparia' Bkbg. = **Neoporteria crispa** (Ritt.) Don. & Rowley.

N. occulta (Sch.) Bkbg. = **Neoporteria occulta** (Sch.) B. & R.

N. odoriflora (Ritt.) Bkbg. = **Neoporteria horrida** (Remy ex Gay)

N. paucicostata & v. viridis (Ritt.) Bkbg. = **Neoporteria paucicostata** (Ritt.) Don. & Rowley.

N. pilispina (Ritt.) Bkbg. = **Neoporteria calderana** (Ritt.) Don. & Rowley.

N. pulchella (Ritt.) Bkbg. *n.n.* = **Neoporteria pulchella** (Ritt.) R.M. Ferryman.

N. pygmaea (Ritt.) Bkbg. = **Neoporteria calderana** (Ritt.) Don. & Rowley.

N. recondita (Ritt.) Bkbg. = **Neoporteria recondita** (Ritt.) Don. & Rowley.

N. reichei (Sch.) Bkbg. = **Neoporteria reichei** (Sch.) Bkbg.

N. residua (Ritt.) Bkbg. = **Neoporteria recondita** (Ritt.) Don. & Rowley.

N. robusta & *v. vegasana* (Ritt.) Bkbg. = **Neoporteria horrida** (Remy ex Gay) D. Hunt.

N. rupicola (Ritt.) Bkbg. = **Neoporteria taltalensis** Hutch.

N. saxifraga n.n. = **Neoporteria iquiquensis** (Ritt) Don. & Rowley.

N. scoparia (Ritt.) Bkbg. = **Neoporteria calderana** (Ritt.) Don. & Rowley.

N. setosiflora & *v. intermedia* (Ritt.) Bkbg. = **Neoporteria setosiflora** (Ritt.) Don. & Rowley.

N. subikii n.n. = **Neoporteria chorosensis** (Ritt.) Don. & Rowley.

N. taltalensis v. flaviflora (Ritt.) Bkbg. *n.n.* = **Neoporteria neohankeana** (Ritt.) R.M. Ferryman.

N. totoralensis (Ritt.) Bkbg. = **Neoporteria totoralensis** (Ritt.) Don. & Rowley.

N. transitensis (Ritt.) Bkbg. = **Neoporteria transitensis** (Ritt.) R.M. Ferryman.

'N. vanbaelii' = **Neoporteria jussieui** (Monv.) B. & R.

N. violaciflora n.n. = **Neoporteria taltalensis** Hutch.

N. wagenknechtii (Ritt.) Bkbg. = **Neoporteria jussieui v. wagenknechtii** (Ritt.) R.M. Hoffmann.

Neogomesia agavoides Castan. = **Ariocarpus agavoides** (Castan.) And.

Neolloydia ceratites (Quehl) B. & R. = **Neolloydia conoidea** (DC) B. & R.

N. conoidea v. ceratites (Quehl) Kladiwa & Fittkau = **Neolloydia conoidea** (DC) B. & R.

N. conoidea v. grandiflora (Otto ex Pfeiff.) Kladiwa & Fittkau = **Neolloydia conoidea** (DC) B. & R.

N. conoidea v. matehualensis (Bkbg.) Kladiwa & Fittkau = **Neolloydia conoidea** (DC) B. & R.

N. erectocentra (Coult.) Benson = **Echinomastus erectocentrus** (Coult.) B. & R.

N. gielsdorfiana (Werd.) Knuth = **Gymnocactus gielsdorfianus** (Werd.) Bkbg.

N. grandiflora (Otto ex Pfeiff.) Berg. = **Neolloydia conoidea** (DC) B. & R.

N. horripila (Lem.) B. & R. = **Gymnocactus horripilus** (Lem.) Bkbg.

N. intertexta (Englm.) Benson = **Echinomastus intertextus** (Englm.) B. & R.

N. johnsonii (Parry) Benson = **Echinomastus johnsonii** (Parry) Baxt.

N. knuthiana (Boed.) Knuth = **Gymnocactus knuthianus** (Boed.) Bkbg.

N. macdowellii (Rebut ex Quehl) H.E. Moore = **Thelocactus macdowellii** (Rebut ex Quehl) C. Glass.

N. mariposensis (Hester) Benson = **Echinomastus mariposensis** Hester.

N. odorata (Boed.) Bkbg. = **Cumarinia odorata** (Boed.) Bux.

N. pseudopectinata (Bkbg.) Anderson = **Turbinicarpus pseudopectinatus** (Bkbg.) Glass & Foster.

N. pulleineana Bkbg. = **Coryphantha pulleineana** (Bkbg.) Glass.

N. saueri (Boed.) Knuth = **Gymnocactus saueri** (Boed.) Bkbg.

N. *smithii* (Muehlpf.) Kladiwa & Fittkau = *'Gymnocactus beguinii'* Bkbg. *nom. inval.*

N. schmiedickiana (Boed.) Anderson = **Turbinicarpus schmiedickianus** (Boed.) Bux. & Bkbg.

N. schmiedickiana v. dickisoniae (Glass & Foster) Anderson = **Turbinicarpus schmiedickianus v. dickisoniae** Glass & Foster.

N. schmiedickiana v. flaviflora (Frank & Lau) Anderson = **Turbinicarpus schmiedickianus v. flaviflorus** (Frank & Lau) Glass & Foster.

N. schmiedickiana v. gracilis (Glass & Foster) Anderson = **Turbinicarpus schmiedickianus v. gracilis** Glass & Foster.

N. schmiedickiana v. klinkeriana (Bkbg. & Jacobs.) Anderson = **Turbinicarpus schmiedickianus v. klinkerianus** (Bkbg. & Jacobs.) Glass & Foster.

N. schmiedickiana v. macrochele (Werd.) Anderson = **Turbinicarpus schmiedickianus v. macrochele** (Werd.) Glass & Foster.

N. schmiedickiana v. schwarzii (Shurly) Anderson = **Turbinicarpus schmiedickianus v. schwarzii** (Shurly) Glass & Foster.

N. subterranea (Bkbg.) F. Moore = **Gymnocactus subterraneus** (Bkbg.) Bkbg.

N. subterranea v. zaragosae (Glass & Foster) Anderson = **Gymnocactus subterraneus v. zaragosae** Glass & Foster.

N. valdeziana (Moell.) Anderson = **Turbinicarpus valdezianus** (Moell.) Glass & Foster.

N. viereckii (Werd.) Knuth = **Gymnocactus viereckii** (Werd.) Bkbg.

N. warnockii Benson = **Echinomastus warnockii** (Benson) Glass & Foster.

Neoporteria andreaeana (Bkbg.) Don. & Rowley = **Pyrrhocactus andreaeanus** (Bkbg.) Ritt.

N. aricensis (Ritt.) Don. & Rowley = **Neoporteria iquiquensis** (Ritt.) Don & Rowley.

N. armata (Ritt.) Krainz = **Neoporteria horrida** (Remy ex Gay) D. Hunt.

N. atrispinosa (Bkbg.) Bkbg. = **Neoporteria villosa** (Monv.) Berg.

N. calderana fa. gracilis (Ritt.) Don. & Rowley = **Neoporteria calderana** (Ritt.) Don. & Rowley.

N. castanea Ritt. = **Neoporteria subgibbosa v. castanea** (Ritt.) R.M. Ferryman.

N. cephalophora (Bkbg.) Bkbg. = **Neoporteria villosa** (Monv.) Berg.

N. choapensis (Ritt.) Don. & Rowley = **Neoporteria horrida** (Remy ex Gay) D. Hunt.

N. curvispina v. aconcaguensis (Ritt.) Don. & Rowley = **Neoporteria curvispina** (Bert.) Don. & Rowley.

N. curvispina v. andicola (Ritt.) Don. & Rowley = **Neoporteria curvispina** (Bert.) Don. & Rowley.

N. curvispina v. carrizalensis (Ritt.) Don. & Rowley = **Neoporteria totoralensis v. carrizalensis** (Ritt.) R.M. Ferryman.

N. curvispina v. echinus (Ritt.) Don. & Rowley = **Neoporteria echinus** (Ritt.) R.M. Ferryman.

N. curvispina v. garaventai (Ritt.) Don. & Rowley = **Neoporteria garaventai** (Ritt.) R.M. Ferryman.

N. curvispina v. heinrichiana (Bkbg.) Don. & Rowley = **Neoporteria heinrichiana** (Bkbg.) R.M. Ferryman.

N. curvispina v. lissocarpa (Ritt.) Don & Rowley = **Neoporteria curvispina** (Bert.) Don & Rowley.

N. curvispina v. transitensis (Ritt.) Don. & Rowley = **Neoporteria transitensis** (Ritt.) R.M. Ferryman.

N. curvispina v. vallenarensis (Ritt.) Don. & Rowley = **Neoporteria vallenarensis** (Ritt.) R.M. Ferryman.

N. eriocephala (Bkbg.) *sensu* Don. & Rowley = **Neoporteria odieri v. malleolata** (Ritt.) R.M. Ferryman.

N. eriocephala v. glaucescens (Ritt.) Don. & Rowley = **Neoporteria echinus** (Ritt.) R.M. Ferryman.

N. fobeana (Mieckl.) Bkbg. = status doubtful.

N. fusca (Muehlpf.) B. & R. = status doubtful.

N. gerocephala Ito = **Neoporteria nidus v. gerocephala** (Ito) Ritt.

N. intermedia (Ritt.) Don. & Rowley = **Neoporteria calderana** (Ritt.) Don. & Rowley.

N. islayensis v. islayensis fa. brevicylindrica (Rauh & Bkbg.) Don. & Rowley = **Neoporteria islayensis** (Foerst.) Don. & Rowley.

N. islayensis v. islayensis fa. grandiflorens (Rauh & Bkbg.) Don. & Rowley = **Neoporteria islayensis** (Foerst.) Don. & Rowley.

N. islayensis v. islayensis fa. minor (Bkbg.) Don. & Rowley = **Neoporteria islayensis** (Foerst.) Don. & Rowley.

N. islayensis v. islayensis fa. mollendensis (Vpl.) Don. & Rowley = **Neoporteria islayensis** (Foerst.) Don. & Rowley.

N. islayensis v. islayensis fa. spinosior (Rauh & Bkbg.) Don. & Rowley = **Neoporteria islayensis** (Foerst.) Don. & Rowley.

N. laniceps Ritt. = **Neoporteria villosa** (Monv.) Berg.

N. lindleyi (Foerst.) Don. & Rowley = **Neoporteria islayensis** (Foerst.) Don. & Rowley.

N. litoralis & v. intermedia Ritt. = **Neoporteria subgibbosa** (Haw.) B. & R.

N. marksiana v. tunensis (Ritt.) Don. & Rowley = **Neoporteria marksiana** (Ritt.) Don. & Rowley.

N. microsperma v. graciana Ritt. = **Neoporteria microsperma** Ritt.

N. microsperma v. serenana Ritt. = **Neoporteria microsperma** Ritt.

N. monte-amargensis (Bkbg.) Don. & Rowley = **Neoporteria odieri v. monte-amargensis** (Bkbg.) R.M. Ferryman.

N. multicolor Ritt. = **Neoporteria nidus v. multicolor** (Ritt.) Hoffmann.

N. napina v. laniger n.n. = **Neoporteria napina v. fankhauseri** (Ritt.) R.M. Ferryman.

N. napina v. mitis (Phil.) Don. & Rowley = **Neoporteria napina** (Phil.) Bkbg.

N. napina v. mitis fa. glabrescens (Ritt.) Don. & Rowley = **Neoporteria napina** (Phil.) Bkbg.

N. napina v. spinosior (Bkbg.) Don. & Rowley = **Neoporteria napina** (Phil.) Bkbg.

N. napina v. spinosior fa. mebbesii (Hild.) Don. & Rowley = **Neoporteria napina** (Phil.) Bkbg.

N. nidus v. matancillana (Ritt.) **Neoporteria nidus** (Sohr.) B. & R.

N. nidus f. senilis (Phil.) Don. & Rowley = **Neoporteria nidus** (Sohr.) B. & R.

N. nigrihorrida vars. major & minor (Bkbg.) Bkbg. = **Neoporteria nigrihorrida** (Bkbg.) Bkbg.

N. odoriflora (Ritt.) Bkbg. = **Neoporteria horrida** (Remy ex Gay) D. Hunt.

N. pilispina & fa. pygmaea (Ritt.) Don. & Rowley = **Neoporteria calderana** (Ritt.) Don. & Rowley.

N. polyraphis (Pfeiff.) Bkbg. = **?Neoporteria villosa** (Monv.) Berg.

N. rapifera Ritt. n.n. = **Neoporteria wagenknechtii** Ritt.

N. reichei v. reichei fa. aerocarpa (Ritt.) Don. & Rowley = **Neoporteria reichei v. aerocarpa** (Ritt.) R.M. Ferryman.

N. reichei v. reichei fa. carneoflora (Kil.) Don. & Rowley = probable hybrid.

N. reichei v. reichei fa. duripulpa (Ritt.) Don. & Rowley = **Neoporteria reichei** (Sch.) Bkbg.

N. reichei v. reichei fa. lembckei (Bkbg.) Don. & Rowley = **Neoporteria reichei** (Sch.) Bkbg.

N. reichei v. reichei fa. neoreichei (Bkbg.) Don. & Rowley = **Neoporteria reichei** (Sch.) Don. & Rowley.

N. reichei v. reichei fa. pseudoreichei (Lemb. & Bkbg.) Don. & Rowley = **Neoporteria reichei** (Sch.) Bkbg.

N. ritteri Don. & Rowley = **Neoporteria jussieui v. wagenknechtii** (Ritt.) Hoffmann.

N. robusta Ritt. = **Neoporteria coimasensis v. robusta** (Ritt.) Ritt.

N. rupicola (Ritt.) Don. & Rowley = **Neoporteria taltalensis** Hutch.

N. scoparia (Ritt.) Don. & Rowley = **Neoporteria calderana** (Ritt.) Don. & Rowley.

N. senilis (Phil.) Bkbg. = **Neoporteria nidus** (Sohr.) B. & R.

N. sociabilis v. napina (Ritt.) = **Neoporteria sociabilis** Ritt.

N. subaiana (Bkbg.) Don. & Rowley = **Neoporteria garaventai** (Ritt.) R.M. Ferryman.

N. subgibbosa v. microsperma (Ritt.) Don. & Rowley = **Neoporteria microsperma** Ritt.

N. subgibbosa v. nigrihorrida (Bkbg.) Don. & Rowley = **Neoporteria nigrihorrida** (Bkbg.) Bkbg.

N. subgibbosa v. orientalis Ritt. = **Neoporteria subgibbosa** (Haw.) B. & R.

N. subgibbosa v. subgibbosa fa. castanea (Ritt.) Don. & Rowley = **Neoporteria subgibbosa v. castanea** (Ritt.) R.M. Ferryman.

N. subgibbosa fa. litoralis (Ritt.) Don. & Rowley = **Neoporteria subgibbosa** (Haw.) B. & R.

N. tuberisulcata (Jac.) Don. & Rowley = **Neoporteria horrida** (Remy ex Gay) D. Hunt.

N. tuberisulcata v. atroviridis (Ritt.) Don. & Rowley = **Neoporteria atroviridis** (Ritt.) R.M. Ferryman.

N. tuberisulcata v. armata (Ritt.) Don. & Rowley = **Neoporteria horrida** (Remy ex Gay) D. Hunt.

N. tuberisulcata v. cupreata (Pos.) Don. & Rowley = **Neoporteria horrida** (Remy ex Gay) D. Hunt.

N. tuberisulcata v. robusta (Ritt.) Don. & Rowley = **Neoporteria horrida** (Remy ex Gay) D. Hunt.

N. tuberisulcata v. vegasana (Ritt.) Don. & Rowley = **Neoporteria horrida** (Remy ex Gay) D. Hunt.

N. vallenarensis Ritt. = **Neoporteria wagenknechtii v. vallenarensis** (Ritt.) Hoffmann.

N. wagenknechtii v. napina Ritt. = **Neoporteria wagenknechtii** Ritt.

Normanbokea pseudopectinata (Bkbg.) Kladiwa & Bux. = **Turbinicarpus pseudopectinatus** (Bkbg.) Glass & Foster.

N. valdeziana (Moell.) Kladiwa & Bux. = **Turbinicarpus valdezianus** (Moell.) Glass & Foster.

Notocactus acutus Ritt. = **Notocactus ottonis** (Lehm.) Berg.

N. agnetae van Vliet = **Notocactus concinnus** (Monv.) Berg.

N. alacriportanus (Bkbg. & Voll) Bux. see under **Notocactus buenekeri.**

N. **allosiphon** Marchesi see under **Notocactus mammulosus**.

N. apricus (Ar.) Berg. = **Notocactus concinnus** (Monv.) Berg.

N. arachnites Ritt. = **Notocactus crassigibbus** Ritt.

N. arechavaletai (Speg.) Hert. = **Notocactus ottonis** (Lehm.) Berg.

N. blaauwianus van Vliet = **Notocactus concinnus** (Monv.) Berg.

N. **brevihamata** (Hge.) Bux. see **Notocactus buenekeri** (Buin.) Bux.

N. bomeljei van Vliet = **Notocactus concinnus** (Monv.) Berg.

N. campestrensis Ritt. = **Notocactus ottonis** (Lehm.) Berg.

N. carambeiensis Buin. & Bred. = **Notocactus ottonis v. tortuosus** (Link & Otto) Berg.

N. eremiticus Ritt. = **Notocactus concinnus** (Monv.) Berg.

'*N. erizo*' = **Notocactus veenianus** van Vliet.

N. erythracanthus Schl. & Bred. = **Notocactus mammulosus** (Lem.) Berg.

N. eugeniae van Vliet = **Notocactus veenianus** van Vliet.

N. floricomus (Ar.) Berg. = **Notocactus mammulosus** (Lem.) Berg.

N. glaucinus Ritt. = **Notocactus ottonis** (Lehm.) Berg.

N. globularis Ritt. = **Notocactus ottonis** (Lehm.) Berg.

N. harmonianus Ritt. = **Notocactus ottonis** (Lehm.) Berg.

N. ibicuiensis = **Notocactus ottonis** (Lehm.) Berg.

'*N. incomptus*' = **Notocactus ottonis** (Lehm.) Berg.

N. laetivirens Ritt. = **Notocactus ottonis** (Lehm.) Berg.

N. linkii (Lehm.) Hert. = **Notocactus ottonis v. tortuosus** (Link & Otto) Berg.

N. **megalanthus** Schl. & Bred. see under **Notocactus mammulosus** (Lem.) Berg.

N. megapotamicus Ost. ex Hert. = **Notocactus ottonis v. tortuosus** (Link & Otto) Berg.

N. minimus Fric & Kreuz. = **Notocactus caespitosus** Speg.

'*N. mueller-moelleri*' Fric = status doubtful.

'*N. muegelianus*' = **Notocactus horstii** Ritt.

N. multicostatus Buin. & Bred. = **Notocactus concinnus** (Monv.) Berg.

N. neobuenekeri Ritt. = **Notocactus sucineus** Ritt.

N. **nigrispinus** (Sch.) Buin. see under **Notocactus leninghausii**.

N. orthacanthus (Link & Otto) Hert. = status doubtful.

N. orthacanthus sensu van Vliet = **Notocactus mammulosus** (Lehm.) Berg.

N. ottonis v. venclusianus Schuetz = orange flowered ?hort. of **Notocactus ottonis**.

N. oxycostatus Buin. & Bred. = **Notocactus ottonis** (Lehm.) Berg.

N. pampeanus (Speg.) Bkbg. = **Notocactus mammulosus** (Lehm.) Berg.

N. paulus Schl. & Bred. = **Notocactus veenianus** van Vliet.

N. pseudoherteri Buin. = **Notocactus herteri fa. pseudoherteri** (Buin.) Herm.

N. pulvinatus van Vliet = clumping form of **Notocactus erinaceus** Haw.

N. purpureus Ritt. = **Notocactus horstii** Ritt.

N. securituberculatus Ritt. = **Notocactus ottonis** (Lehm.) Berg.

N. submammulosus (Lehm.) Bkbg. = **Notocactus mammulosus** (Lehm.) Berg.

N. tabularis (Cels ex Sch.) Berg. = **Notocactus concinnus** (Monv.) Berg.

N. tenuicylindricus Ritt. = **Notocactus caespitosus** Speg.

N. winkleri van Vliet = **Notocactus veenianus** van Vliet.

Oroya species, with the exception of **Oroya borchersii** are all referable to **Oroya peruviana** (Sch.) B. & R.

Parodia agasta Brandt = **Parodia roseoalba** Ritt.

P. agregia Wesk *nom. prov.* = **Parodia dichroacantha** Brandt & Wesk.

P. amblayoensis Brandt = **Parodia microsperma** (Web.) Speg.

P. applanata Brandt = **Parodia schwebsiana** (Werd.) Bkbg.

'*P. atroviridis*' Bkbg. = **Parodia microsperma** (Web.) Speg.

P. aurihamata hort. = **Parodia aureispina** Bkbg.

P. backebergiana Brandt = **Parodia otuyensis** Ritt.

P. belliata Brandt = **Parodia maassii** (Heese) Berg.

P. bermejoensis Brandt = **Parodia maassii** (Heese) Berg.

P. betaniana Ritt. = **Parodia microsperma** (Web.) Speg.

P. bilbaoensis Card. = **Parodia taratensis** Card.

'*P. blancii*' = catalogue name.

P. borealis Ritt. = **Parodia miguillensis** Card.

P. cainena Brandt = **Parodia ocampoi** Card.

P. camargensis Ritt. = **Parodia maassii** (Heese) Berg.

P. camblayana Ritt. *n.n.* = **Parodia maassii** (Heese) Berg.

P. candidata Brandt = hort. hybrid.

P. capillitaensis Brandt = **Parodia spegazziniana** Brandt

P. carapariana Brandt = **Parodia formosa** Ritt.

P. cardenasii Ritt. = **Parodia formosa** Ritt.

P. carminata Bkbg. = **Parodia microsperma** (Web.) Speg.

P. carrerana Card. = status doubtful.

P. castanea Ritt. = **Parodia maassii** (Heese) Berg.

P. catamarcensis Bkbg. = **Parodia microsperma** (Web.) Speg.

P. chaetocarpa Ritt. = **Parodia formosa** Ritt.

P. challamarcana Brandt = **Parodia procera** Ritt.

P. chirimoyarana Brandt = **Parodia formosa** Ritt.

P. chlorocarpa Ritt. = **Parodia microsperma** (Web.) Speg.

P. cintiensis Ritt. = **Parodia maassii** (Heese) Berg.

P. comosa Ritt. = **Parodia miguillensis** Card.

P. compressa Ritt. = **Parodia ocampoi** Card.

P. cotacajensis Brandt = **Parodia ayopayana** Card.

P. cruci-nigricentra (Fric) Sub. = **Parodia faustiana** Bkbg.

P. culpinensis Brandt = **Parodia subterranea** Ritt.

'*P. durispina*' = catalogue name.

P. echinus Ritt. = **Parodia miguillensis** Card.

'*P. ekligiana*' = catalogue name. ?**Parodia procera**.

P. elachista Brandt = **Parodia punae** Card.

P. elata Brandt = **Parodia ayopayana** Card.

P. elegans Fechs. *n.n.* = **Parodia microsperma** (Web.) Speg.

'*P. eriodesa*' = **Parodia schwebsiana** (Werd.) Bkbg.

P. erythrantha (Speg.) Bkbg. = **Parodia microsperma** (Web.) Speg.

P. escayachensis (Vpl.) Bkbg. = **Parodia maassii** (Heese) Berg.

P. firmissima Brandt = **Parodia otuyensis** Ritt.

P. friciana Brandt = **Parodia steumeri** (Werd.) Bkbg.

P. fulvispina Ritt. = **Parodia maassii** (Heese) Berg.

P. gibbulosa Ritt. = **Parodia gibbulosoides** Brandt.

P. gigantea Fric ex Krainz = **Parodia steumeri** (Werd.) Bkbg.

'*P. gigantea v. jujuyana*' = **Parodia spegazziniana** Brandt

P. glischrocarpa Ritt. = **Parodia microsperma** (Web.) Speg.

P. gokrauseana Heinr. = **Parodia steumeri** (Werd.) Bkbg.

P. gracilis Ritt. = **Parodia ocampoi** Card.

P. gummifera Bkbg. & Vol. = **Uebelmannia gummifera** (Bkbg. & Vol.) Buin.

'*P. gutekunstiana*' Bkbg. = **Parodia steumeri microsperma** (Web.) Speg.

P. haageana Brandt = **Parodia maassii** (Heese) Berg.

'*P. higueritas*' = catalogue name.

P. idiosa Brandt = **Parodia otuyensis** Ritt.

P. ignorata Brandt = **Parodia ocampoi** Card.

P. jujuyana Fric ex Sub. = status doubtful.

'*P. kilianana*' Bkbg. = status doubtful. Plants sold as this are usually **Parodia faustiana**.

P. knizei Brandt = **Parodia maassii** (Heese) Berg.

P. koehresiana Brandt = hort. hybrid.

P. krasuckana Brandt = **Parodia tuberculata** Card.

P. lamprospina Brandt = **Parodia maassii** (Heese) Berg.

'*P. lecoriensis*' = catalogue name. ?**Parodia maassii**.

P. legitima Brandt = **Parodia columnaris** Card.

'*P. lixnosa*' = catalogue name. Misspelling of next entry?

P. lychnosa Brandt = **Parodia ocampoi** Card.

P. maassii v. commutans (Ritt.) Don. & Rowley = **Parodia commutans** Ritt.

P. maassii v. commutans fa. maxima (Ritt.) Don. & Rowley = **Parodia maxima** Ritt. (see under **P. commutans** Ritt.)

P. maassii v. subterranea (Ritt.) Krainz = **Parodia subterranea** Ritt.

P. macednosa Brandt = **Parodia miguillensis** Card.

P. matthesiana Heinr. = status doubtful.

P. maxima Ritt. see under **Parodia commutans** Ritt.

P. mazanensis n.n. = **Parodia riojensis** Ritt. & Wesk.

P. mendezana Brandt = **Parodia maassii** (Heese) Berg.

P. mesembrina Brandt = '**Parodia fechseri**' Bkbg.

P. microthele Bkbg. = **Parodia microsperma** (Web.) Speg.

P. minima Brandt = **Parodia schwebsiana** (Werd.) Bkbg.

P. minima Rausch = **Parodia minuscula** Rausch.

P. miranda Brandt = hort. hybrid.

P. muhrii Brandt = **Parodia aureicentra** Bkbg.

'*P. multispina*' = catalogue name.

P. mutabilis Bkbg. = **Parodia aureispina** Bkbg.

P. neglecta Brandt = **Parodia comarapana** Card.

P. neglectoides Brandt = **Parodia comarapana** Card.

P. nigresca Brandt = **Parodia subterranea** Ritt.

P. obtusa Ritt. = **Parodia commutans** Ritt.

P. otaviana Card. = **Parodia maassii** (Heese) Berg.

P. pachysa Brandt = **Parodia formosa** Ritt.

P. papagayana Brandt = **Parodia microsperma** (Web.) Speg.

P. paraguayensis Speg. = status doubtful.

P. parvula Brandt = **Parodia formosa** Ritt.

P. perplexa Brandt = **Parodia maassii** (Heese) Berg.

'*P. peruviana*' = status doubtful.

P. piltziorum Wesk. = **Parodia horrida** Brandt.

'*P. potosina*' = catalogue name. ?**Parodia maassii**.

P. pseudoayopayana Card. = **Parodia ayopayana** Card.

P. pseudoprocera Brandt = **Parodia procera** Ritt.

'*P. pseudosteumeri*' Bkbg. = **Parodia steumeri** (Werd.) Bkbg.

P. pseudosubterranea Brandt = hort. hybrid.

P. purpureo-aurea Ritt. = **Parodia formosa** Ritt.

P. pusilla Brandt = **Parodia formosa** Ritt.

P. quechua Brandt = **Parodia otuyensis** Ritt.

'*P. rauschii*' Bkbg. = **Parodia aureicentra** Bkbg.

'*P. rigida*' Bkbg. = **Parodia dichroacantha** Brandt.

P. rigidispina Krainz = **Parodia steumeri** (Werd.) Bkbg.

P. riograndensis Brandt = hort. hybrid.

P. ritteri Buin. = **Parodia maassii** (Heese) Berg.

P. ritteri v. cintiensis (Ritt.) Krainz = **Parodia maassii** (Heese) Berg.

P. robustihamata Ritt. *n.n.* = **Parodia subterranea** Ritt.

P. rostrum-sperma Brandt = **Parodia maassii** (Heese) Berg.

'*P. rubellihamata*' Bkbg. = **Parodia microsperma** (Web.) Speg.

P. rubida Ritt. = **Parodia maassii** (Heese) Berg.

P. rubricentra Bkbg. = **Parodia steumeri** (Werd.) Bkbg.

'*P. rubriflora*' Bkbg. = **Parodia sanguiniflora** Fric ex Bkbg.

P. rufidihamata Ritt. *n.n.* = **Parodia microsperma** (Web.) Speg.

P. salitrensis Brandt = **Parodia subterranea** Ritt.

P. salmonea Brandt = status doubtful.

P. sanagasta (Fric) Wgt. = **Parodia microsperma** (Web.) Speg.

P. schuetziana Jajo = **Parodia steumeri** (Werd.) Bkbg.

P. scopaoides Bkbg. = **Parodia aureispina** Bkbg.

P. scoparia Ritt. = **Parodia steumeri** (Werd.) Bkbg.

'*P. sebiliensis*' = catalogue name.

P. separata Brandt = **Parodia echinopsoides** Brandt.

P. setifera Bkbg. = **Parodia microsperma** (Web.) Speg.

P. setispina Ritt. = **Parodia formosa** Ritt.

P. sotomayorensis Ritt. = ?**Parodia otuyensis** Ritt.

P. spanisa Brandt = **Parodia microsperma** (Web.) Speg.

P. speciosa Brandt = hort. hybrid.

P. splendens Card. = status doubtful.

P. stereospina Brandt = **Parodia otuyensis** Ritt.

P. sucrensis Brandt = **Parodia tuberculata** Card.

P. superba Brandt = **Parodia microsperma** (Web.) Speg.

P. suprema Ritt. = **Parodia maassii** (Heese) Berg.

'*P. tafiensis*' Bkbg. = **Parodia sanguiniflora v. comata** Ritt.

P. talaensis Brandt = **Parodia macrancistra** (Sch.) Wesk.

P. tarabucina Card. = status doubtful.

P. thieleana Brandt = **Parodia maassii** (Heese) Berg.

P. thionantha Brandt = **Parodia microsperma** (Web.) Speg.

P. tilcarensis (Werd. & Bkbg.) Bkbg. = **Parodia steumeri** (Werd.) Bkbg.

P. tillii Wesk. = **Parodia formosa** Ritt.

P. tojoensis Brandt = **Parodia maassii** (Heese) Berg.

P. tredecimcostata Ritt. = **Parodia echinopsoides** Brandt.

'*P. tuberculosi-costata*' Bkbg. = **Parodia microsperma** (Web.) Speg.

P. uebelmanniana Ritt. = **Parodia microsperma** (Web.) Speg.

P. uhligiana Bkbg. = **Parodia aureicentra** Bkbg.

P. variicolor Ritt. = **Parodia aureicentra** Bkbg.

P. weberioides Brandt = status doubtful.

P. weskampiana Krasucka & Spanowsky = **Parodia microsperma** (Web.) Speg.

P. yamparaezi Card. = **Parodia otuyensis** Ritt.

P. zaletaewana Brandt = **Parodia subterranea** Ritt.

P. zecheri Vasqu. = **Parodia punae** Card.

Pediocactus bradyi v. knowltonii (Benson) Bkbg. = **Pediocactus knowltonii** Benson.

Pelecyphora pseudopectinata Bkbg. = **Turbinicarpus pseudopectinatus** (Bkbg.) Glass & Foster.

P. valdeziana Moell. = **Turbinicarpus valdezianus** (Moell.) Glass & Foster.

Phellosperma tetrancistra (Engelm.) B. & R. = **Mammillaria tetrancistra** Engelm.

Pilocopiapoa solaris Ritt. = **Copiapoa solaris** (Ritt.) Ritt.

Porfiria schwartzii (Fric) Boed. = **Mammillaria coahuilensis** (Boed.) Moran.

Pseudolobivia ancistrophora (Speg.) Bkbg. = **Echinopsis ancistrophora** Speg.
P. aurea (B. & R.) Bkbg. = **Lobivia aurea** B. & R.
P. boyuibensis (Ritt.) Bkbg. = **Echinopsis boyuibensis** Ritt.
P. callichroma (Card.) Bkbg. = **Echinopsis obrepanda** (S–D) Sch.
P. calorubra (Card.) Bkbg. = **Echinopsis obrepanda v. calorubra** (Card.) Rausch.
P. carmineoflora Hoffm. & Bkbg. = **Echinopsis obrepanda** (S–D) Sch.
P. ferox (B. & R.) Bkbg. = **Lobivia ferox** B. & R.
P. fiebrigii (Guerke) Bkbg. = **Echinopsis obrepanda** (S–D) Sch.
P. frankii Bosz. = **Echinopsis obrepanda** (S–D) Sch.
P. hamatacantha (Bkbg.) Bkbg. = **Echinopsis ancistrophora** Speg.
P. kermesina Krainz = **Echinopsis mamillosa v. kermesina** (Krainz) Friedm.
P. kratochviliana (Bkbg.) Bkbg. = **Echinopsis ancistrophora** Speg.
P. lecoriensis (Card.) Bkbg. = **Lobivia ferox** B. & R.
P. leucorhodantha (Bkbg.) Bkbg. = **Echinopsis ancistrophora** Speg.
P. longispina (B. & R.) Bkbg. = **Lobivia ferox v. longispina** (B. & R.) Rausch.
P. luteiflora Bkbg. = **Lobivia aurea** (B. & R.) Bkbg.
P. obrepanda (S–D) Bkbg. = **Echinopsis obrepanda** (S–D) Sch.
P. orozasana (Ritt.) Bkbg. = **Echinopsis mamillosa** Guerke.
P. pelecyrhachis (Bkbg.) Bkbg. = **Echinopsis ancistrophora** Speg.
P. polyancistra (Bkbg.) Bkbg. = **Echinopsis ancistrophora** Speg.
P. potosina (Werd.) Bkbg. = **Lobivia ferox** B. & R.
P. rojasii (Card.) Bkbg. = **Echinopsis obrepanda** (S–D) Sch.
P. toralapana (Card.) Bkbg. = **Echinopsis obrepanda** (S–D) Sch.
P. torrecillasensis (Card.) Bkbg. = **Lobivia arachnacantha v. torrecillasensis** (Card.) Bkbg.
P. wilkeae Bkbg. = **Lobivia ferox v. longispina** (B. & R.) Rausch.

Pyrrhocactus aconcaguensis Ritt. = **Neoporteria horrida** (Remy ex Gay) D. Hunt.
P. aspillagai (Soehr.) Ritt. = **Neoporteria aspillagai** (Soehr.) Bkbg.
P. aricensis Ritt. = **Neoporteria iquiquensis** (Ritt.) Don. & Rowley.
P. armatus Ritt. = **Neoporteria horrida** (Remy ex Gay) D. Hunt.
P. atroviridis Ritt. = **Neoporteria atroviridis** (Ritt.) R.M. Ferryman.
P. calderanus Ritt. = **Neoporteria calderana** (Ritt.) Don. & Rowley.
P. carrizalensis Ritt. = **Neoporteria totoralensis v. carrizalensis** (Ritt.) R.M. Ferryman.
P. chaniarensis Ritt. = **Neoporteria heinrichiana** (Bkbg.) R.M. Ferryman.
P. chilensis (Hildm.) Ritt. = **Neoporteria chilensis** (Hildm.) Don. & Rowley.

P. choapensis Ritt. = **Neoporteria horrida** (Remy ex Gray) D. Hunt.
P. chorosensis Ritt. = **Neoporteria chorosensis** (Ritt.) Don. & Rowley.
P. coliguayensis Ritt. = **Neoporteria curvispina** (Bert.) Don. & Rowley.
P. confinis Ritt. = **Neoporteria confinis** (Ritt.) Don. & Rowley.
P. crispus Ritt. = **Neoporteria crispa** (Ritt.) Don. & Rowley.
P. curvispinus (Bert.) Berg. = **Neoporteria curvispina** (Bert.) Don. & Rowley.
P. dimorphus Ritt. = **Neoporteria jussieui v. dimorpha** (Ritt.) Hoffman.
P. echinus Ritt. = **Neoporteria echinus** (Ritt.) R.M. Ferryman.
P. engleri (Ritt.) Ritt. = **Neoporteria engleri** (Ritt.) Don. & Rowley.
P. eriosyzoides (Ritt.) Ritt. = **Neoporteria eriosyzoides** (Ritt.) Don. & Rowley.
P. eriosyzoides v. domeykoensis Ritt. = **Neoporteria eriosyzoides v. domeykoensis** (Ritt.) R.M. Ferryman.
P. floccosus Ritt. = **Neoporteria echinus v. floccosa** (Ritt.) R.M. Ferryman.
P. floribundus (Bkbg.) Ritt. = **Neoporteria iquiquensis** (Ritt.) Don. & Rowley.
P. glaucescens Ritt. = **Neoporteria echinus** (Ritt.) R.M. Ferryman.
P. glacilis Ritt. = **Neoporteria calderana** (Ritt.) Don. & Rowley.
P. grandiflorus Ritt. = **Neoporteria curvispina v. grandiflora** (Ritt.) Don. & Rowley.
P. heinrichianus (Bkbg.) Ritt. = **Neoporteria heinrichiana** (Bkbg.) R.M. Ferryman.
P. horridus (Remy ex Gay) Bkbg. = **Neoporteria horrida** (Remy ex Gay) D. Hunt.
P. huascensis Ritt. = **Neoporteria huascensis** (Ritt.) Don. & Rowley.
P. intermedius Ritt. = **Neoporteria calderana** (Ritt.) Don. & Rowley.
P. jussieui (Monv.) Ritt. = **Neoporteria jussieui** (Monv.) B. & R.
P. kunzei (Foerst.) Ito = **Neoporteria kunzei** (Foerst.) Bkbg.
P. limariensis Ritt. = **Neoporteria limariensis** (Ritt.) R.M. Ferryman.
P. marksianus & v. tunensis Ritt. = **Neoporteria marksiana** (Ritt.) Don. & Rowley.
P. neohankeanus Ritt. = **Neoporteria neohankeana** (Ritt.) R.M. Ferryman.
P. occultus (Sch.) Ritt. = **Neoporteria occulta** (Sch.) B. & R.
P. odoriflorus Ritt. = **Neoporteria horrida** (Remy ex Gay) D. Hunt.
P. pamaensis Ritt. = **Neoporteria limariensis** (Ritt.) R.M. Ferryman.
P. paucicostatus & v. viridis (Ritt.) Ritt. = **Neoporteria paucicostata** (Ritt.) Don. & Rowley.
P. pilispinus Ritt. = **Neoporteria calderana** (Ritt.) Don. & Rowley.
P. pulchellus Ritt. = **Neoporteria pulchella** (Ritt.) R.M. Ferryman.
P. pygmaeus Ritt. = **Neoporteria calderana** (Ritt.) Don. & Rowley.
P. reconditus Ritt. = **Neoporteria recondita** (Ritt.) Don. & Rowley.
P. residuus Ritt. = **Neoporteria recondita** (Ritt.) Don. & Rowley.
P. robustus & v. vegasanus Ritt. = **Neoporteria horrida** (Remy ex Gay) D. Hunt.
P. rupicolus Ritt. = **Neoporteria taltalensis** Hutch.

P. saxifragus Ritt. = **Neoporteria iquiquensis** (Ritt.) Don. & Rowley.

P. scoparius Ritt. = **Neoporteria calderana** (Ritt.) Don. & Rowley.

P. setosiflorus & *v. intermedius* Ritt. = **Neoporteria setosiflora** (Ritt.) Don. & Rowley.

P. simulans Ritt. = **Neoporteria simulans** (Ritt.) Don. & Rowley.

P. subaianus Bkbg. = **Neoporteria garaventai** (Ritt.) R.M. Ferryman.

P. taltalensis (Hutch.) Ritt. = **Neoporteria taltalensis** Hutch.

P. tenuis Ritt. = **Neoporteria taltalensis** Hutch.

P. totoralensis Ritt. = **Neoporteria totoralensis** (Ritt.) Don. & Rowley.

P. transiens Ritt. = **Neoporteria transiens** (Ritt.) R.M. Ferryman.

P. transitensis Ritt. = **Neoporteria transitensis** (Ritt.) R.M. Ferryman.

P. trapichensis Ritt. = **Neoporteria chorosensis** (Ritt.) Don. & Rowley.

P. truncatipetalus Ritt. = **Neoporteria marksiana** (Ritt.) Don. & Rowley.

P. tuberisulcatus (Jac.) Bcrg. – **Neoporteria horrida** (Remy ex Gay) D. Hunt.

P. vallenarensis Ritt. = **Neoporteria vallenarensis** (Ritt.) Hoffmann.

P. vexatus Ritt. = **Neoporteria recondita v. vexata** (Ritt.) Hoffmann.

P. wagenknechtii Ritt. = **Neoporteria jussieui v. wagenknechtii** (Ritt.) Hoffmann.

Rebutia albiareolata Ritt. = **Rebutia deminuta** (Web.) B. & R.

R. almeyeri Heinr. ex Bkbg. = ?hort. hybrid.

R. arenacea Card. = **Sulcorebutia arenacea** (Card.) Ritt.

'*R. beryllioides*' = **Rebutia wessneriana v. beryllioides** (Buin. & Don.) Don.

R. binnewaldiana Heinr. = status doubtful.

'*R. boliviensis*' = **Rebutia deminuta** (Web.) B. & R.

R. brachyantha (Wessn.) Buin. & Don. = **Rebutia steinmannii** (Solms-Laub.) B. & R.

R. cajasensis Ritt. = **Rebutia deminuta** (Web.) B. & R.

R. calliantha Bewg. = **Rebutia wessneriana v. calliantha** (Bewg.) Don.

R. calliantha v. beryllioides Buin. & Don. = **Rebutia wessneriana v. beryllioides** (Buin. & Don.) Don.

R. canacruzensis Rausch = '**Rebutia pygmaea v. canacruzensis**'.

R. candiae Card. = **Sulcorebutia candiae** (Card.) Buin. & Don.

R. canigueralii Card. = **Sulcorebutia canigueralii** (Card.) Buin. & Don.

R. caracarensis Card. see **Sulcorebutia caracarensis** sensu Rausch.

R. christinae Rausch = '**Rebutia steinmannii v. christinae**'.

R. cincinnata Rausch = '**Rebutia steinmannii v. cincinnata**'.

R. cintiensis Ritt. = **Rebutia fiebrigii** (Guerke) B. & R.

R. colorea Ritt. = '**Rebutia pygmaea v. colorea**'.

R. costata Werd. = '**Rebutia steinmannii v. costata**'.

R. diersiana v. minor Rausch = '**Rebutia pygmaea v. diersiana**'.

R. eos Rausch = '**Rebutia pygmaea v. eos**'.

'*R. espinosae*' = **Rebutia narvaecensis** (Card.) Don.

R. eucaliptana (Bkbg.) Ritt. = **Rebutia steinmannii** (Solms-Laub.) B. & R.

R. fiebrigii v. densiseta (Cullm.) Oeser = **Rebutia fiebrigii** (Guerke) B. & R.

R. friedrichiana Rausch = '**Rebutia pygmaea v. friedrichiana**'.

R. fusca Ritt. = **Rebutia spegazziniana** Bkbg.

R. glomeriseta Card. = **Sulcorebutia glomeriseta** (Card.) Ritt.

R. glomerispina Card. = **Sulcorebutia glomerispina** (Card.) Buin. & Don.

R. gonjianii Kies. = **Rebutia einsteinii v. gonjianii** (Kies.) Don.

R. gracilispina Ritt. = **Rebutia pygmaea** (Fries) B. & R.

R. grandiflora Bkbg. = **Rebutia minuscula v. grandiflora** (Bkbg.) Buin. & Don.

R. hyalacantha (Bkbg.) Bkbg. = **Rebutia wessneriana** Bewg.

R. inflexiseta Card. = **Sulcorebutia inflexiseta** (Card.) Don.

R. iscayachensis Rausch = '**Rebutia pygmaea v. iscayachensis**'.

R. kariusiana Wessn. = pink flowered form of **Rebutia violaciflora** Wessn. or **Rebutia marsoneri** Werd.

'*R. maxima*' = **Rebutia deminuta** (Web.) B. & R.

R. minuscula fa. violaciflora (Bkbg.) Don. = **Rebutia violaciflora** Bkbg.

R. minutissima Ritt. = **Rebutia spegazziniana** Bkbg.

R. mudanensis Rausch = '**Rebutia pygmaea v. mudanensis**'.

R. nazarenoensis Rausch = '**Rebutia pygmaea v. nazarenoensis**'.

R. nigricans (Wessn.) Bkbg. = **Rebutia ritteri** (Wessn.) Buin. & Don.

R. nitida Ritt. = **Rebutia deminuta** (Web.) B. & R.

R. nogalesensis Ritt. = **Rebutia deminuta** (Web.) B. & R.

R. oculata Werd. = **Rebutia euanthema.** (Bkbg.) Buin. & Don.

R. odontopetala Ritt. = **Rebutia pygmaea** '**v. friedrichiana**'.

'*R. oligitiformis*' = **Rebutia pygmaea** (Fries) B. & R.

R. pallida Rausch = '**Rebutia pygmaea v. pallida**'.

R. patericalyx Ritt. = **Rebutia deminuta** (Web.) B. & R.

R. permutata Heinr. = status doubtful.

R. pseudominuscula (Speg.) B. & R. = **Rebutia deminuta** (Web.) B. & R.

R. rauschii Zech. = '**Rebutia steinmannii v. rauschii**'.

R. robustispina Ritt. = **Rebutia spegazziniana** Bkbg.

R. rubiginosa Ritt. = **Rebutia deminuta** (Web.) B. & R.

R. rutiliflora Ritt. = '**Rebutia pygmaea v. diersiana**'.

R. sanguinea Ritt. = **Rebutia spegazziniana** Bkbg.

R. sarothroides Werd. = '**Rebutia einsteinii v. aureiflora**'.

R. singularis Ritt. = **Rebutia padcayensis** Rausch.

'*R. sphaerica*' = **Rebutia ritteri** (Wessn.) Don.

R. tamboensis Ritt. = **Rebutia deminuta** (Web.) B. & R.

R. tarijensis Rausch = ?**Rebutia ritteri** (Wessn.) Don.

R. tiraquensis Card. = **Sulcorebutia tiraquensis** (Card.) Ritt.

R. totorensis Card. = **Sulcorebutia totorensis** (Card.) Ritt.

R. tuberosa Ritt. = **Rebutia deminuta** (Web.) B. & R.

R. vallegrandensis Card. = status doubtful.

R. vulpina Ritt. = **Rebutia spegazziniana** Bkbg.

R. zecheri Rausch = **Rebutia ritteri** (Wessn.) Don.

'*Reicheocactus floribundus*' Bkbg. = **Neoporteria iquiquensis** (Ritt.) Don. & Rowley.

R. pseudoreicheanus Bkbg. = **Lobivia famatimensis** (Speg.) B. & R.

Rodentiophila atacamensis Ritt. *n.n.* = **Eriosyce megacarpa** Ritt.

R. megacarpa Ritt. *n.n.* = **Eriosyce megacarpa** Ritt.

Roseocactus fissuratus (Eng.) Berg. = **Ariocarpus fissuratus** (Eng.) Sch.

R. intermedius Bkbg. & Kil. = **Ariocarpus fissuratus v. lloydii** (Rose) And.

R. kotschoubeyanus (Lem.) Berg. = **Ariocarpus kotschoubeyanus** (Lem.) Sch.

R. lloydii (Rose) Berg. = **Ariocarpus fissuratus v. lloydii** (Rose) And.

Soehrensia bruchii (B. & R.) Bkbg. = **Lobivia bruchii** B. & R.

Solisia pectinata (Stein) B. & R. = **Mammillaria pectinifera** (Stein) Web.

Submatucana aurantiaca (Vpl.) Bkbg. = **Matucana aurantiaca** (Vpl.) Bux.

S. aureiflora (Ritt.) Bkbg. = **Matucana aureiflora** Ritt.

'*S. bagalaensis*' = **Matucana aurantiaca** (Vpl.) Bux.

'*S. calmada*' = **Matucana aurantiaca** (Vpl.) Bux.

S. calvescens (Kim. & Hutch.) Bkbg. = **Matucana aurantiaca** (Vpl.) Bux.

S. currundayensis (Ritt.) Bkbg. = **Matucana aurantiaca** (Vpl.) Bux.

S. formosa (Ritt.) Bkbg. = **Matucana formosa** Ritt.

'*S. grandiflora*' = **Matucana aurantiaca** (Vpl.) Bux.

S. intertexta (Ritt.) Bkbg. = **Matucana intertexta** Ritt.

S. madisoniorum (Hutch.) Bkbg. = **Matucana madisoniorum** (Hutch.) Rowley.

S. paucicostata (Ritt.) Bkbg. = **Matucana paucicostata** Ritt.

S. ritteri (Buin.) Bkbg. = **Matucana ritteri** Buin.

Sulcorebutia albida n. n. = **Sulcorebutia albissima** (Brandt) Pilbeam.

'*S. bicolor*' = **Sulcorebutia steinbachii** (Werd.) Bkbg.

S. caineana (Card.) Don. = **Sulcorebutia breviflora** Bkbg.

'*S. camachoi*' = **Sulcorebutia tiraquensis v. bicolorispina** Knize *nom. prov.*

S. cupreata n. n. = **Sulcorebutia flavissima** Rausch.

S. flavida Brandt = **Sulcorebutia flavissima** Rausch.

S. haseltonii (Card.) Don. = **Sulcorebutia breviflora** Bkbg.

S. hoffmanniana Bkbg. = **Sulcorebutia kruegeri v. hoffmanniana** (Bkbg.) Don.

'*S. koehresii*' = **Sulcorebutia langeri** Neum. & Falk. *nom. prov.*

S. lepida Ritt. = **Sulcorebutia totorensis v. lepida** (Ritt.) Pilbeam ex Don.

S. menesesii v. kamiensis n. n. = **Sulcorebutia menesesii** (Card.) Buin. & Don.

S. muschii Vasqu. = **Sulcorebutia menesesii v. muschii** (Vasqu.) Don.

S. polymorpha (Card.) Bkbg. = **Sulcorebutia steinbachii v. polymorpha** (Card.) Pilbeam.

S. pulchera = incorrectly published name for **Sulcorebutia pulchra** (Card.) Don.

S. seinoiana Vasqu. *nom. prov.* = **Sulcorebutia kruegeri v. hoffmanniniana** (Bkbg.) Don.

'*S. senilis*' = **Sulcorebutia tiraquensis v. bicolorispina** Knize. *nom. prov.*

S. steinbachii v. gracilior Bkbg.
S. steinbachii v. horrida Rausch
'*S steinbachii v. violaciflora*' } = **Sulcorebutia stein-bachii** (Werd.) Bkbg.

S. sucrensis Ritt. *n. n.* = **Sulcorebutia losenickyana** Rausch.

S. taratensis (Card.) Buin. & Don. = status doubtful.

S. tuberculato-chrysantha (Card.) Don. = **Sulcorebutia steinbachii** (Werd.) Bkbg.

S. unguispina Rausch = **Sulcorebutia purpurea** Don.

S. vanbaelii n. n. = **Sulcorebutia kruegeri v. hoffmanniana** (Bkbg.) Don.

S. verticillacantha v. applanata Don. & Krahn = '**Sulcorebutia canigueralii v. applanata**'.

S. verticillacantha v. aureiflora Rausch = '**Sulcorebutia tarabucoensis v. aureiflora**'.

S. verticillacantha v. chatajillensis Oeser & Bred. = **Sulcorebutia alba** Rausch.

S. verticillacantha v. cuprea Rausch = '**Sulcorebutia markusii v. cuprea**'.

S. verticillacantha v. verticosior Ritt. = **Sulcorebutia verticillacantha** Ritt.

'*S. weingartioides*' = **Sulcorebutia pampagrandensis** Rausch.

S. xanthoantha Bkbg. = **Sulcorebutia candiae** (Card.) Buin. & Don.

S. zavaletae (Card.) Bkbg. = status doubtful.

Thelocactus bicolor v. schottii Davis ex Bkbg. = **Thelocactus bicolor** (Gal. ex Pfeiff.) B. & R.

T. bicolor v. texensis Bkbg. *nom. inval.* = **Thelocactus bicolor** (Gal. ex Pfeiff.) B. & R.

T. bicolor v. tricolor Sch. = **Thelocactus bicolor** (Gal. ex Pfeiff.) B. & R.

T. bicolor v. wagnerianus (Berg.) Krainz = **Thelocactus bicolor** (Gal. ex Pfeiff.) B. & R.

T. bueckii (Klein) B. & R. = **Thelocactus tulensis v. bueckii** (Klein) E.F. Anderson.

T. conothelos v. macdowellii Glass & Foster = **Thelocactus macdowellii** (Rebut ex Quehl) C. Glass.

T. flavidispinus (Bkbg.) Bkbg. = **Thelocactus bicolor** (Gal. ex Pfeiff.) B. & R.

T. hexaedrophorus v. fossulatus (Scheidw.) S–D ex Lab. = **Thelocactus hexaedrophorus** (Lem.) B. & R.

T. leucacanthus v. porrectus (Lem.) Bkbg. = **Thelocactus leucacanthus** (Zucc. ex Pfeiff.) B. & R.

T. leucacanthus v. sanchezmejoradai (Meyran) Bkbg. = **Thelocactus leucacanthus** (Zucc. ex Pfeiff.) B. & R.

T. lloydii B. & R. = **Thelocactus hexaedrophorus v. lloydii** (B. & R.) Kladiwa & Fittkau.

T. lophothele (S–D) B. & R. = **Thelocactus rinconensis** (Poselg.) B. & R.

T. lophothele v. nidulans (Quehl) Kladiwa & Fittkau = **Thelocactus rinconensis** (Poselg.) B. & R.

T. matudae Sanchez-Mej. & Lau = **Thelocactus tulensis v. matudae** (Sanchez-Mej. & Lau) E.F. Anderson.

T. nidulans (Quehl) B. & R. = **Thelocactus rinconensis** (Poselg.) B. & R.

T. phymatothelos, '-ele' (Poselg. ex Ruemp.) B. & R. = **Thelocactus rinconensis** (Poselg.) B. & R.

T. rinconensis v. nidulans (Quehl) Glass & Foster = **Thelocactus rinconensis** (Poselg.) B. & R.

T. rinconensis v. phymatothelos (Poselg. ex Ruemp.) Glass & Foster = **Thelocactus rinconensis** (Poselg.) B. & R.

T. sanchezmejoradai Meyran = **Thelocactus leucacanthus** (Zucc. ex Pfeiff.) B. & R.

T. saussieri (Weber) Berg. = **Thelocactus conothelos** (Regel & Klein) Bkbg. & Knuth.

T. schwarzii Bkbg. = **Thelocactus bicolor v. schwarzii** (Bkbg.) E.F. Anderson.

Thelocephala aerocarpa (Ritt.) Ritt. = **Neoporteria reichei v. aerocarpa** (Ritt.) R.M. Ferryman.

T. duripulpa (Ritt.) Ritt. = **Neoporteria reichei** (Sch.) Bkbg.

T. esmeraldana (Ritt.) Ritt. = **Neoporteria esmeraldana** (Ritt.) Don. & Rowley.

T. fankhauseri Ritt. = **Neoporteria napina. v. fankhauseri** (Ritt.) Hoffmann.

T. fulva (Ritt.) Ritt. = **Neoporteria odieri** (Lem.) Berg.

T. glabrescens (Ritt.) Ritt. = **Neoporteria napina** (Phil.) Bkbg.

T. krausii (Ritt.) Ritt. = **Neoporteria odieri v. malleolata** (Ritt.) R.M. Ferryman.

T. lembckei (Bkbg.) Ritt. = **Neoporteria reichei** (Sch.) Bkbg.

T. longirapa Ritt. = **Neoporteria odieri** (Lem.) Berg.

T. malleolata & v. solitaria (Ritt.) Ritt. = **Neoporteria odieri** (Lem.) Berg.

T. napina (Phil.) Ito = **Neoporteria napina** (Phil.) Bkbg.

T. nuda Ritt. = **Neoporteria napina** (Phil.) Bkbg.

T. odieri (S—D) Ritt. = **Neoporteria odieri** (Lem.) Berg.

T. reichei (Sch.) Ritt. = **Neoporteria reichei** (Sch.) Bkbg.

T. tenebrica Ritt. = **Neoporteria napina** (Phil.) Bkbg.

Toumeya papyracantha (Englm.) B. & R. = **Sclerocactus papyracanthus** (Englm.) Benson.

'Turbinicarpus dickisoniae' = **Turbinicarpus schmiedickeanus v. dickisoniae** Glass & Foster.

T. flaviflorus Frank & Lau = **Turbinicarpus schmiedickeanus v. flaviflorus** (Frank & Lau) Glass & Foster.

T. gielsdorfianus (Werd.) V. John & Riha = **Gymnocactus gielsdorfianus** (Werd.) Bkbg.

T. gracilis Glass & Foster = **Turbinicarpus schmiedickeanus v. gracilis** (Glass & Foster).

T. horripilus (Lem.) V. John & Riha = **Gymnocactus horripilus** (Lem.) Bkbg.

T. klinkerianus Bkbg. & Jacobs. = **Turbinicarpus schmiedickeanus v. klinkerianus** (Bkbg. & Jacobs.) Glass & Foster

T. knuthianus (Boed.) V. John & Riha = **Gymnocactus knuthianus** (Boed.) Bkbg.

T. krainzianus (Frank) Bkbg. = **Turbinicarpus pseudomacrochele v. krainzianus** (Frank) Glass & Foster.

T. macrochele (Werd.) Bux. & Bkbg. = **Turbinicarpus schmiedickeanus v. macrochele** (Werd.) Glass & Foster.

'T. polaskii' Bkbg. *nom. inval.* = **Turbinicarpus schmiedickeanus v. schwarzii** (Shurly) Glass & Foster.

T. schwarzii (Shurly) Bkbg. = **Turbinicarpus schmiedickeanus v. schwarzii** (Shurly) Glass & Foster.

T. viereckii (Werd.) V. John & Riha = **Gymnocactus viereckii** (Werd.) Bkbg.

Weingartia aglaia Brandt = **Sulcorebutia tiraquensis v. bicolorispina** Knize *nom. prov.*

W. albaoides Brandt = status doubtful.

W. albissima Brandt = **Sulcorebutia albissima** (Brandt) Pilbeam.

W. ambigua (Hildm.) Bkbg. = status doubtful.

W. backebergiana Brandt = **Sulcorebutia steinbachii** (Werd.) Bkbg.

W. brachygraphisa Brandt = **Weingartia neocumingii** Bkbg.

W. callecallensis Brandt = **'Sulcorebutia tarabucoensis v. aureiflora'**.

W. chilensis (Bkbg.) Bkbg. = **Neowerdermannia chilensis** Bkbg.

W. chuquichuquiensis Brandt = **Weingartia lanata** Ritt.

W. clavata Brandt = **Sulcorebutia steinbachii** (Werd.) Bkbg.

W. corroana Card. 1971 = **Weingartia lanata** Ritt.

W. (Sulcorebutia) croceareolata Brandt = status doubtful.

W. cumingii (S—D) Werd. see **Weingartia neocumingii** Bkbg.

W. erinacea Ritt. = **Weingartia neocumingii subsp. pulquinensis** (Card.) Don.

W. flavida Brandt = **Sulcorebutia flavissima** Rausch.

W. formosa Brandt = status doubtful.

W. gracilispina Ritt. = **Weingartia neocumingii subsp. sucrensis** (Ritt.) Don.

'W. hajekyana' = **Weingartia neocumingii subsp. pulquinensis v. mairanensis** Don.

W. hediniana Bkbg. = **Weingartia neocumingii subsp. sucrensis** (Ritt.) Don.

W. knizei Brandt = **Weingartia neocumingii subsp. pulquinensis** (Card.) Don.

W. lecoriensis Card. = **Weingartia westii** Hutch.

W. longigibba Ritt. = **Weingartia lanata**.

'W. mairanana' Brandt = **Weingartia neocumingii subsp. pulquinensis v. mairanensis** Don.

W. mataralensis Brandt = **Weingartia neocumingii subsp. pulquinensis** (Card.) Don.

W. multispina Ritt. = **Weingartia neocumingii subsp. pulquinensis** (Card.) Don.

W. neglecta Brandt = **Weingartia neocumingii subsp. sucrensis** (Ritt.) Don.

W. nigro-fuscata Brandt = **Sulcorebutia tiraquensis** (Card.) Ritt.

W. oligacantha Brandt = **Sulcorebutia tarijensis** Ritt.

W. platygona Card. = **Weingartia lanata subsp. pilcomayoensis** (Card.) Don.

'W. pruinosa' n.n. = catalogue name = ?**Weingartia neocumingii** Bkbg.

W. pulquinensis Card. = **Weingartia neocumingii subsp. pulquinensis** (Card.) Don.

W. pygmaea Ritt. = **Weingartia kargliana** Rausch.

W. riograndensis Ritt. = **Weingartia lanata subsp. riograndensis** (Ritt.) Don.

'W. rio-orensis' = catalogue name = **Weingartia neocumingii** Bkbg.

W. rubro-aurea = **'Sulcorebutia tarabucoensis v. aureiflora'**.

W. saetosa Brandt = **Weingartia neocumingii subsp. pulquinensis** (Card.) Don.

W. saipinensis Brandt = **Weingartia neocumingii subsp. pulquinensis** (Card.) Don.

W. sucrensis Ritt. = **Weingartia neocumingii subsp. sucrensis** (Ritt.) Don.

'W. tominensis' = catalogue name.

W. torotorensis Card. = **Sulcorebutia torotorensis** (Card.) Bred. & Don.

W. totoralensis Brandt = status doubtful.

W. trollii Oeser = **Weingartia neocumingii subsp. sucrensis** (Ritt.) Don.

W. vilcayensis Card. = **Weingartia westii** Hutch.

Wigginsia arechavaletai (Sch. ex Speg.) D.D. Port = **Notocactus neoarechavaletai** (Sch. ex Speg.) Elsner.

W. corynodes (Otto ex Pfeiff.) S–D = **Notocactus erinaceus** (Haw.) Krainz.

W. erinacea (Haw.) D.M. Port. = **Notocactus erinaceus** (Haw.) Krainz.

W. fricii (Ar.) D.M. Port. = **Notocactus erinaceus** (Haw.) Krainz.

W. horstii Ritt. = **Notocactus neohorstii** (Ritt.) Theun.

W. langsdorfii (Lehm.) D.M. Port. = **Notocactus erinaceus** (Haw.) Krainz.

W. leucocarpa (Ar.) D.M. Port. = **Notocactus erinaceus** (Haw.) Krainz.

'*W. pulvinata*' = **Notocactus erinaceus** (Haw.) Krainz.

W. sessiliflora (Mackie) D.M. Port. = **Notocactus erinaceus** (Haw.) Krainz.

W. stegmannii (Bkbg.) D.M. Port. = **Notocactus erinaceus** (Haw.) Krainz.

W. tephracantha (Link & Otto) D.M. Port. = **Notocactus erinaceus** (Haw.) Krainz.

W. turbinata (Ar.) D.M. Port. = **Notocactus erinaceus** (Haw.) Krainz.

W. vorwerkiana (Werd.) D.M. Port. = **Notocactus erinaceus** (Haw.) Krainz.

Wilcoxia albiflora Bkbg. = **Echinocereus leucanthus** N.P. Taylor.

W. australis hort. *n.n.* = **Echinocereus poselgeri** Lem. (see under Echinocereus leucanthus).

W. poselgeri (Lem.) B. & R. = **Echinocereus poselgeri** Lem. (see under Echinocereus leucanthus).

W. schmollii (Weingart) Bkbg. = **Echinocereus schmollii** (Weingart) N.P. Taylor.

W. tamaulipensis Werd. = **Echinocereus poselgeri** Lem. (see under Echinocereus leucanthus).

PICTURE ACKNOWLEDGEMENTS

Most of the colour photographs in the book have been supplied by Premaphotos, but the publishers would also like to thank the following people who kindly gave permission for their photographs to be reproduced:

L. Bremer 23 *BL*

G. Charles 14 *BL*; 15 *BM*; 16 *TR, BM*; 17 *BL, BM*; 18 *TM*; 19 *TL*; 20 *BL, BM*; 31 *BL, BM, BR*; 32 *TR*; 37 *BR*; 39 *BL*; 41 *BL*; 54 *TR*; 58 *BM*; 62 *BR*; 65 *TR, BM*; 66 *TM, BM, BR*; 67 *TR, BM*; 68 *TR*; 69 *TR*; 71 *TL*; 73 *TL, TM, BM, BR*; 74 *TL*; 75 *TL, TM*; 82 *BM*; 90 *TL*; 106 *BL*; 109 *BL*; 117 *TR*; 118 *TL*; 135 *BL*; 136 *TL, TM, BL, BM, BR*; 137 *TL, TM, BM*; 138 *TL, TM, BL, BM*; 139 *TM*; 144 *TL*; 147 *TL*; 151 *TM*; 154 *BL*; 157 *TL*; 167 *BL, BR*; 188 *BR*; 193 *BM*; 195 *TL, TR, BL, BM, BR*; 196 *TL, TM, TR, BL*

J. Donald 153 *BM*; 156 *BM*; 175 *TR*; 176 *BR*; 177 *BR*

R.M. Ferryman 20 *TR*; 21 *TL*; 22 *BM*; 121 *BM*; 140 *BM*; 141 *BL, BM*; 142 *BM*; 143 *TL, TM*; 144 *TM, TR, BR*; 146 *BR*; 147 *BL, BM*; 148 *BM*; 149 *BM*; 150 *TM*; 168 *TL*

G. Hole 160 *BM*

R. Mottram 59 *BR*; 60 *BM*; 76 *TM*; 105 *TR*; 150 *BR*

D. Parker 33 *BR*

W. Reppenhagen 87 *BL*; 90 *TR*; 92 *TM*; 94 *TL, BR*; 96 *TL, TM, TR*; 99 *BM*; 101 *TM*; 107 *TL*; 108 *BR*; 110 *TM*; 115 *TM*; 116 *TR*; 119 *TM*; 127 *TL*; 130 *BL, BR* (above); 131 *TL*; 133 *BR*; 135 *TL*

P. Smart 84 *TR*; 174 *TL*; 175 *BM*; 184 *TR*; 189 *BL*

N.P. Taylor 57 *TL, TR, BL;* 58 *TL, TM*; 105 *BM*; 109 *TM*; 139 *TL*; 180 *TL*; 190 *BM*

S. Woolcock 86 *BM*

TL=Top Left: *TM*=Top Middle: *TR*=Top Right
BL=Bottom Left: *BM*=Bottom Middle: *BR*=Bottom Right